Greatest Moments
IN BIG TEN FOOTBALL HISTORY

Edited by Mike Bynum

The Unforgetable Coaches, Players and Teams

Autumn Battles Remembered

For more than 110 years, the Big Ten — which got its start as the Western Conference in 1896 — has been the premier college football conference in the country. It was the first conference and through the years it has been the most dominating league.

This is the conference that has had Amos Alonzo Stagg, Fielding Yost, Dr. Henry Williams, Bob Zuppke, Fritz Crisler, Woody Hayes, Duffy Daughtery, Bo Schembechler, Hayden Fry, Barry Alvarez and Joe Paterno as its great coaches.

It is also the league that has given us great players such as Red Grange, Walter Eckersall, Tom Harmon, Nile Kinnick, Bruce Smith, Chic Harley, Alan Ameche, Hopalong Cassady, Archie Griffin, Chuck Long, Bubba Smith, Ki-Jana Carter and Ron Dayne.

The premise of this book was to feature the five biggest games ever played by each of the 12 schools that have been a part of the Big Ten.

Hopefully it will be a trip down memory lane, filled with those special games that our fathers and grandfathers watched on television or listened to by radio, or were perhaps were lucky enough to have seen in person.

These are the big moments that form a school's tradition and link generations.

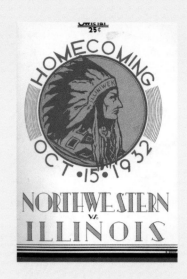

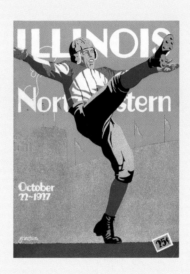

BIG TEN WEEKLY

Western Conference Athletics

Vol. IV.   No. 9

November 18, 1926

10
cents

"Cotton" Wilcox,
Purdue

Photo Credits:

Chance Brockway Photos: 109.
Stephen Carrera: 9, 167.
Getty Images: 156.
The Centre Daily Times: 125, 126, 131, 153, 163.
The Associated Press: 1, 127, 129, 133, 157, 159, 176.
The Columbus Dispatch: 93, 94.
The Detroit News: 165.
The Journal and Courier: 146, 147.
The Herald Times: 151.
Indiana University Archives: 56, 57, 82, 116, 175-right.
Indiana University Alumni Magazine: 114, 117.
Library of Congress: 21-top left, 32.
Michigan State Athletic Dept.: 62, 120, 121-bottom.
Michigan State University Archives: 60-61, 91.
Northwestern University Athletic Dept.: 148, 149, 160, 161.
Northwestern University Archives: 39, 74, 75.
Ohio State University Archives: 17-both, 18, 19, 64, 84, 85, 111, 175-left.
Purdue University Athletic Dept.: 5, 54, 55-both, 80, 81, 86, 87, 97, 104, 105.
Dave Repp: 113.
University of Chicago Archives: 13, 14-both, 15, 16, 28, 29, 30, 31, 33-top, 34, 36.
University of Illinois Archives: 23.
University of Illinois Athletic Dept.: 20, 21-top right, 21-bottom, 102, 103, 139-both, 154, 155.
University of Iowa Archives: 40, 41-both, 43, 73, 107-both, 118, 119, 123-both.
University of Michigan Athletic Dept.: 24, 25, 26, 27, 48, 50, 51, 59-bottom, 79, 88, 89, 121-top.
University of Minnesota Athletic Dept: 12, 45-both, 46, 47, 58, 59-top, 98, 99, 141, 144, 145.
University of Wisconsin Archives: 33-bottom, 53, 66, 67, 69, 70-both, 71, 77.
University of Wisconsin Athletic Dept: 52, 101.
Wisconsin State Journal: 100, 143-all.

The Amos Alonzo Stagg and the Bernie Bierman feature stories are reprinted by the estate of Tim Cohane.

The Anthony Thompson feature story is reprinted by permission of University of Indiana Alumni Magazine.

The Pat Fitgerald feature story is reprinted by permission of the Chicago Tribune.

The Red Grange feature story is reprinted by permission of *ESPN*.

The Big Ten game stories are reprinted from original stories published by the Chicago Tribune, Detroit Free Press, The Detroit News, Minneapolis Star-Tribune, Wisconsin State Journal, The Des Moines Register, Centre Daily Times, The Herald Times, The Journal and Courier, and The Cincinnati Enquirer. Reprinted by permission.

ISBN   1928846-57-2 (hardcover)
        1928846-82-3 (softcover)

Printed in Canada

Photo Imaging: Brian Kelley
Cover and book design: Evan Gilbert, St. Georges, QC
Published by: Canada Hockey LLC

*This book is dedicated to
the late Randy Walker
Northwestern University
Head Football Coach
1999-2005*

Chicago Defeats Badgers to Clinch Conference Title

The Chicago Sunday Tribune

Madison, Wisc. | December 9, 1899

Chicago	12	5	—	17
Wisconsin	0	0	—	0

Chicago holds the championship of the West in football. Amos Alonzo Stagg's Maroons earned the title this afternoon in a bitterly fought but one-sided game, beating Wisconsin, 17 to 0.

There is gloom in Madison. At 2 o'clock the Badgers reigned as heroes and Cardinal flashed as 8,000 students and villagers sang in chorus the jarring yell of Wisconsin, and the bands played as thousands of students marched around the white-lined field chanting premature hymns of victory. Now there is the darkness of defeat.

At the end of the game, the students who had followed Stagg's men to Madison, rushed onto the playing field, lifted them to atop their shoulders and carried them in triumph to the hotel — which was a mile away.

Chicago U. President William Rainey Harper was also captured, lifted to the shoulders of the wild crowd and forced to speak.

While the team was dressing after the game, President Harper told the men not to break training, but to prepare for a trip to California.

The game was fantastic. Madison went football crazy. From end to end the little lake-bound city was covered with cardinal. Every house was draped in cardinal bunting and ribbons. Special trains ran from Chicago and all the Wisconsin towns sent in crowds.

Rain was dripping down dismally and it was cold. But the rain and cold did not stop the crowds. At 1 o'clock the march to the field began. The four classes of the University of Wisconsin, headed by bands and gorgeous with ribbons and banners, paraded to the playing grounds at Camp Randall Field.

Once there, the great grand stand, the field seats and the bleachers were full. Around the field the classes marched, while those making lots of noise rolled down from the seats where the waves of cardinal danced,

Over in the East bleachers a little band of 1,000 Maroon rooters raised the chants of "Chi-ca-go, Chi-ca-go, Chi-ca-go!" but the yells were drowned in the whirlpool of noise from the Badger fans.

It looked all Wisconsin. The teams came on to the field amid a blare of bands and a clash of conflicting yells. Pat O'Dea and Clarence Herschberger, the old Chicago star, gave an exhibition of kicking, then the battle was on.

For six minutes the tide of the game wavered. The crowd roared. And all of a sudden, the maroon struck a vulnerable point in the left side of the Badgers' defense.

Again and again Frank Slaker and Frederick Fell were sent crashing against the Cardinal line, led by E.R. Blair and Ed Cochems. The yells from the Wisconsin faithful lessened as the Maroon forced their way, yard by yard, down the field.

Fourteen minutes into the game, Slaker bruised his way over left tackle for a touchdown.

There was an oppressive silence in the Wisconsin bleachers.

James Henry booted the extra-point kick from a difficult angle to give Chicago a 6-0 lead.

The surprised Badgers kicked off and a moment later fell started the applause by ripping the Wisconsin line for 20 yards. Then came the greatest play of the battle. Walter Kennedy dropped back to punt. Kellogg Speed passed the ball high. Kennedy jumped high into the air to catch it, but before he could get poised to kick the ball, the Badger backs were upon him. Kennedy dodged one man, started across the field, and while in flight, punted sixty yards downfield.

The Chicago crowd went wild. After an O'Dea punt, Chicago, starting near midfield, began to run through a passage between Cochems and Blair. The machine-like work of the Maroons moved Blair away with ease on each play, and Cochems was unable to reinforce him.

Twenty six minutes into the first half, Fell twisted over the goal line in a mass play for a touchdown and the Chicago crowd lost itself in cheering.

Again Kennedy booted a difficult extra-point kick to increase the Maroons' lead to 12-0.

Wisconsin rallied at the start of the second half and the cardinal crowd began to yell. Albert Larson plowed through

A Conference Takes Shape

The early beginnings of the Intercollegiate Conference of Faculty Representatives can be traced to 1894, when Henry Rogers, the president of Northwestern University, who was also a Methodist clergyman, began having informal talks with other presidents at prominent schools in the East and Midwest about the possibility of abolishing college football.

He contacted Charles Eliot at Harvard, James Smart of Purdue and William Rainey Harper at crosstown rival, University of Chicago, and others to get their input and comments about such a drastic move.

President Harper rejected the idea of such a move outright. Smart strongly supported a reform of the game, and Eliot and Smart doubted that any school could pull off such a feat due to the tremendous popularity of the game among their students and alumni.

In the 1880's colleges in both Ohio and Indiana had established athletic conferences similar to those that were already in existence in the East. These alliances attempted to regulate the abuses and violence and unsportsmanlike conduct seen in football and baseball and also attempted to cut down on the tramp athletes that migrated from school to school, or played for a school for four, five or six years without attending classes.

A popular example of this was the 1890 Michigan squad which had seven players who were never enrolled to attend classes.

Another example was the great Yale all-American Pudge Heffelinger in 1890-92. In an interview in 1954, he told his biographer that when he was a high school senior, the University of Minnesota recruited him to play on the Gophers' line in 1887.

So instead of destroying this popularly-growing game, a group of Midwest universities decided to set up an interstate conference made up primarily of public colleges.

Smart, the Purdue president, led this effort. He wrote letters to college presidents in Wisconsin and Illinois, inviting them to a meeting to discuss such an alliance.

Seven schools — Purdue, Illinois, Wisconsin, Chicago, Minnesota, Northwestern and Lake Forest — met on Jan. 11, 1895 at the Palmer House Hotel to listen to Smart and consider the advantages of formalizing such a group.

At a second meeting, Michigan (which had replaced Lake Forest), joined Minnesota, Northwestern, Wisconsin, Illinois, Chicago and Purdue in agreeing to set up the Intercollegiate Conference of Faculty Representatives, which would later become the Western Conference. Following the model of the Indiana Athletic Conference, they agreed to restrict games to college campuses and forbid athletes to accept pay or gifts and set rules by defining eligibility.

Iowa and Indiana joined the Western Conference in 1899, and later that year the group was referred to as "The Big Nine" in a newspaper story.

Michigan would withdraw from the group in 1907. The reason has often been quoted as "institutional control," but the real reason was that Yost, who lived in Ann Arbor part of the year and had many other business interests, objected to the conference's new rules on full-time coaching and scheduling rules.

Ohio State began play in 1913.

When Michigan started playing in the Western Conference again, in 1917, the group was referred to as the "Big Ten" for the first time.

Chicago would quit playing after the 1939 season, and Michigan State filled their slot, and won the Big Ten Conference championship in its first season in 1953.

Penn State became the league's eleventh team and started playing in 1993. They won the conference title and the Rose Bowl the next year.

the Maroon line several times for big gains, and once reached the Chicago 5-yard line. It appeared that O'Dea might kick a field goal, but he didn't and the Badgers lost the ball when the Maroon defense stopped them.

Again Chicago began to march and Slaker got loose on a run around left end. He ran for 30 yards before being brought down by O'Dea. The run was the longest of the game.

As the Maroon offense continued a heart-breaking attack of the left side of the Badgers' defense, Slaker & Co. eventually reached the Wisconsin 7-yard line. The Badgers' defense twice stopped the Maroon onslaught, but on the third try Slaker, who was in the center of a whirling mass, rolled across the Wisconsin goal line with the ball for a touchdown and a 17 to 0 lead. Kennedy's extra-point kick was wide.

From there, the Maroons played to prevent Wisconsin from scoring.

The 1903 Gophers posted a record of 14-0-1 and tied for the Western Conference championship. The tie with Michigan, and a water jug left behind by the Wolverines, was the beginning of the long-running Little Brown Jug rivalry between the two schools.

Gophers & Michigan Finish Marred by Fans

Minneapolis Journal

Minneapolis, Minn. | October 31, 1903

Michigan	0	6	—	6
Minnesota	0	6	—	6

When ten thousand shouting, frantic fans poured out upon the gridiron at Northrop Field and cut short the Michigan-Minnesota football game, they ended one of the greatest games the West has ever seen. The final score was a 6-6 tie.

Michigan coach Fielding Yost's squad entered the contest with a 28-game winning streak and was a 2 to 1 pre-game betting favorite.

Excitement had been brewing all week for the matchup between the Gophers and Michigan. With tickets selling for $3.00 to $5.00 for premium seats, the game was a sellout and attracted a standing-room only crowd of 22,000 — the largest to ever see a football game in Minnesota.

A group of 400 Michigan fans were in attendance and they made themselves conspicuous.

Governor Samuel Van Sant, Cyrus Northrop, the University of Minnesota President, Senator Frederic Snyder, Maj. Haynes and other notables occupied the box seats.

At 2:10 p.m., the Michigan team ran onto the field, and the followers of the maize and blue sent up a husky yell for their favorites. Ten minutes later, Dr. Henry Williams' men appeared and most of the crowd of 22,000 went wild.

Michigan received the opening kickoff, but most of the first half Minnesota had the ball in Michigan territory and reached the Wolverines' 15-yard line on their deepest drive.

The first half ended with the game tied, 0-0.

Michigan got the ball again first in the second half, and Minnesota drove to the Wolverines' 30- and 10-yard lines before these two drives bogged down.

Two series later, Michigan drove from their 36 to score the game's first touchdown, with Willie Heston punching the ball over the final yard for the score. Tom Hammond booted the extra-point kick to give the Wolverines a 6-0 lead.

Minnesota's Sig Harris returned the kickoff to the Gopher 45 and their drive managed to reach the Michigan 32 before the Wolverines defense held their ground.

Two series later, Minnesota returned a Michigan punt to the Wolverines' 38 and drove for a touchdown, with Fred Schacht dashing over left tackle for the final five yards to cut the score to 6-5. Egil Boeckman then added the extra-point kick to even the score at 6-6.

With two minutes left to play, the playing field was overrun by thousands of Gopher fans who were celebrating the team's success. Unable to clear the field, the game was called by Lieut. Nelly, the game's referee.

The 1905 Maroon won its third Western Conference title and first national championship with a 9-0 record.

Stagg's Chicago Is New Football King of the West

Chicago Daily Tribune

Chicago, Ill.	November 30, 1905			
Michigan	0	0	—	0
Chicago	0	2	—	2

The Maroons of the University of Chicago became the Champions of the West this Thanksgiving Day afternoon on Marshall Field in one of the most dramatic football battles in the history of the game.

Fielding Yost's Michigan squad entered the game with a record of 55-0-1 during the past five seasons and had been named the national champions the past four years. They were 12-0 in 1905 and had not been scored on.

The Wolverines' last loss was to Chicago, 15 to 6, in 1900.

Chicago, which was coached by Amos Alonzo Stagg, entered the game with a 9-0 record and had only allowed 5 points scored against them this season. Their last loss had been a 22-12 decision to Michigan last year in Ann Arbor.

It was the biggest game ever played in the West. The winner would be named the champion of the Western Conference and the national champion.

27,000 wildly cheering spectators saw Walter Eckersall make one of the longest punts of his career. It occurred midway through the second half. The ball started at midfield, whirling straight toward the goal posts fifty yards away and barely fell short of sailing over the crossbar.

It was caught back of the goal line by Bill Clark, the Michigan halfback, who made a desperate effort (and a tactical mistake to carry it on the field. He could have played it safe by touching the ball and downing it, but instead opted to run the ball out of the end zone. He eluded two Chicago tacklers. But Chicago's fleet captain, Mark Catlin, who was playing the last game of his football career with a broken rib, was on him like a demon, and threw him back over his goal line and forced a safety to give Chicago its two points — the only score of the game.

A key point in the contest was the ejection of Michigan's Joe Curtis from the game after he plowed into Eckersall, following Eckersall's punt, with his knee and shoulder, which hurled Eckersall to the ground 12 yards away.

The game then became a punting duel between Eckersall and Michigan's Johnny Garrels.

A crowd of 27,000 packed Marshall Field on Thanksgiving Day to watch the biggest game ever played in the Midwest.

Garrels also had the game's longest run — a 35-yarder — in the second half. He got around Chicago's left end and only had Eckersall between him and the Chicago goal line. But Eckersall robbed him of the touchdown.

Then came the game's biggest moment with Eckersall's punt that Clark tried to run back, but instead got thrown for a safety.

Chicago's Hugh Bezdek drove the Maroon to inside the Michigan 30 before halftime and Eckersall attempted several dropkicks for field goals — but none were close.

Mark Catlin (left), the Maroon captain, assisted on the tackle that gave Chicago the 2-0 win. Walter Eckersall (right) put on an impressive punting exhibition.

The First Game of the Century

By Amos Alonzo Stagg

The game was played November 30, 1905, at Marshall Field (later Stagg Field) in Chicago. There was tremendous interest in the game and the largest crowd in the history of football in the Middle West to that time — 25,791 — paid see it.

The background of this titanic struggle was that in five years (1901 to 1905) Fielding Yost's Michigan teams had rolled up 2,821 points to 40 for the opposition. In eleven games that season they had not been scored on while making 495 points. Chicago also had a great team. It had played nine games and won them all, scoring 243 points to the opponents' 5.

The enthusiasm of the crowd was unbounded throughout. The field was in perfect condition, protected by many tons of hay. With my approval, after the game the hay was set on fire with a gigantic blaze. Dr. J.E. Raycroft, later of Princeton fame, started the blaze.

The game was played under the old rules — the year before the introduction of the forward pass and the opening up of the game. Five yards had to be gained in three downs (for a new first down). The size of the playing field was 110 yards, with goal posts on the goal line and no end zones. A ball kicked over the goal line and touched down for a touchback was brought out to the 25-yard line. The length of the game was 70 minutes, divided into halves of 35 minutes each.

Michigan was the heaviest team I had ever seen. Adolph (Germany) Schulz, the all-American center, weighed 220 pounds. Octopus Graham, the guard, weighed 245. Henry Shulte, the other guard, 195, and Joe Curtis, the team captain, at left tackle was a giant from Colorado.

The game was played on Thanksgiving. The weather was clear and 25,791 spectators paid $35,000 at the gate. The Atlantic Coast had discovered us. Among the Eastern delegation were Walter Camp and Caspar Whitney, the all-America team selectors.

From the start of the game it was shown that the teams were evenly matched. The first half was played almost entirely in the center of the field. Chicago penetrated into Michigan territory three times while Michigan crossed the center of the field only once. The nearest we got to the Michigan goal was their 35-yard line; their nearest to ours, the 50-yard line. It was punt, punt, punt, with John Garrels, later an Olympic hurdler, holding his own against Walter Eckersall. Both kicked magnificently. The defense was so strong that it looked as though a lucky break or a bad mistake would be the only

Amos Alonzo Stagg

chance of producing a score.

The play changed somewhat in the second half, for Chicago was six times in possession of the ball in Michigan territory, including once on their 32-yard line. Eckersall, who had kicked five goals against Illinois in our preceding game, attempted a drop kick for a field goal from the 37. It was partially blocked.

Once Garrels got off a tremendous punt which Eckersall recovered on Chicago's 15-yard line. We immediately suffered a penalty of half a distance to the goal line, putting the ball near the Chicago 8-yard line. Here Eckersall's clever thinking took Chicago out of immediate danger with the most daring play I ever saw in a championship game. Standing behind the goal line in punt formation, and with Michigan's linemen rushing through to hopefully block the punt, Eckersall circled to the right and ran between the goal posts and was run out of bounds at Chicago's 22-yard line.

This feat heartened Chicago, and it was not long until the Maroon was in Michigan's territory. After three more downs, Michigan's defense fought fiercely and Eckersall punted the ball over their goal line.

Bill Clark, instead of touching the ball down and bringing it out to the 25-yard line, attempted to run it out, circling wide behind the goal posts, and was hit by our right tackle, Art Badenoch, just after Clark crossed the goal line. Then, Mark Catlin, our right end, tackled him high and they threw him back across the goal line for a safety that won the game for us, 2 to 0.

Eckersall & Co. Rout Illini

Chicago Sunday Tribune

Chicago demonstrated what new football is capable of doing under even fairly favorable conditions today by burying Illinois under a score of 63-0 at Marshall Field.

On a gridiron which was dry enough to permit accurate handling of the ball, although too slippery from recent soakings to afford sure footings, the Maroons turned loose a small portion of the new plays which had been developed behind locked gates this year, but was unable to use last Saturday against Minnesota. The result was the most spectacular and brilliant game of the season.

Before the game was three minutes old, Walter Eckersall shot a long pass to Wally Steffen, who was far out beyond the opposing end and had an open field for an 85 yard-yard sprint to the goal line.

But that was only the beginning. The Maroons rolled up a total of twenty-two points in the first half and added forty-one more in the second half.

Illinois fought gamely to the last, but was powerless against Chicago's speed and daring. Only once did Illinois have a real chance to score. A fumble right at the beginning of the second half gave the visitors the ball the ball only 12 yards from the Maroon goal and in two plays moved the ball to the Chicago 2-yard line. But the Maroon defense stiffened and kept the Illini out of the Chicago end zone.

After the ball was given over to Chicago, Eckersall booted it out of danger and Illinois' opportunity was gone.

Steffen redeemed himself for the poor showing he made against Minnesota in last week's 4-2 loss. Twice he made runs of 75 yards or more, while runs of 15, 20 and 25 yards were like ice cream and cake for him. Steffen scored half of Chicago's touchdowns today.

Eckersall was successful on only one of three field-goal dropkicks.

Fred Walker and Edwin Parry were prominent factors in the success of Chicago's passing and onside kicks.

Walker made nine of the 10 point-after kicks he attempted.

A few minutes after Steffen's opening score, Eckersall

Chicago, Ill. | November 17, 1906				
Illinois	0	0	—	0
Chicago	22	41	—	63

booted a drop kick from the Illini 20-yard line to give the Maroon a 10-0 lead.

Using a series of double and triple passes, Chicago was again within striking distance of the Illini end zone.

Eckersall, on a delayed pass, ran from the Illini 22 to reach the 2-yard line. A fumble cost them 12 yards. Steffen then dodged in and out on his way to a touchdown. Walker booted the ball squarely to boost Chicago's lead to 16-0.

When the Maroon got the ball again, Eckersall gained 15 yards. The Chicago trio of Steffen, Eckersall and Sherman Finger added runs of 7, 11, 12 and 20 yards, then Finger dived over for the touchdown. Walker's extra-point dropkick made it 22-0 with halftime just a few minutes away.

Illinois opened the second half with its best effort to score after Steffen fumbled a Charles Moynihan kickoff. The Illini drove from the Maroon 12 to the 2 on a one-yard carry by Frank Pinckney and nine more yards by Lion Gardiner on a shift play. Pinckney added another yard and Gardner got it to the six-inch mark, but at this point the Chicago defense showed its muscle and didn't allow the Illini offense into the end zone.

Steffen chalked up the next touchdown on a long run and Walker's drop kick for a 28-0 lead.

Steffen then exploded on a 75-yard sprint for a touchdown and Walker added another touchdown on a 30-yard run. His dropkicks gave the Maroon a commanding 40-0 lead.

Steffen scored next when he got loose on a 60-yard run. Finger's touchdown run made it 52-0.

Eckersall, who perhaps thought he was overworking his backs, scored the next touchdown. Walker's dropkick gave Chicago a 58-0 cushion.

Harry Schott, one of the lesser scrubs in the Chicago lineup, scored the final touchdown on one-yard smash. Walker then missed his only point-after kick.

Wally Steffen

All-American halfback Chic Harley (left) and Pete Stinchcomb led the Buckeyes to their first ever win over Michigan.

Buckeyes' Win Puts an End to Michigan Jinx

By THE ASSOCIATED PRESS
The Cincinnati Enquirer

The Ohio State Buckeyes celebrated the burial of the Michigan jinx. Led by the sensational play of all-America halfback Chic Harley, the Buckeyes defeated Michigan, 13-3, before a crowd of 25,000 at Ferry Field this afternoon.

It was the Buckeyes' first ever win over Michigan.

Ohio State had never won a game against the Wolverines in 22 years since the first game was played in 1897, which the Wolverines won easily, 34-0. The closest score in the series was a 0-0 tie in 1900.

Michigan was unable to pick up much yardage on the ground except on rare occasions.

In the third quarter, with the Buckeyes ahead, 7-3, Harley slipped past three tacklers and dashed 50 yards for an impressive touchdown.

Harley's touchdown romp was set up by a 17-yard run by

Ann Arbor, Mich.	October 25, 1919					
Ohio State	7	0	6	0	—	13
Michigan	0	3	0	0	—	3

Pete Stinchcomb on a quarterback sneak.

The point-after kick failed, which resulted in the final score of 13-3.

The Buckeyes' first touchdown came in the first quarter when left tackle Iolas Huffman broke through the Wolverines' line and blocked a punt. The ball rolled over the goal line and Jim Flower, the Ohio State right end, pounced on it for a 6-0 lead.

Cliff Sparks, the nifty Michigan quarterback, booted a 43-yard field goal in the second quarter for the Wolverines' only points all afternoon.

Michigan coach Fielding Yost tried to get his squad back into the contest, by directing his backs to pass the ball 18 times — but none were successful.

Michigan's 19-0 upset of the Buckeyes in the Ohio Stadium dedication game was the Wolverines' biggest ever win.

Michigan Defeats Buckeyes in New Stadium Opener

BY HARRY BULLION
The Detroit Free Press

Columbus, Ohio | October 21, 1922

Michigan	3	7	6	3	—	19
Ohio State	0	0	0	0	—	0

There is a great spoltch on the brand new 80,000-plus stadium that Ohio State University, amid much pomp and ceremony, dedicated this afternoon.

And tonight the old town is raining with the cheers of the maddening throngs from Michigan, whose football warriors today lowered the proud Scarlet and Gray of the Buckeye school before a crowd never before equalled at a game on a gridiron of the West. If ever a triumph was sweet to the Wolverines, this 19-0 victory this afternoon was. For three years Fielding Yost and his loyal followers have been burning for the revenge they achieved on this, the red letter day in all the history of the Western Conference.

Ohio State was whipped to a standstill, damaged as no team coached by John Wilce ever had been before, and there is a deep thick pall hanging over every supporter of the Scarlet and Gray. In one blow, the Wolverines whipped out the fruits of Ohio State's triumphant years; pushed back again the chesty Buckeyes, and while about it, jumped again on a position that will command the esteem of the West.

Before the third period was concluded it was a foregone conclusion that the Ohioans were in over their heads against the dashing attack and defense of the Wolverines and many in the vast throng began to make their way to the exits.

Those who stayed were struck with awe by the Wolverines' precision in executing plays. For once, the spirit of Ohio State was killed and her supporters were almost speechless with the horror of the catastrophe.

Walter Camp was in the press box. He came to see the greatest football field in the country, and the caliber of pigskin toters in the wild and wooly West.

He saw Kipke, a blizzard in action; Goebel, Kirk, Roby, Cappon, Muirhead and Uteritz outwit, outplay, and with the help rendered by their teammates, virtually crush the Ohio State battle front that its legions of followers boasted would win over Michigan through superior intellect, better coaching and psychology, which they believed was created by three straight wins over the Wolverines.

Michigan's defense stopped every OSU attack. OSU gave them thrust for thrust. Ohio State tried every phase of football she knew, but seemed dumbfounded when the men of Yost solved every trick and actually led the Buckeyes to their doom.

Michigan scored two touchdowns and a pair of field goals this afternoon. Paul Goebel put the Wolverines in the lead in the first quarter with a field goal from Ohio State 11-yard mark. In the final period, Harry Kipke booted a dropkick from the 38-yard line. The touchdowns came in between, in the second and third quarters.

Both touchdowns were scored by Kipke. The first one came on a double pass that sucked the whole Buckeye defense over to the left while Kipke, taking the ball from Doug Robey, sped around right end for 25 yards and the first Michigan touchdown scored against the Buckeyes in four years.

Ohio State had not fully recovered from that blow when, in the third quarter, the little blond marvel of the Wolverines speared a pass out of the air and ran 35 yards to cross the Buckeyes' goal line again.

Like a unit, the Michigan line constantly attacked the enemy. Her ends nailed the Ohio State backs almost in their tracks and the tackles, particularly Stanley Muirhead, were as venerable as the Rock of Gibraltar. And realizing early that Ohio State could do nothing to stop Michigan's charging defensive from reaching quarterback Vince Workman — who it is said, can hit a dime with a forward pass — the Buckeyes began to fill the air with passes.

Only once was Ohio State dangerous, but the alertness of the Wolverines' defensive backfield thwarted the Buckeyes' design. This happened in the third period, the toughest spot in the whole game for Michigan, and one where the Yostmen were confronted by two serious ordeals.

Ohio State had the ball on the Michigan 10-yard line, with

fourth down and two yards to gain.

Workman elected to try a pass that fell safely in Wilmer Isabel's hands, but Herb Steger tackled him so hard that the ball, slipping from his hands, fell into Frank Honaker's. Only Frank Cappon stood between the Buckeye end and the Michigan goal line and it looked as though the Michigan fullback would not be able to get past the Buckeye blockers. But he dodged two burley linemen, swung around in front of Honaker and brought him down.

Kipke immediately kicked out of danger. Later in the quarter, Workman, favored by a slight wind, kicked the ball dead inside the Michigan 5-yard line.

The Wolverines tried one play around end to get away from the uprights and Kipke booted the ball out of danger.

The Michigan contingent was on hand early — nearly 18,000 strong. Special trains from Ann Arbor and Detroit were fully loaded and the roads were black with automobiles, each draped in the colors of the Wolverines. One party made the trip from the University seat of the Wolverine state in an ancient car and tethered the machine to a hitching post just outside The Deshler Hotel by employing a halter. The car, from front lights to rear bumper, was smeared with yellow and blue paint.

Victory for Michigan means "hell" in this place tonight.

COPYRIGHT 1924
KAUFMANN & FABRY CO.
425 S. WABASH AVE.
CHICAGO.
ALL RIGHTS RESERVED.

DEDICATION HOMECO
UNIVERSITY OF ILLINOIS MEMORI
OCTOBER 18, 192-
ILLINOIS 39, MICHIC
ATTENDANCE 67

A crowd of 67,000, the largest ever to see a game in the Midwest, were treated to a scoring exhibition by Red Grange.

Illini's Grange Opens Memorial Stadium With Unforgettable 5 TD Show

BY JAMES CRUSINBERRY
Chicago Sunday Tribune

Champaign, Ill.	October 18, 1924						
Michigan	0	7	0	7	—	14
Illinois	27	0	6	6	—	39

Michigan never knew Red Grange, the Illinois wildcat, until today. Now Michigan knows him well. The great runner of Bob Zuppke's football team ran all over Michigan in the first quarter of their grid battle today at the new Illinois stadium and crushed the Ann Arbor boys before they realized they were in a contest. The final score was 39-14 in favor of the boys of Illinois, but was 27-0 at the end of the first quarter when Grange raced down the field four times for touchdowns in less than 12 minutes of play. He would finish with 402 yards total offense — 212 rushing, 64 passing and 126 kickoff returns.

A total of 67,000 jammed into the new $1.7 million Memorial Stadium — it was the largest crowd to ever see a game in the West.

Grange, who ran and dodged with the speed of a deer, had torn Michigan to pieces before the game had gone more than 15 seconds because he received the first kickoff and from his 5-yard line ran and dodged and tore his way 95 yards for a touchdown.

Right then and there Michigan knew it was up against something it hadn't seen in football before.

Three more times in the first period Grange got loose for long runs for touchdowns. His second one came after about five minutes of play and was a 67-yard romp.

The joyful Illini rooters were hardly through cheering that thrilling play before the red-headed Wheaton lad got loose for

Illinois' Red Grange (right) ran for 5 TD's and passed for another in the 39-14 win against Michigan.

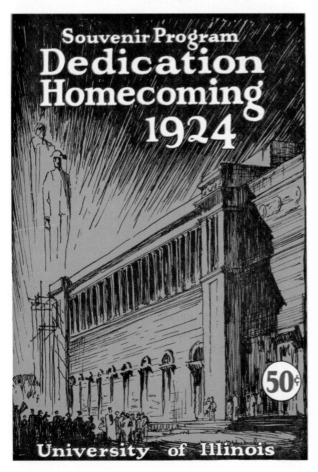

Souvenir Program
Dedication
Homecoming
1924

50¢

University of Illinois

Bob Zuppke's Illini teams won national championships in 1914, 1919, 1923 and 1927.

another touchdown — for 56 yards.

Before the quarter was over, Grange took the ball on the Michigan 44-yard line and dashed through the entire Wolverines defense for a fourth touchdown.

Grange's four touchdown runs were as sensational open field runs as have been seen in years. He carried the ball for a total of 262 yards on the four TD runs.

It is doubtful if anything near his equal has been seen in the West since the days of Walter Eckersall at Chicago. Most sportswriters in the press box called it the greatest perform-ance ever seen on an American gridiron.

Zuppke pulled Grange for the second quarter, and the Michigan squad seemed to regain its strength, holding the Illini scoring machine in check. But Grange returned in the second half and scored on an 11-yard run in the third quarter.

In the fourth quarter, Grange connected with Marion Leonard on a short pass for the final Illini touchdown.

Michigan's Herb Steger scored on a 15-yard run in the second quarter and F.A. Rockwell added a 1-yard TD run on a quarterback sneak to wrap up the scoring.

Illinois' Galloping Ghost: The Best There Ever Was

By Larry Schwartz
ESPN

Chris Berman on ESPN Classic's *SportsCentury* series once explained, "I was interviewing George Halas and I asked him who is the greatest running back he ever saw. He said, 'That would be Red Grange.' And I asked him if Grange was playing today, how many yards do you think he'd gain. And he said, 'About 750, maybe 800 yards.' And I said, 'Well, 800 yards is just okay.' Halas then sat up in his chair and he said, 'Son, you must remember one thing. Red Grange is 75 years old.' "

Pro football came of age by selling the popularity of college legend Red Grange.

In sport's Golden Age of the 1920's, he was football's golden boy. Red Grange was the name, though he was commonly known as The Galloping Ghost. While it's a shame they don't make nicknames like that any more, it's even more disappointing they don't make many players like the three-time All-American halfback.

"This man Red Grange of Illinois is three or four men rolled into one for football purposes," wrote Damon Runyon. "He is Jack Dempsey, Babe Ruth, Al Jolson, Paavo Nurmi and Man O' War. Put together, they spell Grange."

If you made a football movie and the star scored four touchdowns, covering an incredible 262 yards, in just 12 minutes, would anyone think it was anything but fiction? But that's what Grange accomplished against one of the best defenses in the country. That 1924 game against Michigan so inspired Grantland Rice to give Grange his nickname and write:

A streak of fire, a breath of flame
Eluding all who reach and clutch;
A gray ghost thrown into the game
That rival hands may never touch;
A rubber bounding, blasting soul
Whose destination is the goal.

Then less than a week after the remarkable No. 77 completed his college eligibility in 1925, he was breathing life into the struggling professional game. While it was a

national television contract four decades later that eventually made the National Football League truly major league, it was Grange who first gave the pro game legitimacy. His exhausting coast-to-coast 67-day barnstorming tour with the Chicago Bears filled stadiums and newspaper space.

Not big at 5-foot-11 and 175 pounds, his philosophy was simple: "If you have the football and 11 guys are after you, if you're smart, you'll run." And while he could run like the wind, he also could shimmy his hips like an exotic dancer, becoming as elusive as an invisible man.

"I will never have another Grange, but neither will anyone else," said Bob Zuppke, his coach at Illinois. "They can argue all they like about the greatest football player who ever lived, but I was satisfied I had him when I had Red Grange."

The storybook life of Harold Grange began on June 13, 1903 in Forksville, Pa. After his mother died when he was five, his father, Lyle, a foreman for a lumber company, moved the family to Wheaton, Illinois, where four brothers had settled.

While Lyle switched professions and worked his way up to chief of police at Wheaton, his son starred in athletics. At Wheaton High School, the redhead earned 16 letters in football, baseball, basketball and track (a four-time sprint champion).

Working summers as a helper on an ice truck enhanced his physical development. Eventually, he would be given the nickname, "The Wheaton Iceman." Despite scoring 75 TD's and 532 points in high school, Grange considered skipping football at Illinois and competing in basketball and track. But some fraternity brothers got Grange to change his mind with the use of a large wooden paddle.

In his first game, Grange scored three touchdowns, including a 66-yard punt return, against Nebraska in 1923. In seven games as a sophomore he ran for 723 yards (5.6 average) and scored 12 TD's in leading unbeaten Illinois to the national championship.

But it wasn't until the Michigan game on Oct. 18, 1924, that Grange reached legendary status. He returned the opening kickoff 95 yards for a touchdown. Then he scored on runs of 67, 56 and 44 yards. All this in the first 12 minutes. The four touchdowns were as many as Michigan had allowed in the two previous seasons. Tired, he took a rest, but came back to

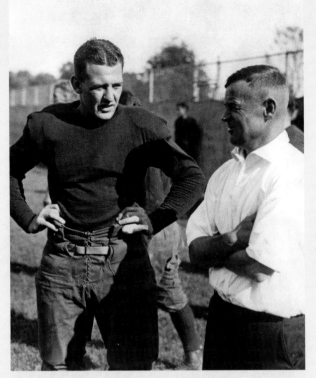

Red Grange (left) and his coach, Bob Zuppke, led the Illini to its greatest era in college football.

run 11 yards for a fifth touchdown and passed 20 yards for a sixth score as Illinois won, 39-14, to end Michigan's 20-game unbeaten streak. He totaled an amazing 402 yards — 212 rushing, 64 passing and 126 on kickoff returns.

As a senior, in a 24-2 upset of Penn in Philadelphia, Grange rushed for a career-high 237 yards through ankle-deep mud and scored three touchdowns, including runs of 56 and 13 yards. With rumors of Grange turning pro swirling, he helped Illinois win its season-finale, 14-9, over Ohio State.

In his 20-game career, he ran 388 times for 2,071 yards (5.3 average), caught 14 passes for 253 yards and completed 40-of-82 passes for 575 yards. Of his 31 touchdowns, 16 were from at least 20 yards, with nine from more than 50 yards.

The day after the Ohio State game, Grange announced he was turning pro. C.C. Pyle, a Champaign theater owner and promoter, negotiated an elaborate deal with Bears owner and coach George Halas in which Grange was guaranteed a reported $3,000 per game and a percentage of the gate.

Grange's jump to play for pay brought credibility to the pro game and shocked the collegiate world. "I'd have been more popular with the colleges if I had joined Capone's mob in Chicago rather than the Bears," Grange said.

While 7,500 attended the Bears' last non-Grange game, a standing-room only crowd of 36,000 jammed into Cubs Park (now known as Wrigley Field) on a snowy Thanksgiving to see Grange's pro debut. It was reported that Halas cried while counting the receipts. Grange ran for 96 yards and had an interception in a 0-0 tie with the Chicago Cardinals.

The Bears concocted a hybrid schedule — part regular season, part exhibitions — in which they played 19 games in 67 days. The frantic tour began with 10 games in 18 days in the East and Midwest. After an 11-day break the Bears played nine games in the South and on the West Coast.

While some games drew fewer than five figures, others attracted huge crowds, such as the more than 65,000 that attended contests in New York and Los Angeles. Grange played in 17 games (injury kept him out of the other two) and when the tour ended on Jan. 31, 1926, he went home to Wheaton weary but wealthy, driving a new $5,500 Lincoln and wearing a $500 raccoon coat. Pyle also made his client richer by getting him numerous lucrative endorsement deals.

When a bid by Grange and Pyle to buy a piece of the Bears was rejected by Halas, the two formed their own league, the American Football League, in 1926, with Grange playing for the New York Yankees. The league folded after a year. The Yankees, though, joined the NFL, but in the third game of the 1927 season, Grange suffered such a severe knee injury against the Bears that he never was the same dashing runner he had been.

After missing the 1928 season, he returned to the Bears in 1929, when he suffered a big financial hit in the stock market crash. Playing six more years, he became more valuable as a defensive back than as a running back in this era of one-platoon football.

In the NFL's first scheduled championship game, his touchdown-saving tackle late in the fourth quarter preserved the Bears' 23-21 victory over the New York Giants in 1933.

In the twenties, Grange made two films and a movie serial, called *The Galloping Ghost*. After his retirement from football, he became successful in the insurance business, real estate and as a motivational speaker. He became an analyst on Bears games for 14 years until 1963 and on network television college games.

A charter member of both the College and Pro Football Halls of Fame, he died of pneumonia on Jan. 28, 1991 in Lakes Wales, Fla. He was 87.

When asked about his success in football, Grange said, "They built my accomplishments way out of proportion. I never got the idea that I was a tremendous big shot. I could carry a football well, but there are a lot of doctors and teachers and engineers who could do their thing better than I."

Yost Showed Michigan the Way to Big-Time Glory

BY JOE LAPOINTE
Special to The Detroit Free Press

One hundred-five years ago, when Fielding Yost started coaching football at the University of Michigan, the sport was a rough version played by men without helmets. The ball was much larger and rounder. Linemen would play with loops attached to their belts so they could tow ball carriers through enemy lines. Touchdowns and field goals counted for five points each.

One of Yost's most famous plays, "Old 83," required a fake in which the halfback would take the center snap, fall down after faking a pitch to a runner, then get up and pitch to a different back who would run around the other end. This play would be illegal today, as the play is over once a ball carrier is down.

"Football in those days was a man-to-man fight on the field," Yost told sportswriter Grantland Rice in a 1922 interview. "Almost anything went. Today the rules have changed most of this. There are penalties for clipping, for piling on, for roughing the kicker, for striking with the palm of the hand for anything that looks like intentional roughness."

In 1986, then-Michigan coach Glenn E. (Bo) Schembechler was asked about Fielding H. (Hurry-up) Yost at a press luncheon in Ann Arbor. Though they coached decades apart, Yost and Schembechler have something in common. Both rank among college football's most prominent coaches of all time.

Schembechler (194-48-5 at U-M) recalled that, when he took the Michigan job in 1969, his wife, Millie, became a friend of Eunice Yost, Fielding Yost's widow.

"I went up to his house," Schembechler said. "He lived not far behind where I lived. I went up there several times. Walked around to see all the artifacts on Fielding Yost, Stagg and Pop Warner — those were the real pioneers. 'Hurry-up' Yost. Must have been a heck of a guy!"

You could say that. The spirit of Yost is not only an Ann Arbor ghost. Yost was something of a football Johnny Appleseed at the turn of the century, helping to spread through the Midwest and West Coast the popularity of a sport that was as undefined as it was rugged.

Walter Camp (left) and Fielding Yost visit at practice before the 1903 Michigan-Chicago game in 1903.

Born in West Virginia in 1871, the son of a Confederate Civil War soldier, Yost never saw a football game until he was a young adult, but he soon found he had a knack for playing and coaching the game.

Although he had a law degree, Yost quickly took to coaching football. At first he was a wanderer, playing line at West Virginia in 1895 and 1896, then coaching at Ohio Wesleyan (7-1-1 record in 1897), Nebraska (7-3 in 1898), Kansas (10-0 in 1899) and Stanford (7-2-1 in 1900).

He later explained he wanted "to see as much of the country as I possibly could" and that football was a good way to see it.

He found a football home at the University of Michigan in 1901, living there part-time (during football seasons) for two decades and full-time from 1921 until his death in 1946.

Yost was U-M's athletic director from 1921 to 1941. He quit coaching in 1926 with a 165-29-10 record.

In addition, he was a lawyer and businessman involved in a cement company, a furniture firm and a bank in Tennessee.

He was a military history buff, often visiting the site of Custer's Last Stand and interviewing Indians who had fought the battle. He looked beneath land, too, in speculative enterprises for various minerals.

"In fact," he once wrote in a letter to a friend, "I actually had a fling at oil, gas, coal, gold, flurospar, silver, bauxite, graphite, asbestos and copper."

Aside from coaching and private business, Yost's greatest success came as an athletic director. On the campus at Ann Arbor, he built a golf course, the huge Michigan Stadium and the Yost Field House, now known as Yost Ice Arena, home of the hockey team. To compare him to modern Michigan men, he was something of a combination of Schembechler and athletic director Don Canham.

"He was a tremendous genius from the standpoint of management of an athletic department," Canham says. "He made Michigan (sports program) what it is. Looking at the minutes of the meetings (of his era) he was pretty autocratic. He had to be."

When Yost supervised construction of what is now a 111,000-seat, single-deck football stadium, he included footings that would support a second deck, Canham said.

When Yost coached, it was at smaller stadiums called Regents Field and Ferry Field. His most famous teams, from 1901-05, were called the "Point-a-Minute" teams because they outscored their foes 2,841 to 42 in 57 games. Only one

of those games was a defeat (2-0 to Chicago, in the last game of 1905). He won the first Rose Bowl, in 1902, with a 49-0 victory over Stanford.

This was in an era right before a crackdown on the sport that came from the White House and President Theodore Roosevelt. Educators of the time said the sport had become excessively brutal. They wanted to curb the practice of tramp athletes moving from campus to campus, transferring their services almost as professionals.

"Sure, Yost recruited," Schembechler said with a chuckle, recalling that some of Yost's early stars played for him at different schools.

At the time, not everyone regarded these tactics as violations. One such incident, which came to light in 1935, took placed in 1899 when Yost coached at Kansas. A player named George Krebs showed up there, tried out for football, became a starting lineman and led the team to a victory over Nebraska. Krebs had graduated that spring from West Virginia, where he had starred with Yost on the football team.

"(Yost) wrote me, asking me to play on his (Kansas) team," Krebs said in a 1935 interview. "That was all right in those days, you know."

Yost himself had left the West Virginia team for one game to play for Lafayette against Pennsylvania. And when Yost was coaching at Wesleyan in Ohio in 1897, he brought his team north to play the Michigan Wolverines.

When he arrived, Yost — a 6-foot, 195-pound college graduate with a law degree — explained that he had been able to find only 10 players. Would it be all right, Yost asked, if he filled in on the line?

Michigan's 1905 Point-a-Minute team's 56-game unbeaten streak came to a halt after a 2-0 loss to Chicago.

Yost visits with his 1926 stars Bennie Oosterbaan (left) and Benny Freidman (right).

Permission was granted. And Yost helped the team to a scoreless tie.

"This was in the so-called barbarian days of football," journalist Westbrook Pegler once wrote of Yost, "long before Mr. Yost distinguished himself for his ethical piety at the University of Michigan."

Yost, born April 30, 1871, was the son of Permenus Esley Yost and Elzena Jane Ammons Yost. He was a farm boy who later taught rural school and worked as a deputy sheriff in a mining county. He was large in built for his era and wore a handlebar mustache as a young man (in the era called "The Gay 90's.") He attended Ohio Normal, a Methodist university in Ada, Ohio, and played first base on the baseball team, before he studied law and played football at West Virginia.

Later, Yost was frequently seen with an unlighted cigar in his mouth. Cartoonists frequently drew his shock of unruly white hair falling across the top of his forehead.

Writers of his era sometimes quoted him in dialect. Yost would go in to an alumni meeting and tell the grads:

"Doncha know I believe you men are behind me, but too far behind me."

Yost didn't drink alcohol and opposed the repeal of prohibition in 1933. "Some people can drink alcohol and it does them no harm," he frequently said, "but alcohol never helped anyone." It seems he knew how to talk to people.

"He was a politician," says Will Perry, Michigan's associate athletic director, who has written a book about Michigan football. "He had a great sense of public relations. He would go up to The Michigan Daily (the student newspaper) and help them write headlines."

His brother, Ellis Yost, wrote in 1948 that Yost was "a lover of the outdoors. Fielding was fond of hunting both big and little game. He bagged big game in the West Virginia mountains, California and Canada."

One animal that particularly interested him was the wolverine. Yost was envious that supporters of the University of Wisconsin brought a live badger to their games. So he searched for a year and finally got 10 live wolverines from Alaska. They grew so vicious that Yost had to give them up, keeping one at a campus zoo.

When Yost was courting his future wife in Nashville, Tenn., she introduced him to her father and, after Yost had left, asked what he thought of Yost.

"There," pronounced the father, "is a man."

Most of all, however, the man was known as a football coach.

"He believed in defense," Schembechler said earlier this week. "They didn't score very often on him."

Yost's first Michigan team didn't allow a point scored against them; his first five teams shut out 50 of their 57 opponents.

Yost believed in punting as a weapon, not only as a surrender of the ball when the offense failed to move it. He advocated surprise quick kicks on third down, saying that field position was sometimes more important than ball possession.

In a 1948 article, Detroit lawyer Charles F. Delbridge recalled Yost's football philosophy.

"How often have we heard him say: 'Pass, punt and pray,' " Delbridge wrote. "What's the easiest way to gain ground? Pass or punt her way down the field. Then hold 'em and pray for a break. If they fumble, fall on it. If they pass, grab it. Hold 'em. Take the ball away from them deep in their territory. If ya can't take it away from 'em, you can't win anyway. Then you're in 'po-zee-shun.' In po-zee-shun to use a scoring play. Only yardage that really counts is that one yard across the goal line, y'know. 'Why risk losing the ball on a short or lateral pass, the distance ain't worth it, y'know?' "

Yost (far right) and (left to right) Pop Warner, Knute Rockne, Babe Ruth, Christy Walsh and Tad Jones gathered in New York City to attend the Coachmen's Dinner in 1925.

Bennie Oosterbaan, who played end on Yost's last two teams in 1925 and 1926, recalled Yost as a "very likable, loveable person who knew his stuff.

"A very good teacher who could get it across with a smile on his face," Oosterbaan, a pallbearer at Yost's funeral, said in an interview. "Bo is a different personality. Yost never raised his voice. Most coaches do."

He wrote the book *Foot Ball for Player and Spectator*, published in 1905. He had one losing season at Michigan, in 1919, with a 3-4 record. He won 10 conference championships.

He left coaching for one season, 1924, then returned for two seasons before leaving the job for good. Yost then concentrated on supervising the building of athletic facilities on the campus and supervising the program until he retired on July 1, 1941, at the age of 70. He died five years later.

One of Yost's chief rivals was Amos Alonzo Stagg of the University of Chicago. Yost was not especially fond of Knute Rockne, the Notre Dame coach. When the University of California at Berkeley asked Yost's opinion of Rockne for a possible job, Yost wrote a letter that said in part: "Knute Rockne is a graduate of Notre Dame University but is a Protestant. My information is that he is interested only in competitive athletics. In my opinion, he would 'fret' under the administration and restrictions as exist in our Western Intercollegiate Conference Universities."

And now, in the list of football's legendary names Stagg, Rockne, Yost and Warner there is another, a modern one: Schembechler.

Chicago's Austin "Five Yards Per Carry" McCarthy bursts through the line for the Maroon at Stagg Field.

Chicago 21, Grange 21 in Memorable Thriller

BY ROBERT M. LEE
Chicago Sunday Tribune

Chicago, Ill.	November 8, 1924					
Illinois	0	14	7	0	—	21
Chicago	7	14	0	0	—	21

If all of the superlatives could be summoned together by some witches' trick and each encouraged to smite a gong extolling the grandeur of today's football game between Chicago and Illinois, wherein they strove to a tie of 21 to 21, even such a multiplicity of the utmost were doomed to fade idly in the human ear as a sound too frail and insufficient to express the emotions of the 32,000 and more at Stagg's Field.

Amos Alonzo Stagg's Chicago squad started quickly with Austin McCarty ripping through the Illini defense for 15 yards, then for another 15 yards. Harry Thomas burst through on two impressive runs. McCarty, who carried the ball on eight of the first dozen plays, led the Chicago advance that reached the Illinois 5-yard line. The only thing that stopped them was McCarty's fumble, which was recovered by Frank Rokusek.

When the Maroon got the ball again at the Illinois 28, McCarty continued as if nothing had happened. It took seven carries, and McCarty had the ball on six of those. He smashed over the center of the Illini line for a 1-yard touchdown. Robert Curley entered the game in place of William Abbott and drop-kicked the extra point for a 7-0 lead.

Before the Illinois kickoff, Stagg called McCarty to the sidelines and replaced him with Walter Marks.

After fielding the kick, Chicago started from its 20 and marched downfield with the trio running tandem of Marks, Harry Thomas and Graham Kernwein. Fourteen plays later, Kernwein pounded the middle of the line and the ball rested inches away from the Illinois goal line.

On the first play of the second quarter, Thomas crossed over left tackle for Chicago's second touchdown and the west stands were a riot of students. In the east stands, where the Illinois fans sat, there was silence.

The Maroons collected the extra point when Curley faked a drop kick and tossed a pass to Harrison Barnes in the end zone for a 14-0 lead.

It would take Illinois 10 plays to reach the Chicago goal line. On eight of these plays Harold (Red) Grange was either running around end or cutting inside the tackles, or passing. Two of the passes went for 31 yards. After a Grange pass for 16 yards to Charles Kassell that reached the Chicago 4, the Phantom sent tearing across the field to his left and charged forward to cross the goal line to cut Chicago's advantage to 14-6. Earl Britton's extra-point kick made it 14-7.

Following an Illini punt Thorpe Drain fielded it at the Chicago 25 and ran down the sidelines to reach midfield. Eight plays later, Thomas reached the Illinois 5-yard line. Eugene Francis, who replaced Marks, ran through a big gap in the Illinois defense for Chicago's third touchdown. Drain drop-kicked the extra-point to boost Chicago's lead to 21-7.

But Grange still wasn't finished.

Starting from the Illini 26, Grange for ran 14 and 12 yards to reach the Chicago 48. After gaining only one yard on the next two carries, Britton tossed a beautiful pass to Grange put the ball on the Chicago 25-yard line. After Grange picked up 8 yards on two plays, the Illini went into a kick formation and uncorked a double pass that put the ball on the Chicago 4-yard line.

It was pulled off when Britton dropped back as if to kick. Instead he passed to Kassell, who passed backward to Grange and he raced to the 4.

On the next play, Grange swung to his left and bolted toward the goal line for his second touchdown. Britton's extra-point kick made it 21-14.

In the third quarter, Grange picked up a Chicago punt at his 20, shot around the left end, down the sideline, and then back toward the center of the field and crossed the Maroon goal line to complete his 80-yard romp — and third touchdown of the game. Britton's kick evened the score at 21-21.

In the fourth quarter, Chicago drove to the Illini 17 on the strong running of Thomas and Francis, whose open-field run for 20 yards would have been a touchdown if Clarence Muhl had not pulled him down at the Illini 31. After a pair of short runs by Thomas and Francis, and a 5-yard gain by Philip Barto, Kernwein shot a pass across the middle that was intercepted by Kassell on the 10.

Neither team would get any closer to scoring.

Austin McCarthy, a senior halfback, scored the Maroon's first TD against Illinois.

Stagg: The Grand Old Man of the Midway

BY TIM COHANE

Amos Alonzo Stagg was the greatest innovator in the history of college football.

He entered Yale in the fall of 1884 and graduated in 1891. He was a star pitcher and led Yale to five straight championships. Six National League teams made him offers to pitch in the pros. The largest was from New York at $4,200 per year. But Stagg turned it down to hopefully become a preacher.

One sportswriter later described Stagg's reasoning: "So long as a pitcher gets $4,200 for six months and a preacher gets $600 for a year, there will be good pitching and bad preaching."

In 1888, Stagg joined the Yale football squad and played end. He was named an all-American in 1889.

After graduating from Yale, Stagg coached football, basketball and baseball at Springfield College for 2 seasons.

He then accepted an offer to coach at the newly-built, Rockefeller-financed University of Chicago in 1892 from Dr. William Rainey Harper, the school's new president and Stagg's former advisor at Yale.

During his 41-year tenure at Chicago, he coached the Maroons to seven Big Ten championships: 1896, 1899, 1905, 1907, 1908, 1913 and 1924. His 1905 and 1913 Maroons were named national champions.

Stagg is the first coach to ever use the pass. In a 1954 interview with The Associated Press, that was later recounted in Allison Danzig's football classic, *Oh How They Played the Game*, Stagg recounted the first use of the pass. He explained that in 1894 — 12 years before the forward pass was legalized — he instructed Frank Hering, who used to throw the football like a baseball pitcher, to make a long lateral pass to an end on certain plays when he received a kick. This was the season when Stagg's squad played a 15-game schedule, then traveled to the West Coast to play four more games.

"He was the first man I ever saw throw a football that way. The regular method was to curl the ball against the forearm and throw it out with a sidearm pass."

Two years later, in 1896, Hering became the first full-time

Amos Alonzo Stagg coached Chicago for 41 years. His teams won 7 Big Ten titles and 2 national championships.

coach at Notre Dame, putting together a record of 12-6-1 in three seasons.

In 1906, when the forward pass was legalized, Stagg installed 64 pass patterns. These new pass plays included a pass by a reversing wingback after a handoff, single- and double-flanker receivers, a guard eligible after a shift, a "sleeper" to the sidelines, and a fake pass and run. He didn't overlook much.

Stagg also invented the onside kick, the quick kick, the short punt formation, the fake kick, the huddle, putting numbers on the backs of jerseys, the numbering of plays, the hidden-ball play, practicing under lights (and a white football was used for greater visibility), padded goal posts, the lateral pass, man in motion, the Statue of Liberty play, blocking dummys, and the blocking sled. His 1891 team at Springfield College played the first indoor football game. It was played at Madison

Square Garden against a team of former Yale players.

Stagg was also instrumental in shaping the modern T formation. He had four distinct contributions to this long-standing style of playing the game: the stand-up quarterback lining up behind center; the split buck play, the man-in-motion and the quarterback keeper.

In 1930, when Rockne's teams were putting together back-to-back national championship seasons, he was asked where the famous Notre Dame shift came from. Rockne explained, "Where everything else in football came from."

He then added: "Yale."

But what Rockne should have added was that he had been taught the shift by his former coach at Notre Dame, Jesse Harper, who had learned it as a Chicago quarterback under Stagg. All Rockne introduced was the flexing of the end to get a blocking angle on the tackle.

Stagg's innovations, however, were not limited to football. While at Chicago, while coaching the Maroons basketball team in 1895, he was the first coach to play with five players on the court. This innovation would later get him inducted into the Basketball Hall of Fame.

As a baseball coach, he was the first one to develop a batting cage for his players.

In 1905, powerhouse Michigan invaded Chicago's Marshall Field with a 56-game undefeated streak that had begun in 1901. They were coached by Fielding Yost, whose teams were known as the "Point-a-Minute" Wolverines after scoring 2,821 points in 56 games. They had defeated Chicago the past four seasons by scores of 22-0, 21-0, 28-0 and 22-12.

At a track meet in the spring of 1905, Yost — a brilliant coach, who was also a nonstop talker and sometimes abrasive — got into an argument with Stagg and promised Chicago another beating in football that fall. "We'll give you plenty!" Yost warned, and six months later at five minutes before the 1:45 kickoff, Stagg told his players, "Don't let him cram this game down my throat."

The game was a defensive struggle, with plenty of punting by both teams.

After the first half, as his team retreated to their locker room, a lady member of the Chicago faculty gave him a message from President Harper. He was dying of cancer but was listening to the game on a special telephone hookup. His message was, "You must win for me."

Through a furious, sullen second half, the defensive and kicking struggle raged on. With time running out, Walter Eckersall punted from midfield, driving the ball low and hard behind a head wind into the end zone. Bill Clark tried to clear it for Michigan, but a pair of Chicago defenders, Mark Catlin and Art Badenoch, tackled him for a safety. It was the only points scored on the Wolverines all season, but the 2-0 victory was enough to give Chicago the Western Conference title and national championship.

Stagg's 1899 team won its second Western Conference championship with a record of 12-0-2.

Stagg watches the 1901 Chicago-Michigan game from the sidelines, which featured his new "Whoa Play."

There would be four more Big Ten championships, with a lag of eleven years between the last two. The 1921 and '22 teams missed the conference crown because of a seven-point loss the first year and a tie game the second.

In 1923, Illinois finished first in the conference with a 5-0 record, Chicago was second at 5-1. The Illini won their match with the Maroon, 7-0, on a 60-yard run by Harold (Red) Grange. That run gave Illinois the win and denied Chicago the Big Ten title.

In 1924, Chicago won the Big Ten with a conference record of 3 victories, 1 loss and 3 ties. The key was a 21-21 tie with Illinois.

The Illini invaded Stagg Field on November 8. Three weeks before, on October 18, at the dedication game of the Illini's new Memorial Stadium, Illinois ran over Michigan, 39-14. Or rather Grange had. He had run back the opening kickoff 95 yards for a touchdown, and broke three touchdown runs of 67, 56 and 44 yards — all in the first 12 minutes of the first quarter. In the second half, he ran 15 yards for a touchdown and passed 23 yards to Marion Leonard for a sixth TD.

Stagg had sent his former star end and young assistant, Herbert Orrin (Fritz) Crisler to scout the game. Crisler would later win coaching laurels of his own at Princeton and Michigan.

Stagg's strategy was to slow down Grange by not letting him have the ball. How do you do that? By controlling, by keeping possession, by moving it.

On this windy, snowy day against Grange and Illinois at Stagg Field, the Maroon back who would make the difference was Austin "Five Yards" McCarthy.

Five yards was his shortest gain as he hammered out 56 yards in six plays on the opening kickoff, behind a big, strong Chicago line. The drive was aborted when Illinois recovered a fumble on its 4-yard line, but after Earl Britton punted on first down, back came McCarthy, pounding out gains of five yards or more on a march of 49 yards for a touchdown and a 7-0 lead.

Unimpressed, Illinois kicked off again, and Chicago and McCarthy shook the Illini for a second touchdown to take a 14-0 lead. So far Stagg's plan had worked perfectly. It was well into the second quarter and Illinois had possession of the ball for only one play. Grange had yet to handle the ball.

Illinois opted to receive the ball this time. And Grange got the ball. In eight plays he gained 69 yards, scoring from the 4-yard line. On the next Illini possession, Grange gained 40 yards in 9 runs, mixed with two passes he caught for 44 yards. He scored from the 5.

But at halftime, Chicago led the contest, 21-14.

In the second half, Bob Zuppke, the Illinois coach, changed to a seven-man line and box defense that shut down McCarthy's five-yard advances. Grange would break loose on an 80-yard touchdown run to tie the game at 21-21 and had another 55-yard run called back for holding.

When it was over the score stood at Chicago 21, Grange 21 and the Maroon would win their seventh conference title. Grange, however, had still managed to run for 300 yards, passed for 177 and scored three touchdowns in the game.

After the 1932 season, Stagg was forced to retire at the age of 70.

His team had begun to decline beginning in 1929. His successor, Clark Shaughnessy, would guide the program for seven more years, but the once-powerful Maroons would become the breather on the schedule for Big Ten teams. Following the 1939 season, Chicago would drop football and would withdraw from the Big Ten in 1945.

In 1933, Stagg moved to the West Coast to take over coaching the University of the Pacific at the age of 71. During 14 years there, his record was 60 wins, 75 defeats and 7 ties. His best teams had a record of 7-3 in 1938 and 7-2 in 1943.

At the age of 84, he joined the staff at Susquehanna College to assist his son, Amos Alonzo Stagg Jr., who was the school's head football coach.

Stagg would finally retire at the age of 90, when he moved back to California. However, Stockton College gave him an honorary title of "kicking coach."

When he died in 1965, Stagg was 102 years old.

Chicago's new president, William Rainey Harper, hired Stagg in 1892 to build the athletic program at the Rockefeller-financed school.

Stagg's 1913 Maroon routed the Wisconsin Badgers, 19-0, en route to its second national championship.

Jay Berwanger accepts the All-America Captain's Cup from Christy Walsh and Mrs. Knute Rockne in 1935.

The Best Who Was the First

BY COOPER ROLLOW

If Grantland Rice had needed a fifth horseman to go along with the four members of the Notre Dame team Rice once canonized, the honor might well have gone to Jay Berwanger.

Jay who?

Jay Berwanger, the University of Chicago's incredible "one-man gang," who gained more than a mile from scrimmage before becoming the very first winner of the Heisman Memorial Trophy in 1935. How good was Berwanger? Rice, the legendary sportswriter, recalled hearing Berwanger's high school coach in Dubuque, Iowa, say, "If Berwanger isn't another Jim Thorpe, there'll never be one."

Rice went on to quote Red Grange, the Galloping Ghost of Illinois: "Back of a good line, Berwanger would still be running in every game he played."

Berwanger, a two-time all-America halfback for Chicago when the Maroons were still members of the esteemed Big Ten Conference, was recognized as the best football player not only in the Midwest, but also in the nation. However, the trophy he prized most the year he won the Heisman was the Silver Football presented to him by The Chicago Tribune as the Big Ten's most valuable player of 1935.

The bronze statue from New York was just one more accolade. It had not yet been named the Heisman when it was won by Berwanger. The original Heisman award was called The Downtown Athletic Club Trophy and was to be given to the best college football player at a school located east of the Mississippi River. The award was given only in 1935. The name of the trophy was changed the next fall after the death of John Heisman, the first athletic director of the DAC.

Berwanger, who was senior class president at Chicago's

prestigious south side university and was becoming accustomed to hearing his athletic exploits extolled, recalled that he wasn't overly thrilled when he returned to the Psi Upsilon fraternity house on a blustery November day in 1935 and found a telegram telling him of his latest honor.

"It said I had won some trophy," Berwanger said, "and that there would be two tickets to take a guest and me to New York. It didn't seem like a real big deal. No one at school said anything much to me about it. I was more excited about the trip than the trophy because it was my first flight."

Berwanger selected his coach, Clark Shaughnessy, as his guest on the trip to New York. Berwanger learned nearly as much about the eastern metropolis as he had learned about football from Shaughnessy, one of the game's great innovators and strategists. The two took toured the city, watched a performance of the Rockettes and had lunch at the 21 Club.

Still, the occasion was little more than a sightseeing trip to Berwanger. The trophy from New York meant little to him until another dozen or so years, when Heisman winners began cashing in on the award when negotiating rich professional football contracts.

"I never dreamed the Heisman would ever be so important," Berwanger explained during lunch at his golf club in Hinsdale, Ill. "When television came on the scene and college football began getting exposure, it became a big deal that I won the first one."

"The difference between winning the first Heisman in 1935 and winning it now is like the difference between nothing and a million dollars. For 20 years, I had no requests for autographed pictures. Then, after World War II, I started getting 10 or 12 letters a week. I have a good supply of pictures. I autograph them and send them out myself."

Berwanger's trophy disappeared, to all intents and purposes, for nearly a decade after he received it. The huge bronze statue, which weighed 25 pounds but felt like 50, became a nuisance for Berwanger to lug around the Chicago campus and he couldn't find a convenient storage space at the fraternity house. So he asked his Aunt Gussie to keep it for him until after graduation.

Aunt Guusie's coffee table wasn't big enough and her mantle wasn't wide enough to accommodate the monster trophy. She finally found a use for it, and for nearly 10 years the trophy served as Aunt Gussie's doorstop, providing her house off Lake Michigan with cool breezes. It also became a convenient floor-level hat rack for Berwanger and other quests.

Berwanger was 6-foot-1 and 195 pounds as a triple threater leading the Maroons to an 11-11-2 record in three varsity campaigns. During his Heisman season of 1935, he rushed for 577 yards on 119 carries and completed 25 of 67 passes for 405 yards.

A true all-around performer, Berwanger did the Maroons' punting and kicking, scored six touchdowns, caught two passes, intercepted four, and returned punts and kickoffs.

"Shaughnessy was wonderful for me," Berwanger said. "He was able to see my potential. We had eight or nine offensive formations, mostly running, which was my strongest suit.

"I loved defense," Berwanger added. "People were hitting me, and playing defense gave me a chance to hit them back."

Berwanger weighed only 150 pounds when he made his first touchdown for Dubuque High School in 1929. "I just caught the ball from center, looked for a hole in the line, closed my eyes and ran," he recalled. "I carried the ball from center, looked for a hole in the line, closed my eyes and ran," he recalled. "I carried the ball three times with my eyes shut, I was so scarred. Then someone yelled, 'Okay, Jay, you're over.' "

Even though handicapped by the weakest team in the Big Ten, Berwanger racked up a career yardage total of 1,839 yards — an average of 4.19 per rush. He also completed 51 passes for 926 yards and scored 22 TD's.

Small wonder that Amos Alonzo Stagg, whose coaching career spanned 40 years at Chicago, said upon turning the team over to Shaughnessy before Berwanger's sophomore year, "My greatest regret at leaving the Midway for a California post is that I won't have the chance to handle Berwanger. Jay is a complete player."

Berwanger hardly dared leave the field. The Maroons had virtually no chance to win without their "one-man gang." And the Chicago football program, history shows, had virtually no chance of surviving without the brilliant halfback. To borrow a popular pro football expression, Berwanger was Chicago's "franchise player." Four years after he played his last game, during which Chicago won only one Big Ten contest, the school dropped football.

When Berwanger learned that his alma mater was considering canceling its Big Ten varsity program in 1939, he protested vigorously. At the University of Chicago, academics came first and football second — a distant second.

No other Big Ten school, not even Northwestern, emphasized academics over athletics so heavily. The Maroons were lucky to enroll 20 football candidates a year while opponents were successfully recruiting 50 or 60. During Berwanger's era, the Maroons' game plan was simple: If Berwanger could keep the game close, maybe Berwanger could win it.

The university president at the time, Robert M. Hutchins, said the school had several choices. "We could buy a team," he said, "but the Chicago Bears were not for sale. We could

Jay Berwanger won the first Heisman Memorial Trophy in 1935.

Berwanger reversed his field three times, eluded 10 Buckeyes, just missed going out of bounds on either sideline, stopped dead twice so that his interference could form, and finally picked up a blocking convoy to the end zone.

Despite Berwanger's artistry, Ohio State went on to win. But the free-wheeling halfback, showing Heisman form without knowing of the existence of the trophy series he was soon to inaugurate, beat Illinois in his college finale, returning a punt 50 yards to the 1-yard line, diving over for a touchdown and kicking the extra point in a 7-6 Chicago victory.

Berwanger launched not only the Heisman, but also the National Football League draft. He was the first player ever drafted by the NFL, and one of the few ever to outwit the Chicago Bears' venerable, tight-fisted owner-coach, George Halas.

The Philadelphia Eagles drafted Berwanger in 1936, but Halas obtained signing rights to him. Papa Bear accosted Berwanger at The Palmer House in Chicago soon after and politely asked the Chicago star, "How much money would you like to play for the Bears, Jay?"

Berwanger, who had no interest in pro ball and had already mapped out a business future in manufacturing that was to make him a millionaire, replied, "Twenty-five thousand dollars over two years."

"We'll see you around, Jay," said Halas, whose highest-paid Bear, Bronko Nagurski, was making $7,000 a year and being paid in i.o.u.'s.

"I gave him a figure I knew he wouldn't agree to," Berwanger said, "I've never regretted the decision. The depression was on, and I didn't think I could get a "good job" while playing pro football."

"Halas held no grudge against me. We became friends in later years. He left $25,000 in his will to the University of Chicago for athletic facilities."

Berwanger's "good job" with a sponge rubber company paid $25 a week. After serving in the Navy Air Force during World War II, he started his own manufacturing business, selling molded rubber and plastics.

"My strengths were speed and elusiveness," Berwanger said. "A fullback is a brave man. He likes to run over people. A halfback, by nature has to be a coward. He runs away from others. I had a 9.9 speed in the 100-yard dash, so I ran away. "

No opponent who ever faced Berwanger considered him a coward. That would have been still another first.

drop down a level, or we can drop football altogether."

Hutchins listened to both sides, then made a decision. The Maroons would drop big-time football entirely.

Berwanger's first year of varsity football was stunning. He played every minute of every Big Ten game.

In the eight games of the 1933 season, he scored eight times and kicked seven extra points. He rushed for 667 yards, did half of Chicago's passing, backed up the line on defense, and punted. The team went 3-3-2 and Berwanger was named to the All-Big Ten team.

His finest moments in football came in his senior year. Berwanger nearly beat Ohio State himself.

He scored both touchdowns to give the Maroons a 13-0 lead early in the second half. On one TD, an 85-yard dazzler,

Berwanger's Heroics Beat Illinois in Thriller to Rap Up Banner Career

By Harvey Woodruff
Chicago Sunday Tribune

Champaign, Ill. | November 23, 1935

Chicago	0	0	0	7	—	7
Illinois	0	6	0	0	—	6

As the timekeeper's gun barked the finish of the fortieth Illinois-Chicago football game at Memorial Stadium this afternoon, Jay Berwanger was hoisted to the shoulders of admirers and carried from the scene of his last collegiate appearance to the Maroon dressing room as Chicago celebrated its 7-6 victory over the Illini.

It was a fitting finale to the career of the sensational senior who matriculated to Chicago from Dubuque High School nearly 4 years ago and has been the bulwark of Midway football hopes since his sophomore year.

With defeat impending, 6-0, Berwanger late in the third quarter received a punt from Les Lindberg at midfield and shook off five Illinois tacklers along the route of a 49-yard run to Illinois' 1-yard line, where he went to his knees as the result of Ken Nelson's final dive.

Then, Berwanger, who also calls the signals, generously elected to give Warren Skoning, who had made short, sure gains through the opposing line all afternoon, the ball for the touchdown dive. Twice Skoning dived into a pack of desperately charging Illini, but the goal line was still a football away. On third down, Berwanger vaulted high over the line and rolled into the end zone for the tying touchdown.

Now came the important point after touchdown. With Omar Fareed holding the ball, Berwanger booted the extra-point kick. It sailed straight and true over the bar for the point that spelled Chicago's victory. Even the majority of Illini rooters among the 12,000 fans present did not begrudge the Chicago leader his hour of triumph in his final appearance.

Berwanger entered the game lacking 33 yards short of a mile of ball-toting while wearing the Maroon of Chicago. Within 9 minutes after the opening kickoff, he reached this magical figure. He finished the afternoon with 101 yards rushing on 26 carries.

The Chicago squad overpowered Illinois, with 192 yards total rushing as compared to Illinois' 23. The Maroon also led the game in first downs, 11 to 3.

Ewald Nyquist, who was also playing his final game, intercepted 3 Illini passes in the fourth quarter.

It was Lindberg, the Illinois star player, who booted a beautiful, booming 72-yard punt that feel dead on the Chicago 3-yard line, who put the Maroons in the hole and paved the way for the Illinois touchdown in the second quarter. The Maroons did not get back into Illini territory during the remainder of the first half.

Following a Maroon punt, Illinois had the ball on the Chicago 30. There were about two minutes left in the second quarter. Twice the Maroon defense knocked down a pair of Lindberg passes. On third down, Lindberg passed to little Bobby Grieve, the track sprinter from Lombard, Ill., who scooted past the Maroon secondary and hauled in the pass at the Chicago 10-yard line, then ran the final 10 yards for a touchdown and a 6-0 lead. Lindberg's extra-point kick was low and wide.

Shortly after the Illini touchdown, the Maroon attempted to get a scoring match started with a pass from Berwanger to Bill Gillerlain. But it was intercepted by Ken Nelson, who sped downfield 25 yards and dived for the goal line marker on the sideline. The ball then fell from his grasp and landed in the end zone, where it was recovered by a Chicago player.

After a conference of officials, it was ruled that Nelson went out of bounds at the Chicago 1-yard line, but the ball had fallen from his arms before he left the field of play and that Chicago's recovery of the loose ball made it a touchback.

The Maroon would reach the Illini 26 later in the second quarter. Early in the third quarter, they drove to the Illinois 22-yard line.

Then came Lindberg's booming 72-yard punt which set up the game's climax.

Northwestern Ends No. 1 Minnesota's Reign

BY WILFRID SMITH
Chicago Tribune

Evanston, Ill.	October 31, 1936						
Minnesota	0	0	0	0	—	0
Northwestern	0	0	0	6	—	6

The four-year reign of No. 1-ranked Minnesota's mighty men ended on the muddy, rain-swept gridiron of Dyche Stadium today as a band of fighting Wildcats presented Northwestern's greatest homecoming throng with a stirring 6 to 0 victory.

By one touchdown, a short, smashing drive by Steve Toth on the second play of the fourth quarter of this bitter struggle, the Wildcats raised their Purple flag to the top of the Western Conference rankings.

That touchdown, produced by an alert team which capitalized on a fumble and subsequent penalty on Minnesota for roughness, ended the Gophers' string of 21 consecutive victories.

It was Minnesota's first defeat since Harry Newman of Michigan kicked a field goal in 1932 for a 3-0 win that gave the Wolverines their last Big Ten title.

The greatest crowd to jam its way into Dyche Stadium since 1930 — a paid attendance of 48,347 — saw the end of the Minnesota era. Thousands of these came from the Twin Cities to cheer for the Gophers.

Tonight Northwestern students paraded through Evanston in honor of their heroes.

The intangible factor — team spirit — was the basis of Northwestern's bid for victory. The Wildcats, outrushed from scrimmage, refused to yield and Minnesota's longest gains could not be linked together to carry the Gophers to the Wildcats' goal line.

Fighting fiercely on defense, and watching the ball every minute in anticipation of the dreaded Minnesota laterals, Northwestern broke up the Gophers' desperate last quarter rallies. Twice after Minnesota's fatal fumble the Wildcats followed Gopher laterals and recovered the ball.

Weather conditions probably were a handicap to Minnesota, whose backs prefer a fast field.

Northwestern had its first opportunity to score near the end of the third quarter. Don Heap's 8-yard run around the Gophers' left end on a reverse reached the Minnesota 20-yard line. It was the Wildcats' longest run of the game.

The burly Gophers held and three thrusts netted Northwestern only seven yards. Then Don Geyer, whose place kicks had whipped Ohio State, went back to the 20-yard line and, with Heap holding, tried to boot a field goal that could make the difference in victory. But the ball shot to the right and the score remained 0-0.

Andy Uram, the Gophers' fleetest back, failed to pick up yardage, then Minnesota was penalized five yards for delay in the huddle. Jules Alfonse smashed into the line and as he hit an immovable Northwestern defensive wall, the wet ball slipped from his grasp. Dewitt Gibson, the Wildcats' tackle, fell on it at Minnesota's 13-yard line.

On the first play, Heap fumbled and recovered the loose ball, losing two yards. Then Geyer punctured the line for two yards, and after he was stopped, Ed Widdseth, the Minnesota left defensive tackle, was penalized for roughness. The referee moved the ball to the Gophers' 1-yard line.

Geyer cracked through for one-half yard. It was the last play of the third quarter.

As the teams plodded their way to the south goal, Toth replaced Geyer in the backfield. On the next play, Toth moved the ball to within inches of the Minnesota goal line. On third down, Toth took the ball and smashed behind Mike Calvano, Bob Voights and John Zitko. He then slid outside the Gophers' defensive left tackle, eluded a pair of Gophers and sprawled face down over the goal line. Toth's extra-point kick was blocked.

Three times in the remaining 14 minutes the Gophers would hammer into Northwestern territory, reaching the Northwestern 39, 17 and 37 — each time the Wildcats' defense stiffened.

Minnesota's deepest advance into Northwestern territory was in the first quarter, when the Gophers' reached the Wilcats'15-yard line.

Minnesota had a 9 to 7 lead in first downs and in total yardage, 248 to 148.

Northwestern 6	Illinois - - - 9	Indiana - 13	Temple - - - 3
Minnesota - - 0	Michigan - 6	Iowa - - - 6	Holy Cross - 0
Notre Dame - 7	Chicago - - 7	Purdue - 7	Fordham - 0
Ohio State - - 2	Wisconsin - 6	Carnegie - 6	Pitt - - - - 0

Chicago Sunday
Herald and Examiner Sports

BUSINESS AND MARKETS

PART TWO

SUNDAY, NOVEMBER 1, 1936   ★★★★

NORTHWESTERN WINS!

THE GUN SOUNDS! THE GAME IS OVER! AND 48,307 PURPLE FANS AND TEAM GO INTO A FRENZY. TUG WILSON IS ON EXTREME LEFT; COACH WALDORF CENTER IN RAINCOAT.

MAROONS BEAT BADGERS FOR FIRST WIN, 7 TO 6

Bill Gillerlain's Point Kick Provides Chicago Margin; Skoning, Bellin Score.

By Geo. Morgenstern.

MADISON, Wis., Oct. 31—One point stood between Chicago and Wisconsin today, and the point—and the victory were Chicago's.

Coming to life surprisingly, after three disappointing games, the Maroons got into the Big Ten winning list with a 7 to 6 victory over the Badgers before a homecoming crowd of 18,000 that sat through a steady downpour in Camp Randall Stadium.

The Maroons scored in the first four minutes, twice again were within a few yards of other scores, and topped off their comeback with a 75-yard march in the final minutes that chilled Wisconsin's chance of stealing the ball game from the fire.

MUFF TWO CHANCES.

Wisconsin had two fourth quarter chances and made good on one of them after a fumble on the Maroon 13-yard line had given them their opening. But, on the decisive try that meant the difference between winning and losing, Wisconsin just didn't have it.

The point that put Chicago over was constituted by Bill Gillerlain, while Ed Christianson missed on what he had the chance of equalizing matters with his try after

Turn to Page 4, Column 2.

Irish Humble Ohio Again Despite Bad Breaks, 7-2

55,000 Watch McCormick Score

By Warren Brown.

SOUTH BEND, Ind., Oct. 31.— Football history almost repeated itself—with reverse English—a Notre Dame eked out a 7 to 2 victory over Ohio State before a rain-swept Stadium jammed by 55,000 here today.

It was distinctly a "battle of the breaks," that all the Wolverines rolling up thirteen first downs to the winners' two, and outgaining them in yardage, 244 to 52.

The alert Illini stunned a homecoming crowd of 35,000 by striking twice in the second period, with a field goal and a touchdown, after stopping a 56-yard Michigan march nine yards short of the goal in the opening period. The field goal resulted from a

Turn to Page 2, Column 6.

Battle of Breaks as—
ILLINI OVERCOME WOLVERINES, 9-6

ANN ARBOR, Mich., Oct. 31.—(A.P.)—A wily band of fighting Illini from the University of Illinois ambushed the University of Michigan Wolverines along football's comeback trail today and won their first Western Conference game of the season, 9 to 6.

It was distinctly a "battle of the breaks," that all the Wolverines rolling up thirteen first downs to the winners' two, and outgaining them in yardage, 244 to 52.

The alert Illini stunned a homecoming crowd of 35,000 by striking twice in the second period, with a field goal and a touchdown, after stopping a 56-yard Michigan march nine yards short of the goal in the opening period. The field goal resulted from a

Turn to Page 2, Column 6.

GOES OVER FOR IRISH!

BUNNY M'CORMICK—Halfback ace saves day for Irish!

BIG TEN STANDING

	W.	L.	T.	Pct.	Pts.	OP
Northwestern	4	0	0	1.000	51	3
Minnesota	3	1	0	.667	50	6
Indiana	2	1	0	.667	27	19
Ohio State	2	1	0	.667	72	14
Chicago	1	2	0	.333	14	41
Illinois	1	2	0	.333	21	31
Purdue	1	2	0	.333	13	31
Iowa	1	2	0	.333	13	33
Wisconsin	1	3	0	.250	12	39
Michigan	0	2	0	.000	6	43

SATURDAY GAMES.
Wisconsin at Northwestern.
Iowa at Minnesota.
Chicago at Ohio State.
Michigan at Pennsylvania.
Syracuse at Indiana.
Purdue at Fordham.

GOBLINS FROM INDIANA 'SCARE' IOWANS, 13 TO 6

Oze as Wicked Witch Frightens Hoosiers, but They Win at Halloween Party.

By Wayne K. Otto.

BLOOMINGTON, Ind., Oct. 31. —Bo McMillan's football goblin from Indiana put on a Halloween party this afternoon before a homecoming crowd of 15,000 celebrants by subduing Iowa, 13 to 6, but only after a very spirited exhibition.

With Oze Simmons, the ebony flash of the Corn Staters, appearing in the wicked witch role, Bo's boys had many a nervous moment chiefly because Oze threatened to wreck them and off all afternoon. Twice Simmons got away with runs of 40 yards, or slightly more to open attacks that the Hoosiers had to stave off on their 3-yard line.

OZE THREATENS AGAIN.

In the final period Oze returned a punt 40 yards but the charge went to pieces again on Indiana's 3-yard line when Osmaloski made a bad pass that Oze had to drop on back at the 23-yard stripe. However, Simmons passed to H. Harris and the game ended for Iowa's only score.

Indiana's first touchdown came in the second quarter when Roy Eads intercepted a pass from Frank Balazs and galloped 35 yards to the Iowa goal. The second touchdown was scored by George Fowler who plunged over in the third period to climax a smart and well directed aerial attack by Indiana's triple-threat star, Vernon Huffman.

Iowa provided the first bit of action during the afternoon and Oze Simmons was the principal in the show. Oze intercepted one of Huffman's passes and sped back 41 yards to Simmons who was pushed out of bounds on the Hoosiers' 6-yard

DEFENSE STIFFENS.

Here Indiana's defense stiffened but on fourth down Hid lateralled to Simmons who was pushed out of bounds on the Hoosiers' 6-yard

Turn to Page 2, Column 7.

Gopher Victory String Ends
Toth Wins for Purple, 6-

STEVE TOTH—His touchdown whips Gophers.

In the Dressing Room—
Wildcats Celebrate Great Victory

By Edgar Munzel.

We have witnessed clubhouse victory celebrations over a period of ten years in baseball world series and every other sport, but there was none that ever surpassed the bedlam of enthusiasm that hit the dressing room of the Northwestern University football team after yesterday's triumph over Minnesota at Dyche Stadium.

Faces smeared with mud, the Wildcats stormed into the dressing room like a pack of wild maniacs. If there was hysteria among the fans in the stands, who stood up to a man in the west section to thunder their ovation as the new conquerors of the gridiron world trotted off the field, these boys who trailed the victory were completely berserk.

WILD SCENE.

They threw their headgears at each other, scrambled over locks, slapped one another on the back and whooped and hollered in a deafening discord that nevertheless was sweet music to all the coaches and those lucky enough to gain admittance to the room.

In a world series the players

Turn to Page 3, Column

Vanzo Calls Real Hero of Game

By Harry MacNamara

Northwestern beat Minnesota yesterday! And as long as love history will be dated that rainy, murky last day of October, 1936, whenever and wherever football lore is discussed.

Northwestern won, 6 to 0, the score didn't matter much—the capacity gathering of 48,000 jammed into the limited confines of Dyche Stadium, Evanston.

They came harboring faint suspicions that this Wildcat team coached by Lynn Waldorf, might achieve the impossible—beat mighty Golden Gophers. However, their suspicions were fathered purely by the hope that is posed to spring eternal in human breast.

SUFFER NOT IN VAIN.

They sat there through a raging rain and suffered silently exposure as the battle was raging down there in the mud, but saw what they came to see—the fall of a mighty champion. They saw Northwestern's valiant and inspired Wildcats win, and that's all that mattered.

The Wildcats won this game, a dramatic, fiercely tested combat, right after the

Turn to Page 3, Column

Red Raiders Snap Army String, 14-7

WEST POINT, N. Y., Oct. 31.— (A.P.)—Colgate, badly beaten in the first half, came from behind with a great display of its football hocus-pocus today to topple Army from the ranks of the undefeated with an unexpected 14 to 7 victory.

—Vote American—

Navy Defeated by Pennsylvania, 16-6

PHILADELPHIA, Oct. 31.—(A.P.)—Off to a quick lead through the first-period touchdown and field goal, Penn's rugged Quakers scored their first victory in four years over Navy today, defeating the Midshipmen 16 to 6.

In a world series the players

Turn to Page 2, Column 2.

The Herald and Examiner's headline says it all: The Wildcats' win over Minnesota was their biggest in the school's history.

Nile Kinnick addresses the Downtown Athletic Club of New York City after accepting the Heisman Trophy in 1939.

A Hero Beyond the Field

BY RICK WARNER

John Greenleaf Whittier, the noted American writer of the 1800's once wrote: "Of all sad words of tongue and pen, the saddest are these: 'It might have been!'" Nile Clarke Kinnick Jr. lived only 24 years, but he was already a legend when he died.

Kinnick was a modern-day Renaissance man, an exceptional student-athlete who loved poetry and politics as much as football. In 1939, Iowa's "Cornbelt Comet" won The Heisman Memorial Trophy and was named the Male Athlete of the Year by The Associated Press, beating out Joe DiMaggio and Joe Louis. But Kinnick, the grandson of a former Iowa governor, had ambitions that went far beyond sports.

World War II, however, ended those plans. When the Navy fighter pilot was lost at sea in 1943, the nation may have lost a future senator, Supreme Court justice, or — as some predicted at the time — a president. "There is no calculating what he might have done ...," said Wiley Rutledge, an Iowan who was a U.S. Supreme Court justice in the 1940's.

Kinnick was president of his senior class at Iowa and graduated with honors as a Phi Beta Kappa. He turned down a lucrative offer to play pro football in order to attend law school at Iowa, but with war looming in 1941, he joined the Navy and was called to active duty three days before the Japanese attacked Pearl Harbor.

"Every man whom I've admired in history has willingly and courageously served in his country's armed forces in time of danger," Kinnick wrote in his dairy. "It was not only a duty but an honor to follow their example as best I know how."

"May God give me the courage and ability to so conduct myself in every situation that my country, my family and my friends will be proud of me."

Family, friends and teammates always took pride in Kinnick's accomplishments, which included playing almost every minute of the 1939 season until he was hurt in the final game. Though they were usually undermanned, undersized and underdogs, Kinnick and his fellow "Ironmen" went 6-1 that year, including an upset of mighty Notre Dame.

"He was the most disciplined young man I have ever met in my life," said Al Couppee, the quarterback of the 1939 squad. "Nile knew exactly what he wanted and how he wanted to get there ... His dedication was to be the best he possibly could be. Nile was the only person I ever saw in my life who was trying to do that every day and every minute."

Kinnick and his two younger brothers grew up on a farm in Adel, Iowa. Although he was small for his age, Kinnick developed into an all-around sports star and once played on the same Junior Legion baseball team with future Hall of Famer Bob Feller, who was from nearby Van Meter.

During the Depression, the family was forced to leave the farm and move to Omaha, Neb., where Kinnick's father got a job with the Federal Land Bank. At Benson High, Kinnick was an 'A' student and made all-state in football and basketball.

Kinnick's father, Nile Sr., played football at Iowa State, but Nile Jr. decided to attend the University of Iowa, which at the time was a doormat team in the Big Ten. The Hawkeyes continued to struggle in Kinnick's first two seasons, winning a total of two games, but it wasn't his fault. A triple threat as a runner, passer and kicker, he was All-Big Ten as a sophomore and played most of his junior year on a severely injured ankle. Still, Kinnick blamed himself for the Hawkeyes' problems, telling his parents in a letter: "Your son should have stuck to ping-pong and parlor games."

The Hawkeyes' fortunes began to change when Coach Irl Tubbs was replaced by Dr. Eddie Anderson after the 1938 season. Anderson, an Iowa native, played under Knute Rockne at Notre Dame and then went to medical school while playing pro football for the Chicago Cardinals. He came to

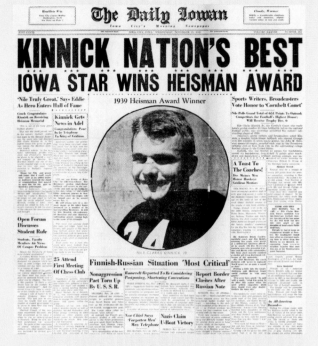

Kinnick won three of college football's top prizes: the Heisman, Maxwell and the Big Ten's Silver Football.

Iowa from Holy Cross, where his teams had gone 47-7-4 during the previous six seasons.

Anderson was a demanding coach who put his teams through intense physical training. "He's the only physician I've ever known who thought the cure for everything from a hangnail to appendicitis was 'running it off,' " said George (Red) Fyre, a center and linebacker on his 1939 team.

Kinnick was Anderson's kind of player. Despite his small stature (5-foot-8, 170 pounds), Kinnick was one of the strongest men on the team. "Tough as an iron post," Anderson said. "Slap him in the stomach and he'll break your wrist."

Kinnick displayed his toughness — and versatility — as Iowa opened the season with a 41-0 rout of South Dakota. He ran for three touchdowns, including a 65-yard dash, passed for two more and drop-kicked five conversion points.

He was spectacular again the following week in a seesaw 32-29 victory over Indiana — Iowa's first win over the Hoosiers in 18 years. Kinnick tossed three TD passes, ran for another, set a school record by returning nine punts for 201 yards and had 171 yards in kickoff returns.

Iowa lost its next game, 27-7, to Michigan and Tom Harmon, who would win The Heisman Memorial Trophy the following year. Iowa's only score came on a 71-yard touchdown pass from Kinnick to Floyd (Buzz) Dean. "Kinnick was as tough a competitor as any man I played against," Harmon said. "I don't care how bad you had Kinnick down, he came back at you."

After beating Wisconsin and Purdue, the Hawkeyes shocked undefeated, No. 3-ranked Notre Dame, 7-6, in Iowa City. Once again, Kinnick was the hero, running over two tacklers to score Iowa's only touchdown just before halftime. Notre Dame scored in the fourth quarter but missed the extra point, and Iowa held on for the huge upset.

Next up was mighty Minnesota. The Golden Gophers led, 9-0, in the fourth quarter before Kinnick rallied the Hawkeyes with two touchdown passes — a 45-yarder to Erwin Prasse and a 28-yarder to Bill Green with three minutes left. Kinnick clinched the 13-9 victory with an interception in the closing seconds and was carried off the field by joyous fans in his final home game.

"There's a golden helmet rising on a human sea across Iowa's football field in the twilight here," wrote James S. Kearns of The Chicago Daily News. "Now the helmet rises as wave upon wave of humanity pours onto the field. There's a boy under the helmet, which is shining like a crown upon his head. A golden No. 24 gleams on his slumping, tired shoulders.

"The boy is Nile Clark Kinnick Jr., who has, just now, risen above all the defenses that could be raised against him ... Here was Kinnick at the peak of his great career, leading a frenzied little band of Iowa football players to a victory which was impossible. They couldn't win, but they did."

Kinnick had played every minute of his last six games. The streak was stopped in the season finale against Northwestern when he injured his shoulder. The game ended in a 7-7 tie that cost Iowa the Big Ten championship, but it didn't dim the enthusiasm for the school's best team in 15 years.

"We couldn't go anywhere without people cheering us," Couppee said. "They even stopped movies to turn on the lights and cheer us. We were forever the Ironmen."

The biggest cheers were for Kinnick, who set 14 school records and was involved in 107 of the 130 points Iowa scored that season. Along with his offensive contributions, Kinnick led the team with eight interceptions.

So it was no surprise when Kinnick swept all of the major postseason awards, including The Heisman Memorial Trophy. In his memorable acceptance speech, Kinnick alluded to the war that would eventually take his life. "I thank God that I was born to the gridirons of the Middle West and not to the battlefields of Europe," he said. "I can say confidently and positively that the football players of this country would rather fight for the Heisman than foe the Croix de Guerre."

Kinnick played one more football game, throwing two touchdown passes for the College All-Stars in a 45-28 loss to the NFL champion Green Bay Packers on Aug. 29, 1940. He turned down a $10,000 offer from the NFL's Brooklyn Dodgers so he could study law and pursue other interests, including politics. That fall, he introduced Republican presidential candidate Wendell Wilkie at a rally in Iowa Falls. During the speech, many people in the crowd chanted, "We Want Kinnick!"

But a possible law and political career was interrupted by World War II.

On June 2, 1943, Kinnick took off on a training flight from the U.S.S. Lexington in the Caribbean Sea. The plane started to leak oil, and Kinnick was forced to make a water landing four miles from the ship. Ensign Bill Reiter, who was flying next to Kinnick's plane, said he saw Nile in the water. Although no one is sure what happened, there was speculation that Kinnick drowned after being knocked unconscious during the landing.

Kinnick's brother, Ben — a Marine pilot — was killed 15 months later when he was shot down over the Pacific.

More than sixty years after his death, Nile Kinnick remains a hero in his home state. Iowa's football stadium now bears his name and a statue of the Hawkeye star stand outfront. A park in his hometown of Adel is also named for Kinnick. His face is on the coin tossed by officials at the start of every Big Ten game.

"There was just an aura about him," Couppee said. "He didn't try to create it, it was just there. You really had the feeling you were in the presence of someone very special."

Iowa halfback Nile Kinnick (24) scores on a 4-yard touchdown run against Notre Dame in 1939.

The Game Breaker

BY ANDREW THOMAS AND ROBERT McG. THOMAS JR.

The date and place was Dec. 9, 1941, New York City. A young man climbs the steps of The Downtown Athletic Club. Inside, more than 900 people wait to pay tribute to him as the nation's outstanding college football player. Tonight, though, Bruce Smith has more than football on his mind. So do the 900 who have come to honor him.

In football, Smith's ears were used to the roar of the crowd. This evening they are still ringing from air-raid warnings, prompted by the bombing of Pearl Harbor two days earlier.

Yet a father still finds time to be proud this night, just as thousands of fathers would be made proud by sons defending their country in the years to come. For just as the nation has a score to settle, Smith had settled a score for his father well before the first Japanese bombs rained down on the U.S.S. Arizona and the other American ships which were caught by surprise.

As memories begin to fade back to another time and place, suddenly it is Nov. 19, 1910, in Ann Arbor, Mich. A young man is glaring across the line of scrimmage. He is wearing a University of Minnesota uniform. Those across the line wear the colors of the University of Michigan. Lucius Smith is angry, and he is frustrated, for he has seen an uncanny tide of misfortune befall his Golden Gophers on this day.

Indeed, such is the Michigan Wolverines' bizarre windfall and the Gophers' anguish, that rules will be changed drastically the next year. This, however, will be little solace to the gritty defensive lineman whose anger turns to disgust when he cannot make a tackle on Michigan's winning touchdown play.

Defeat is bitter. Especially at the hands of your arch rival. Especially when it is the last time you and they will go toe to toe. You dream of one last shot, but it can never be — unless the torch is passed.

Time and those memories then move fast forward. It is now Nov. 11, 1939, in Ann Arbor, Mich. A young man wearing No. 54 on his University of Minnesota jersey races up and down the field in such a dazzling display of raw ability that his Golden Gophers upset the mighty Wolverines, 20-7.

It is sophomore tailback Bruce Smith's first year on the varsity. He will be named honorable mention all-America by season's end. His father's revenge has only just begun.

Now, however, as the young man they call the Game Breaker prepares to receive the 1941 Heisman Trophy, few are speaking of the tailback or his incredible heroics between the goal posts. This is fine with Smith, the Faribault, Minn., native, who has out-pointed his nearest competition for the award in the same fashion he carries himself off the field — modestly. Smith had topped Angelo Bertelli, Notre Dame's sophomore quarterback, 554-345, in the closest Heisman vote to date.

True to form, Smith gives most of the credit to his teammates and to his coach, Bernie Bierman, when everyone at the ceremony knows that without No. 54, the Golden Gophers wouldn't have come close to their awesome back-to-back undefeated, untied seasons or their back-to-back national championships. While Smith knew when to be humble, he certainly knew when to shine.

Like the time his junior year when he ran wild through a tough Ohio State defense, racking up 139 yards and scoring both touchdowns in a 13-7 Minnesota victory. Or the day his senior season when he watched the first quarter of the Iowa game from the sideline due to an injury. The Gophers couldn't even get a first down. In the second quarter, Smith limped onto the field. He touched the ball only seven times the rest of the day, accounting for every Gophers touchdown by running or passing in a 34-13 victory.

Although game-breaking displays like those are the reason for the gathering at The Downtown Athletic Club, much of the talk this night is understandably on the United States' entry into World War II. In fact, the speeches are cut short so that those in attendance can listen to President Franklin D. Roosevelt's radio address from the White House.

Too bad Roosevelt couldn't have heard Smith's address.

"Those Far Eastern fellows," he begins, "may think that American boys are soft, but I have had, and even now have, plenty of evidence in black and blue to show that they are making a big mistake. I think that America will owe a great debt to the game of football when we finish this thing off. It keeps millions of American youngsters like myself hard and able to take it and come back for more."

Bruce Philip Smith was built to take it. A high school standout in football, basketball and golf, it seemed only fitting that the 6-foot, 200-pound athlete with the blond hair and blue eyes and rugged good looks chose to pursue football in college. His play in the Minnesota backfield dazzled fans from 1939 to 1941.

Bruce Smith led the Golden Gophers to a 16-0 record in 1940 and 1941 and a pair of national championships. In 1941, he earned all-America honors and won the Heisman Trophy.

Although to look at him, one would assume his style of running would be to blast right through defenders, Smith was more a finesse runner, able to cut sharply in an instant and leave the opposition grasping at air. He did not have blinding speed, yet he fully utilized any interference, instinctively knowing where his blockers were. As a tailback in Bierman's single-wing attack, Smith also had to be adept at passing, kicking and receiving. It didn't take long for Bierman to praise Smith as the "greatest halfback I've ever seen play."

For all of the big plays in his college career, the exclamation point came in Smith's junior year against Michigan. Could a father ask for more?

In 1940, the Wolverines were led by their senior all-American halfback, Tom Harmon. On his way to winning The Heisman Memorial Trophy, Harmon was determined to prove that Minnesota's victory the year before had been a fluke.

Now it is Nov. 2, 1940, in Minneapolis, Minn. A heavy mist falls as the two undefeated teams slug it out on a field thick with mud. Curiously, the Wolverines are having little trouble moving the ball. They have the Gophers repeatedly back on their heels. Michigan is ahead, 6-0. On this dreary day, however, six points may as well be 36, for unlike Michigan, Smith's squad appears stuck in the mud.

Again, the Wolverines bulldoze their way inside the

Minnesota 10, but just as it appears the Harmon gang is closing in on the kill, a Michigan pass is picked off in the end zone. Minnesota takes over on its own 20.

Bierman, blessed with not one, but two outstanding backs in Smith and senior George Franck (who would finish third to Harmon in the 1940 Heisman race), decided to try something different. Smith is sent in at the wing position as Franck lines up in Smith's tailback slot. Franck has tremendous speed and everyone expects his number to be called. It is not.

Smith takes a handoff on a weakside reverse, catching the Wolverines off guard just long enough to slant off his left end and break into the secondary, dodging and feinting his way past no fewer than six defenders as he makes his way downfield.

The seventh is the safety, Harmon, himself, but this is Lucius Smith's little boy coming his way. Harmon never has a chance. He later calls Smith's 80-yard touchdown run "one of the finest the game of football has ever seen." The Game Breaker has struck again. The extra-point kick is good, and Michigan suffers its only defeat of the season, 7-6.

It was Harmon's last chance to beat his arch adversary, yet Michigan's prolific scorer was not able to make the debate even close. He was shutout in both the 1940 and '41 games. The second loss was especially bitter since it cost Michigan

The 1941 Minnesota Gophers won the national championship with an 8-0 record. It was their fourth title in 8 years.

both an undefeated season and a sure national championship — which went to Minnesota.

Michigan didn't have Harmon in 1941, but once again the Wolverines entered the Minnesota game undefeated, and once again it was Smith who made the difference, breaking open a scoreless tie, this time with a pass that set up the only touchdown in the 7-0 Gophers victory. And once again, it was Michigan's only loss of the season.

Between making ferocious tackles on defense, and absorbing the hard hits when he carried the ball, Smith played with a lot of pain. He was just as valuable to his teammates displaying his courage at walking onto the field injured as he was at making a big score or a vital first down. If their captain could play in pain, so could they.

Smith saved his greatest performance for the final game of his all-America senior season. In an all-out assault on Wisconsin, Smith, while playing on a banged-up knee, was a one-man marvel. In succession, he threw a 45-yard pass, setting up his own 18-yard touchdown run; faked a pass and ran 42 yards before lateraling to a teammate for the last five yards of the second touchdown play; set up the third touchdown by intercepting a pass and running it back 43 yards to the Badger 11; and then threw a farewell 20-yard touchdown pass before being helped off the field, leaving it to his inspired teammates to fill out the 41-6 victory.

It was a Hollywood ending to a brilliant career, so much so that Hollywood coaxed him into starring in a movie based on his life, *Smith of Minnesota* — which was similar to a film made on his Heisman predecessor, Harmon.

It was not a time of make-believe, however, and Smith backed up his words of Dec. 9 by enlisting in the Naval Reserves in Feb. 1942.

Determined to serve his country, he passed all of his physicals despite having severely-torn cartilage in his right knee, which, typically, he kept quiet about. He received his fighter pilot's wings while continuing to dominate the game of football, being named captain of the East squad in the 1942 East-West Shrine game, the MVP in the College All-Star Game later that summer, and later the Armed Services' Player of the Year.

After the war, Smith joined the National Football League. He played four injury-plagued seasons with the Green Bay Packers and the Los Angeles Rams, where it was apparent his numerous ailments had taken their toll.

And so, at the age of 29, Smith retired from the game and became the first Heisman winner to have his college number retired. In 1972, he was elected to the College Football Hall of Fame — posthumously.

After working hard as a salesman, Bruce Smith died of cancer on August 28, 1967, at the age of 47. He left behind a wife and four children.

On Sept. 28, 1970, Lucius Smith presented his son's Heisman Trophy to the University of Minnesota. Bruce Smith had always said it belonged to the 1940 and '41 teams.

On that day, a father harkened back 30 years. Just as America had the last laugh in World War II, old Lucius had his in an old grudge, thanks to his son, a fellow they called the Game Breaker.

Smith's Run, Mernik Kick Topples Michigan

By Charles Johnson
Minneapolis Star Journal

Minneapolis, Minn. | November 9, 1940					
Michigan	0	6	0	0 —	6
Minnesota	0	7	0	0 —	7

A gallant, fighting Minnesota football team refused to become frightened in any of the many tight spots this afternoon and edged out the best Michigan football team in 10 years by a score of 7 to 6 on a rain-soaked Memorial Stadium field before 63,894 drenched customers.

Yes, that's right. The score was Minnesota 7, Michigan 6.

For the second time in three years, those Gophers, unbeaten in the parade to the Western Conference and possibly to the national championship, gave the Wolverines of Fritz Crisler some of their own medicine — a one-point defeat.

It was the Gophers' third-straight win against Michigan and their seventh straight win in the series while playing on home turf.

But don't think the outpouring of Minnesota rooters didn't say their prayers often on this rainy afternoon.

They had to. On four occasions, this brilliant Michigan football combination, had to throw back Minnesota goal-line attacks — some of them inches from paydirt.

Smith, of Faribault, Minn., a mudder if there ever was one, was the boy who outshone Michigan's Tommy Harmon and the Gophers' George Franck — both all-American bidders.

He raced 80 yards for a touchdown on a straight off-tackle slant at Michigan's right side. In came Joe Mernik to replace Smith, the hero, and he booted the game-deciding kick.

Harmon was a remarkable performer here and you don't have to look to the statistics for confirmation. You had to see him run to appreciate his abilities in the mud.

The Minnesota players appreciated him in a big way. And when the final gun sounded, they rushed onto the field, and swarmed all over him to congratulate him on his performance. It was the finest demonstration one group of football players ever gave to a rival player.

Michigan had five scoring opportunities, but only crossed the Minnesota goal line once. In the second quarter, Harmon marched his Wolverines from their 45 to the Minnesota 34, then punted to it out of bounds at the Michigan 6. Gophers halfback Bill Daly fumbled in the Minnesota 6.

After two failed rushing plays, Harmon connected on a pass to Evasheveski, who was in the end zone, for the touchdown, but his extra-point kick failed.

Michigan's Tom Harmon (98) attempts to cut back against the Minnesota secondary in their 1940 memorable game.

Tom Harmon, Michigan's two-time all-American halfback, won the 1940 Heisman and Maxwell trophies.

Not Even the Enemy Could Bring Him Down

By Gene Wojciechowski

The year was 1940 and Michigan tailback Tom Harmon had just led the Wolverines to a 40-0 victory against Big Ten arch-rival Ohio State at Ohio Stadium. In what was his final — and perhaps finest — performance for Michigan, Harmon ran for 139 yards and two touchdowns. He completed 11 of 12 passes for 151 yards and another two scores. He had four extra-point kicks and averaged 50 yards per punt.

Afterward, as he left the field, Harmon heard an unexpected sound from the crowd of 73,000 Buckeye fans. It was applause ... For him a Michigan man. Go figure.

In the rarest of tributes, Harmon received a standing ovation in Columbus. The only greater honor would have been to let him dot the "i" during the Buckeye band's halftime show.

The audience had seen greatness that day and it knew it. So in a strange and unexpected acknowledgement, each fan stood and applauded Thomas Dudley Harmon, better known as "Old 98."

Heisman Memorial Trophy voters knew it, too, which is why Harmon was the easy choice when the ballot results were announced on Nov. 27, 1940. New York Times reporter William D. Richardson, commenting on the Heisman outcome, put it perfectly when he wrote that Harmon "scored standing up, just as he had done so many times during his career on the Michigan team."

The 6-foot, 195-pound Harmon, powerful and fast (he ran the 100 in 9.8 seconds), carried every voting section of the country, except the Southwest, which was partial to runner-up John Kimbrough, the Texas A&M fullback. Harmon finished with 1,303 points, a comfortable 462 more than Kimbrough received.

On the night of the Heisman dinner, which was held then in The Downtown Athletic Club gymnasium, Harmon listened as Walter P. Holcombe, the president of the D.A.C., delivered a brief lecture about the award's signifigance.

"You have won a great distinction," Holcombe said, "but I remind you that in so doing you have acquired a great responsibility as well — that of setting for our American boys as fine an example in afterlife as you thus far have shown them as a student, an athlete, a sportsman and a gentleman."

Harmon remembered every word. Years later, when considering the meaning of the trophy, Harmon spoke as if Holcombe were standing on his shoulder.

"I suppose that if we were in England this honor would be the equivalent of knighthood because these young men have certainly proved their character on the field of battle. And I say to the winner ... this is an honor that is not to be taken lightly ... because from this day on ... whatever you go ... whatever you do ... the honor of being the Heisman Trophy winner will remain your constant responsibility."

Harmon was the keeper of the Heisman flame as well as anyone. Born on Sept. 28, 1919, in Gary, Ind., the bubble-gum chewing son of Louis and Rose Harmon dreamed of winning the award as early as his freshman year at Horace Mann High School. His boyhood idol was none other than Jay Berwanger, the University of Chicago halfback who won the first Heisman Trophy in 1935.

"I had so much respect for him," Harmon once said. "He had no help at Chicago. I wanted to become the player he was, a 60-minute man. I saw him in a newsreel, receiving the Heisman Trophy. I heard the announcer say that the trophy went to the outstanding college football player in the country. That struck with me. I've always been goal-oriented, and from that day on. I had my eye on the Heisman."

It was at Horace Mann High that Harmon might or might not have earned the nickname that stayed with him throughout his entire career, both as a player, an Air Force fighter pilot and as a broadcaster.

The story goes that Harmon, the actual winner of a Gary-sponsored bubble gum blowing contest, showed up at practice one day with a wad of the stuff in his mouth. As Coach Doug Kerr conducted the first day of practice, Harmon blew a giant-sized bubble that caught the attention of everyone, including a peeved Kerr, who told the freshman to immediately leave the field and return his uniform to the team manager.

"I'm not turning in my uniform," Harmon said. "I came out here to play football."

"Oh, you did, did you?" said Kerr. "We'll see about that."

So Kerr assigned Harmon to the kickoff return team, where

the freshman promptly ran for a touchdown against the varsity. Kerr ordered another kickoff and again Harmon returned it for a score.

Guess who made the team as a freshman?

Told later to choose a jersey for the first game, Harmon picked a number, but was forced to change when informed it belonged to an upperclassman.

"I went to pick another jersey, but there was only one left," Harmon would say. "It was old, tattered, with holes in it."

Old 98.

About five years later, as a tailback in Michigan's single-wing formation, Harmon recalled the gentle ribbing he would take from Forest Evashevski, his lead blocker and roommate. "At practice, Evy would say, 'Come on, Old 98, let's get it in gear.'" Harmon said.

By today's standards, Harmon's statistical accomplishments aren't overpowering. In 1938, his first season on the Wolverines varsity, Harmon rushed for 398 yards and passed for 310. The next season he gained 1,356 yards, scored 14 touchdowns and 102 points to lead the nation and finished second in the Heisman balloting. In his senior year, Harmon accounted for 1,346 total yards, 16 touchdowns and 117 points. As usual, he punted, returned punts, returned kickoffs, played defensive back, kicked extra points and won a Heisman.

For his career, Harmon gained a total of 3,438 yards, which, for historical comparison, was nearly 600 yards less than Brigham Young quarterback Ty Detmer, the 1990 Heisman winner, had in a single season.

But numbers don't always measure the player, as Evashevski, Harmon's best friend, once tried to explain.

"A lot of modern backs are comparable with Tom as far as running ability goes," Evashevski said. "He had change of pace, good balance, quickness and some trout in him to elude tacklers. But how can you compare them to him as a back? When he played, there was one platoon. If you couldn't play defense, you didn't play — and Tom was a great defensive back. He played it in the pros for two years because his legs had been scarred so bad in his last dogfight in the war that he couldn't have taken the pounding on offense.

"Tom was our passer, too. Back then, if you threw two incompletions in a row, it was a five-yard penalty, and you had to be at least five yards behind the line of scrimmage to throw. So there were a lot fewer passes. And there were a lot fewer plays period because the clock never stopped. Plus, Tom kicked off for us and kicked our points after touchdowns."

There was more, of course. Freshmen weren't eligible. The schedule was only eight games. There were no bowl games. In fact, Harmon's records were established in just 24 games

Harmon and his roommate, Forest Evashevski, in 1939.

— about half as many as a four-year Wolverine starter plays these days.

Statistics or no statistics, Harmon was a player for the ages, a person to make the D.A.C. proud. As a junior, he scored two touchdowns, threw for two others, kicked three extra points and one field goal in the first half of Michigan's 85-0 victory against Chicago. The next season, Chicago dropped the entire program.

Sorry, Mr. Berwanger.

Harmon once recorded a 63-yard touchdown run against Penn that observers said, after counting all the weaving and backtracking done, actually covered more than a hundred yards and took at least a minute or so to compete.

Against California on Sept. 28, 1940 — Harmon's birthday — the senior tailback was on his way to a third touchdown when Harold Brennen, a former San Francisco end in 1929, dashed from Berkeley's Memorial Stadium stands and tried tackling him at the Cal 2-yard line.

After all, no one else could.

Recalled Brennan: "The kid looks at me kinda funny and says, 'What the hell do you think you're doing?' And I said, 'I'm tackling you.' The next thing I know two men have got me by the neck and doggone if it isn't two cops.'"

Like the Golden Bears themselves, Brennan missed. Most everyone did. And by the way, Harmon later convinced the police to free the overzealous Cal fan.

After graduating from Michigan, Harmon, a speech major, announced that he had no intention of playing professional football. Instead, he wanted to pursue a career in radio broadcasting.

Harmon appeared in the movie, *Harmon of Michigan*, which was a semibomb, but earned him $25,000, enough to pay for a new home in Ann Arbor for his parents.

The Chicago Bears, the most powerful team of the day and

owned by the legendary George Halas, made Harmon the No. 1 pick in the 1941 NFL draft. Harmon declined the offer, joined a Detroit radio station and later played a single professional game for the New York Americans of the American Football League.

"I was beating my guards to the hole and decided this was no place for me," he said.

In December of that year, Harmon enlisted in the Army Air Corps and later earned his wings as a pilot of a twin-engined B-25 bomber. In April of 1943, while en route to a combat zone, Harmon and his crew were forced to bail out of their plane (named "Old 98") somewhere over Dutch Guiana in South America. Harmon was the only survivor, as he spent four days alone in swampy rain forests before being found by natives.

After recovering from his injuries, Harmon was transferred to China, where he flew P-38 fighters until being shot down during an Oct. 30 battle over Kiukiang, a Yangtze River port. He suffered multiple burns during the dogfight, but was rescued by Chinese guerrillas who escorted him back to his base.

Shortly after returning to the United States, Harmon proposed to Elyse Knox, a movie actress and model. They were married in 1944 at the same University of Michigan chapel where a special Mass had been said for Harmon following his first air crash. Elyse's wedding dress was made from the silk of the parachute that saved Harmon's life in China.

Harmon — mostly because he needed money to pay off a tax bill from his earlier movie fees — played two seasons for the Los Angeles Rams. That done, he pursued his first choice of careers — broadcasting. For the next 20 years, Harmon covered almost every major sporting event.

On March 15, 1990, Harmon suffered a heart attack not long after playing golf at the Bel Air Country Club in Los Angeles. He was 70.

It was Harmon's son, Mark (Harmon also had two daughters, Kelly and Christie), who one day asked about the Heisman Trophy that set on a desk inside the house. The answer was vintage Harmon.

"My dad's explanation was simple," recalled Mark. "Awarded once a year to the best college football player in the country ... and that he couldn't have accomplished any of it without his teammates. Those were the important moments for me ... the concept of teamwork, for sure, but the idea that this very football player was also my father."

Harmon (98) ran and passed for 3,438 yards and scored 30 TD's during his 3-year career at Michigan.

Hirsch & Badgers Humble No. 1 Ohio State

By Willard R. Smith
Wisconsin State Journal

Madison, Wisc.	October 31, 1942					
Ohio State	0	0	0	7	—	7
Wisconsin	0	10	0	7	—	17

Wisconsin toppled mighty Ohio State, 17-7, today before a record sellout crowd of 45,000 to remain the only undefeated football team in the Big Ten conference.

It was Wisconsin's first win over the Buckeyes since 1918.

The game was billed as a fullback's battle between Pat Harder of Wisconsin and Gene Fekete of Ohio State and the results stoodout in the following statistics: Harder — 21 tries for 97 yards; Fekete — 20 tries for 65 yards.

The difference was not just Harder, but also Dave Schreiner, Wisconsin's all-America end and acting captain, and a line which showed itself superior and stopped the blasts of the Buckeyes time after time.

Ohio State's fast left halfback, Paul Sarringhaus, was completely eclipsed by Wisconsin's sophomore back, Elroy Hirsch, who gained 118 yards was nearly double the yardage Sarringhaus had, but on the same number of carries.

Hirsch streaked 59 yards to set up Wisconsin's first touchdown in the second quarter. Running like a scared jackrabbit in the desert with only sagebrush and cactus to hinder him, Hirsch started around right end at his 20, hurdled a tackler at the 30 and was finally brought down by Tommy James on the Buckeyes' 21. A few moments later, Harder scored the touchdown on a dive from the six-inch mark.

Harder not only booted the extra-point kick, but also added a sharply-angled field goal from the Ohio State 27 to give the Badgers a 10-0 lead before halftime.

The Buckeyes were no match for Wisconsin in the first half. Only twice did they cross midfield, reaching the Wisconsin 38 on one occasion and the 47 on another trip.

The Buckeyes were at their best late in the third quarter. With James playing in Sarringhaus' spot, Ohio State drove from its 4-yard line to the Badgers' end zone in 17 plays. When the Buckeyes got inside the Wisconsin 11, Sarringhaus and Fekete re-entered the game and Sarringhaus scored on a 3-yard run. Fekete added the extra-point kick to cut Wisconsin's lead to 10-7.

After receiving the kickoff, Wisconsin marched from its 34 for a touchdown. Twice Hirsch passed to Schreiner — first for a 12-yard gain, then a 14-yarder, which the all-American grabbed in the end zone for the Badgers' second touchdown. Harder's extra-point kick gave Wisconsin a 17-7 lead.

With eight minutes left to play, the Buckeyes attempted a futile flurry of long passes. Hirsch intercepted one of these and returned it from his 6-yard line to the 30.

The game was also broadcast on short-wave radio to stations around the world, with 11 stations in South America, two in Ireland, one in Iceland, two in Alaska, two in Hawaii, three in England and three in Australia to American troops.

It was the second loss in 14 games for Paul Brown since he took over as the Buckeyes' coach.

Dave Schreiner was Wisconsin's first All-America end, earning the honor in 1941 and 1942.

Wisconsin's Elroy Hirsch (40) sweeps right end behind the block of fullback Pat Harder (34) for a 59-yard gain.

Bob DeMoss (50), Ed Cody (25) and Bill Canfield (70) celebrate after Purdue's 35-13 win over Ohio State.

Isbell's Boilermakers Blast No. 1 Buckeyes

By GORDON GRAHAM
The Journal and Courier

Columbus, Ohio	October 20, 1945						
Purdue	6	16	6	7	—	35
Ohio State	0	0	0	13	—	13

The proud Buckeyes of Ohio State "got the buck" by a fierce charging and perfectly prepared Purdue football team here today as 73,585 shocked spectators saw Coach Cecil Isbell's Boilermakers roll over Carroll Widdoes' heralded eleven, 35 to 13.

Purdue defeated a Buckeyes team which had won 12 straight games and had not given up a single point this season. The Boilermakers shoved a foot firmly into the national football picture and at the same time became a co-favorite with Minnesota to win the Big Ten championship.

In many ways the spectacular triumph goes down as the most important in Purdue football history.

Probably the fact that Purdue had 22 points before the befuddled Ohio State team could make its first down best indicates the superiority of the blazing Boilermakers. That's how good they were at Ohio Stadium today — and all Buckeye coaches, players, sports writers and fans admitted it.

Just 18 seconds before the first quarter came to a close Ed Cody finished a 58-yard drive by plunging four yards into the end zone for a 6-0 lead.

Isbell's gang was "off to the races." Desperately, Widdoes rushed Paul Sarringhaus into the game, but despite the latter's fine performance, the Buckeyes went from bad to worse.

A short punt by Oliver Cline went out of bounds on the OSU 42 a fews plays after the second quarter began. Three plays later, an awed capacity crowd was watching a second Purdue touchdown. It came on a 38-yard pass from Bob DeMoss to Bill Canfield. Tom Hughes kicked the extra point for a 13-0 lead.

Ohio State began to come apart at the seams. The confused Buckeyes managed to be offsides, to be in motion and finally to fumble on the Buckeyes' 43 in four plays after the kickoff. Marvin Crowe recovered the fumble for Purdue.

Less than three minutes later, DeMoss tossed a pass to Canfield at the OSU 8-yard line and Canfield raced into the end zone. Hughes' extra-point kick made it 20-0 with 7:55 remaining in the first half.

It didn't take quite a minute for the Boilermakers to score again. Hughes' kickoff was not fielded by a Buckeye until it reached the 1-yard line. Cline finally decided to pick up the flopping football, but as he did he was catapulted back into his end zone by a solid wall of battling Boilermakers. However, the ball was ruled dead at the 1.

Cline went deep into his end zone, but it wasn't enough as Hughes and blocked the kick, causing a safety to give the Boilermakers a 22-0 lead.

Before halftime, Ohio State settled down long enough to put together a pair of first downs but the drive bogged down and Purdue took over at their 38.

In the third quarter, after two failed drives by the Buckeyes, Purdue marched 67 yards for a touchdown, which put the game out of reach. DeMoss connected on a 40-yard pass to Bob Heck and then threw a 19-yard TD pass to Cody for a 28-0 lead.

The Buckeyes finally got on the scoreboard in the fourth quarter following a Purdue fumble at the Boilermakers' 36. Ohio State's Harold Daugherty whipped a long pass to Carlton Kessler, who caught the ball at the Boilermakers' 2-yard line, then raced across the goal line for the touchdown. The extra-point kick was blocked.

Striking with amazing power, Purdue showed it could still shatter the Buckeyes defense. Cody found gaping holes in the Ohio State defense, and led a 69-yard advance.

On three plays, Cody ran 22, 8 and 39 yards for his third touchdown. Hughes' extra-point kick made it 35-6 with eight minutes left to play.

Daugherty again was the leader as Ohio State clicked for its second touchdown. His 31-yard pass to Tom Watson put the ball deep in Purdue football. A Charles Gandee to Alex Verdova lateral scored from the 14-yard line to cut the Boilermakers' lead to 35-13.

Ed Cody (top) ran for 3 touchdowns and Bob DeMoss (above) passed for 2 TD's against the Buckeyes.

Bo McMillin's 1945 Indiana Hoosiers celebrate their 26-0 win against Purdue and the school's first Big Ten title.

Hoosiers Rout Purdue, Win First Big Ten Crown

BY GRADY BENNETT
The World-Telephone

Bloomington, Ind. | November 24, 1945					
Purdue	0	0	0	0	—	0
Indiana	0	0	13	13	—	26

The greatest Indiana University football team of all time now rules the Big Ten Conference.

This afternoon the Coach Alvin Nugent (Bo) McMillin-mentored Hoosiers rocketed to glory before a record crowd which was bigger than the entire population of Bloomington. The Crimsons did this by the process of practically chasing an amazed Purdue eleven off the snow-flaked Memorial Stadium gridiron in the second half after playing a scoreless first two quarters in the nation's No. 1 pigskin classic of the day.

In scoring their stunning 26-0 victory over their arch rivals, before a roaring crowd of 27,000, the battling Hoosiers sandwiched between Thanksgiving and Christmas a bright finish which probably will mark the beginning of a new era in IU football.

It was the Hoosiers' first Big Ten football championship. And the first time an IU eleven completed an undefeated season.

The Hoosiers played before the biggest audience ever jammed into Memorial Stadium. And it was the most important win any IU team has ever earned.

Indiana once again has possession of the Oaken Bucket. It is their fifth win over the Boilermakers in the past six seasons.

After battling Purdue to a scoreless draw in the first half, the Hoosiers added 13 points in the third quarter and another 13 points in the fourth to finish off Purdue.

And then Coach McMillin, a banquet and pep session speaker of renown, delivered his three-word post-game address in the Hoosier lockerroom. It was: "Nice goin' boys."

He sort of choked up afterward.

The fans who paid scalpers 15 dollars or more per ticket were getting big bargains. They saw enough football in that one game to far more than repay them for the hundreds of miles of icy highway many of them drove to see Indiana's thrilling victory.

Purdue was completely whipped. For every first down Purdue gained, Indiana had five. The Hoosiers picked up 79 yards through the air compared to none for Purdue. Indiana also had stolen 3 Boilermaker passes — compared to none for the Hoosiers.

Following the game, the students get a Victory Vacation Day on Monday and the Indiana Board of Trustees voted to give Coach Bo McMillin a new 10-year contract.

Following a between-the-halves lecture by McMillin, the Hoosiers came out and scored its first touchdown, became inspired over this breaking of the ice, then caught fire and became unbeatable.

Indiana's first touchdown was set up by a 30-yard pass from Ben Raimondi to George Taliaferro that reached the Boilermakers' 1-yard line. Two plays later, Pete Pihos smashed over behind guard for the touchdown. Charles Armstrong's extra-point kick made it 7-0.

Two minutes later, Ted Kluszewski recovered a Black and Gold fumble on the Purdue 1-yard line. Pihos pile-drived over for his second touchdown to give Indiana a 13-0 lead. Armstrong's extra-point kick failed.

In the fourth quarter, Mel Groomes and Taliaferro led the Hoosiers' advance from their 35 to the Purdue 39. Raimondi tossed a pass to Taliaferro that reached the 24. Taliaferro then ripped with the ball to Purdue 10. Raimondi passed to Kluszewski, who hurdled a pair of frantic Purdue players to reach the end zone and give Indiana a 19-0 lead. Armstrong's extra-point kick again failed.

With five minutes left to play, Raimondi intercepted a long pass on his 45-yard line and ran it back to the Purdue 34. Five rushing attempts reached the 21. A Raimondi pass to Bob Ravensberg reached the Purdue 4. Three plays later, Raimondi fired the final touchdown pass to Louis Mihajlovich. Armstrong booted the extra-point kick to give Indiana a 26-0 lead with 1 minutes 40 seconds left to play.

Raimondi finished with seven completions on 11 attempts for 79 yards. Groomes ran for 68 yards on 12 carries and Pihos, who was injured on the first play of the fourth quarter, toted the ball 11 times for 50 yards. Ravensberg also intercepted a pair of Purdue passes.

Indiana's Mel Groomes (57) outraces four Boilermaker defenders. He finished with 68 yards rushing on 12 carries.

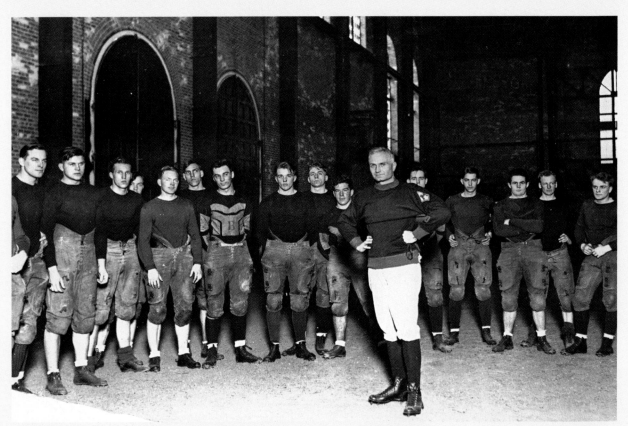

In his ten seasons at Minnesota, Bernie Bierman led the Gophers to 6 Big Ten titles and 4 national championships.

The Hammer of the North

BY TIM COHANE

Bernie Bierman didn't have much to say in public, but his teams spoke for him. From 1932 to 1941, his Minnesota Golden Gophers won 64, lost 11 and tied 5. They were undefeated five times, won six Big Ten titles — 1934, '35, '37, '38, '40 and '41 — and won national championships in 1934, '36, '40 and '41.

A 28-game undefeated streak was broken by a 6-0 loss to Northwestern on a muddy field in 1936. That game cost Minnesota the Big Ten title, but it was ranked No. 1 at the end of the season by The Associated Press in their first national poll.

Before returning to his alma mater in 1932, Bierman coached at Montana, Mississippi State and Tulane. At Tulane, his 1929 team went undefeated and the ''31 team went 11-0 in the regular season, then lost, 21-12, in the 1932 Rose Bowl to Howard Jones' great Southern Cal squad.

After he retired from coaching, Bierman called his 1934

Minnesota team his best ever. It was blessed with great talent — Pug Lund, the captain and all-American halfback; Glen Seidel at quarterback; Frank Larson, the all-American end; Billy Bevan, the all-America guard; Bob Tenner, the all-America end; and future coaches Bud Wilkinson (of Oklahoma) and Milt Bruhn (of Wisconsin) at guard.

Harry Kipke, the Michigan coach, spoke for a majority when he described the 1934 Gophers' talent-laden squad, "It is the greatest team I ever saw or played against as a coach. Their reserves would beat almost any team in the country."

Bierman was an all-around star at Litchfield High and entered the University of Minnesota in 1912. He won seven varsity letters — three each in Football and track and one in basketball.

Bierman was captain and halfback of Minnesota's 1915 conference champions, and his approach to the game was deeply influenced by Dr. Henry Williams, who coached the Gophers from 1900 to '21.

Probably the greatest single clinical play in Bierman's

dynasty was an extemporaneous lateral of a punt that brought victory when a scoreless tie seemed imminent. Wilkinson, who was an outstanding guard for Bierman in 1934 and '35, was shifted to quarterback in 1936, where he was a standout player. He engineered the beginning of the play. Dick Cullum, the ace football writer of the Minneapolis Times, described it:

"There were 68 seconds left to play against Nebraska in 1936 ... the Cornhuskers had the ball on their 43-yard line ... Sam Francis, Nebraska's best kicker, had been replaced by sophomore Ron Douglas. He punted a short, high kick to Wilkinson, who fielded it at the Minnesota 28. Wilkinson caught the ball near the sideline, and took the first step to the inside and backwards, drawing all the tacklers toward him.

"It was not until one of them had him by one leg that he let the ball go. Andrew Uram caught it on the 25-yard line and ran through a broken field 75 yards for a touchdown. It was unquestionably one of football's finest plays. At one stage of the play, every Nebraska player had a hand on Uram, but he shook them off and scored the touchdown to lead the Gophers to a 7-0 victory.

On defense, Bierman's Minnesota teams were nearly impregnable. In three games, 1938-40, Tommy Harmon, Michigan's famed No. 98, failed to get into the Gophers' end zone. Of the five defeats incurred by Fritz Crisler's Michigan teams between 1938 and 1941, four came from Minnesota.

The headline rivalry of Bierman's pre-World War II years was against pappy Waldorf's Northwestern teams from 1935 to 1941. Minnesota won four of these contests, Northwestern won three.Minnesota's margins were 21-13, 7-0, 13-12 and 8-7; Northwestern's were 6-0, 6-3 and 14-7. The total points were Gophers 59, Northwestern 58.

His last national championship team of 1941 completed an 8-0 year with trouncings of Iowa and Wisconsin.

During World War II, he served as a marine colonel for three years and did some coaching at Iowa Pre-Flight.

In 1945, he returned to the University of Minnesota, where he replaced Dr. George Hauser, who had put together a record of 15-11-1 in three seasons. Bierman had been offered the job at Southern Cal, but he turned it down because he was sure he could rebuild at Minnesota.

After a 4-5 record in 1945, Bierman's squad improved to 5-4 in '46 and 6-3 in '47, then put together a pair of 7-2 seasons in 1948 and '49. But after a disappointing 1-7-1 record in 1950, Bierman retired to serve in the Gophers' athletic department and worked on the WCCO radio football broadcasts. He later retired to live in Laguna Hills, Calif.

During his first tenure at Minnesota, in 1932-41, Bierman's teams posted a record of 8-1-1 against Minnesota in the battle for the Little Brown Jug.

Illini Defeat No. 1 Bucks

By WILFRID SMITH
Chicago Tribune

The Fightin' Illini twice struck through the air this afternoon to whip Ohio State, 14-7, before 71,119, who jammed Memorial Stadium to capacity. The Buckeyes were the No. 1-ranked team in the country.

Don Stevens, the speedy back, who had never scored for Illinois, caught two passes for touchdowns. Perhaps the Buckeyes also forgot about Stevens. They now know that he was the swiftest man on the field, the only Illinois runner to average more than 5 yards per carry. Stevens' total of 78 yards was exceeded only by Vic Janowicz, who handled the ball seven more times.

Early in the second quarter, Fred Major, the Illini quarterback, connected with Stevens on a 38-yard pass for Illinois' first touchdown. Stevens caught the ball in full flight and outran Ray Hamilton, the Buckeyes defender.

A few minutes later, following an Ohio State fumble that was recovered by linebacker Joe Hall at the Ohio State 47, the Illini struck again. Johnny Karras picked up 12 and 8 yards on two-straight runs, then Stevens ran for nine yards on a double reverse to move the ball to the Ohio State 18.

Stevens added 3 yards on a dive play and Majors passed to Tony Klimek for 10 yards to move the ball to the 5-yard line. He then threw to Stevens, who was in the end zone for the touchdown. Sam Rebecca booted his second extra-point kick to give Illinois a 14-0 lead.

Before halftime, Janowicz smashed the middle of the Illinois defense for 16 yards on three straight plays to cut the Illini lead to 14-6. Janowicz added the extra-point kick to make it 14-7 — but that would be the end of the scoring for both teams.

Late in the third quarter, Ohio State drove from its 20 to the Illini 10, but the drive got halted when Walt Klevay fumbled a pass from Janowicz that was recovered by Elie Popa.

Champaign, Ill.	November 18, 1950					
Illinois	0	14	0	0	—	14
Ohio State	0	7	0	0	—	7

Don Stevens, a receiver who had never scored, caught 2 passes for touchdowns for the Illini.

A stingy Michigan State defense wrapped up halfback Bob Hurley (33). They held Michigan to 81 yards rushing.

State's 'Bowl Hawks' Feed on Wolverines

By Hal Middlesworth
Detroit Free Press

East Lansing, Mich. | November 14, 1953						
Michigan State	0	7	7	0	—	14
Michigan	0	0	0	6	—	6

Don't close that Rose Bowl gate in Michigan State's face — not yet. The Spartans kept a foot in the opening today when they scored their first gridiron home victory of all time over Michigan, 14 to 6, while Wisconsin was upsetting Illinois, 34 to 7.

It was the Spartans' final conference game of their first official season in the Big Ten, giving them a 5-1 record and clinching at least a tie for the championship.

Illinois, which still must play Northwestern next week, and which tumbled Michigan, 19 to 3, last week has a 4-1 mark in the Big Ten.

If Michigan State and Illinois finish in a deadlock in league standing, it will take a Conference vote to pick the Big Ten's Rose Bowl representative.

The second biggest crowd in Michigan State's history — a sun-bathed gathering of 52,324 — saw the Spartans score twice on short passes after long marches for their fourth-straight victory over Michigan. It tied the longest winning string in the ancient series.

Michigan's only score came in the final period after a Spartan fumble on the four-yard line.

The Spartans marched 89 yards for their opening score in the second quarter. Sophomore Earl Morrall sparking the final 30 yards and passing five yards to Jimmy Ellis for the touchdown.

They rolled back 66 yards for another touchdown in the third quarter, with Bert Zagers throwing the first pass of his college career for the score.

Zagers, in the Spartans backfield as a fill-in for the ailing Billy Wells, southpawed a four-yard toss to Ellis Duckett on a play which fooled the Wolverines completely.

Evan Slonac kicked both of the Spartans' extra points.

Ellis, a specialist on punt returns, gave the underdog Wolverines their scoring chance when he ran a fourth-quarter punt out of the end zone and dropped it on the four-yard line.

Lou Baldacci, Michigan's sophomore quarterback, sneaked across from the one-yard line three plays later, but missed the extra point.

The Wolverines then scared the Spartans by driving back to their four-yard line after intercepting a pass, but State stiffened and threw the challengers back to the 14 before taking the ball away from them.

Michigan's best all-around performance of the season wasn't good enough to keep intact the Wolverines' record of never losing in East Lansing.

But it kept the stout-hearted Wolverines in the running right up to the final few minutes of a game which some expected them to lose in a lopsided fashion.

Lack of an adequate passing attack prevented Michigan State from rolling up the score in a contest marked by the absence of thrilling long runs or passes.

The longest bites of yardage for the Spartans were a couple of 11-yard runs by quarterbacks trapped on passing attempts.

The lightweight legs of halfback Leroy Bolden carried the Spartans to their important victory.

Although he only weighs 157 pounds, the Flint firecracker popped the Wolverines from every angle — wide sweeps, cutbacks and straight-ahead plunges — for a net gain of 75 yards on 23 rushing attempts.

State's Slonac added 62 yards on 18 carries.

Michigan scattered its ball-carrying but wound up with only 81 yards to State's total of 194.

Although the Spartans scored both their touchdowns on passes, they hit only four out of 13 for a measly 22 yards, while Michigan collected 78 yards on a 7-for-14 record.

Michigan, going down to its third defeat of the season (all in the Big Ten) against five victories, suffered when Dick Balzhiser, the fullback-linebacker, was injured in the first quarter and failed to return.

The Spartans, beaten only by Purdue this season in a stunning upset, had no losses.

Players from both sides, however, required frequent treatment during the rugged battle witnessed by something like 60 million television fans as well as the near-record crowd.

State started its first scoring drive after Baldacci boomed a 59-yard punt to the Spartans' 11-yard line late in the first quarter.

It took 19 plays for the green-shirted hosts to reach scoring territory. They arrived at Michigan's 34 as the first quarter ended and Morrall replaced Tom Jewcic at the throttle.

His arrival seemed to perk up the Spartans and a reserve backfield including Morrall, Ellis, Travis Buggs and Gerry Planutis used nine plays for a score. On the touchdown pass, Ellis maneuvered behind Gene Knutson, the Michigan defender, and took Morrall's five-yard toss as they both tumbled to the turf.

Slonac's extra point made it 7 to 0 at the half as fumbles stalled attacks for each side.

Zagers intercepted a pass by Ted Kress to start the Spartans toward their second touchdown early in the third period.

This was a Bolden production, with the little speedster showing his heels to the Wolverines on nine of the 19 plays in the 66-yard thrust.

The turning point was a fourth-quarter plunge in which Bolden hit for four yards to Michigan's 14. It was only a question of time then — and Zagers supplied the answer on a fourth-down pass from the four, the first he ever tried in college.

Duckett and Bolden both were in the end zone and Duckett took it in the left-hand corner for a lead which became 14 to 0 when Slonac made his extra-point kick.

When Ellis fumbled Baldacci's fourth-quarter punt, it put some starch in the Wolverines. Guard Dick Beison recovered for Michigan and Baldacci sneaked across from the MSU 1-yard line after two thrusts by Bob Hurley, who was filling in for the injured Balzhiser.

Bob Topp intercepted a Morrall pass soon after and Michigan moved down to the four-yard line on a 16-yard pass from Danny Cline to Baldacci, but that was as far as they got. A running play and a pass attempt was stopped and the Spartans took over.

Ohio State's Bobby Watkins (45) pulls in a pass to set up the Buckeyes' second touchdown against Wisconsin.

Cassady & Buckeyes Upset No. 2 Wisconsin

BY LOU SMITH
The Cincinnati Enquirer

Columbus, Ohio	October 23, 1954					
Wisconsin	0	3	7	21	—	31
Ohio State	0	7	0	7	—	14

Ohio State was up. Wisconsin was "upset." The battling Buckeyes picked themselves off the sod to rip from behind a halftime deficit and conquer highly touted Wisconsin, 31-14-before an overflow crowd of 82,636 — the third largest crowd in the history of historic Ohio Stadium.

Combined with the bulling smashes of all-America halfback Alan Ameche, this was the slashing assault which had catapulted the Badgers through the season without a loss — until they ran into the Buckeyes.

Wisconsin led, 7-3, after baffling the Buckeye defenders with a brilliant scoring play in the final minutes of the first half to overcome a three-point deficit, which was the result of a second-period field goal by Ohio State's Tad Weed.

With brilliant Howard (Hopalong) Cassady leading the way, the Buckeyes slammed over four touchdowns in nine minutes to break the game wide open. Cassady, a standout candidate for all-America honors, turned the game into a rout with a spine-tingling 88-yard run of a pass interception in the closing minutes of the third quarter for a 10-7 lead.

This electrifying dash completely demoralized the Badgers. In the final period the Buckeyes, heading for their first undefeated season under Woody Hayes, racked up three more quick touchdowns.

Sophomore Hubert Bobo bulled over from the Badgers' 4; Dave Leggett got into the scoring act with a 27-yard run, after which Jerry Harkrader of Middletown, Ohio, added insult to injury by racing 10 yards for the final Ohio State score. The final three Ohio State touchdowns were run off in exactly five minutes and 14 seconds.

Weed also was in the spotlight. He booted a 29-yard field goal in the second quarter and added two extra-point kicks to run his string of consecutive conversions to 16 over a two-year period.

Following Weed's field goal that gave the Buckeyes a 3-0 lead, Wisconsin's Miller intercepted a John Borton pass with less than five minutes left in the second quarter at the Badgers' 46 and returned it to the OSU 37.

It would take Wisconsin only two plays to get on the scoreboard. Miller blasted his way through the middle for five yards. On the next play, he flipped a 10-yard pass to Pat Levenhagen, who sprinted 22 yards for the touchdown. Glen Wilson's point-after kick gave Wisconsin a 7-3 lead.

Ohio State's "break" that broke the game wide open was Cassady's 88-yard run of a pass interception with three minutes left in the third quarter. It would break the game open for the Buckeyes.

The mercury-footed Cassady picked off Miller's pass on the OSU 12. He needle-threaded his way stright up the field for 20 yards and then cut for the sidelines. He gave one would-be Badger tackler the hip at midfield.

This left only Levenhagen, the Badger defender, between him and the Wisconsin goal line. Cassady out-maneuvered the young Badger back at the 20 to go the rest of the way with no trouble.

Bobo set up OSU's second touchdown by recovering Levenhagen's fumble on the Badgers' 31 after dropping the sophomore with a jarring tackle. Cassady broke off tackle for 39 yards to Wisconsin's 31. En route to the Badger end zone, Leggett nailed Watkins with an 18-yard pass and Bobo powered over the final four yards for the touchdown. Weed's extra-point kick made it 17-7.

The Bucks made it 24-7 shortly afterward when Leggett broke over his own left guard and rambled 27 yards. Bob Watkins added the extra-point kick to make it 24-7.

A Wisconsin fumble set the stage for the final Buckeye touchdown with 9:09 left to play in the fourth quarter. Don Swartz recovered the loose ball for the Bucks on the Wisconsin 10-yard line. On the first play, Harkrader sprinted 10 yards for the TD and Watkins' extra-point kick put Ohio State on top, 31-7.

The Badgers picked up a consolation TD in the final two minutes with Bob Gingrass capping an 80-yard march with his one-yard TD run. Gingrass's extra-point kick made it 31-14.

Alan Ameche (35) bulled over for 2 TD's against Minnesota to wrap up his journey to the 1954 Heisman Trophy.

Badgers Rip Minnesota in Ameche's Last Game

By HENRY McCORMICK
Wisconsin State Journal

Madison, Wisc. | November 20, 1954						
Minnesota	0	0	0	0	—	0
Wisconsin	7	13	7	0	—	27

Wisconsin's 1954 football team saved its best 60 minutes for the final game of the season, and that was enough to bring the Badgers a 27-0 victory over longtime rival Minnesota at Camp Randall before a capacity crowd of 53,131.

The victory enabled the Badgers to finish in a tie with Michigan for second place in the final Big Ten standings and gave Wisconsin its second best overall record during Coach Ivy Williamson's regime. The win gave the Badgers a 5-2 record in the Big Ten and an overall record of 7-2.

Following the game, nine Badgers seniors hoisted an embar-

rassed Alan (The Horse) Ameche on their shoulders and carried him off the field.

Ameche had played on a sprained ankle and was not in top condition, but he performed heroically on defense and scored 2 touchdowns on goal-line runs. He reinjured his ankle late in the third quarter and was forced to the bench for the remainder of the afternoon.

The Badgers set a new Big Ten team record with seven pass interceptions. Clarence Bratt got four of these, which was a new Big Ten individual record.

Bratt had a career day. He swiped four Minnesota passes, scored a touchdown, ran for 67 yards on 10 carries, returned one kickoff for 16 yards and returned two punts for 34 yards.

Jimmy Miller, the Badgers quarterback, intercepted a pass, completed four of eight passes for 41 yards and ran for 61 yards on 13 carries.

Miller went four yards off tackle for the Badgers' first touchdown in the first quarter. Ameche rammed a yard for Wisconsin's second TD on the first play of the second quarter, then scored on a 3-yard run less than three minutes later.

Bratt scored the Badgers' fourth touchdown on a 4-yard burst in the third quarter.

Minnesota made only two first downs and never got inside the Wisconsin 40-yard line during the first half.

The Gophers did better in the second half, but its deepest advance was to the Wisconsin 17-yard line.

Bratt made three of his record four interceptions in the second half, along with Gary Messner grabbing an errant Gopher pass. Bobby Gingrass, Bratt and Miller picked off Minnesota passes in the first half.

The shadow of things to come was seen on Minnesota's third play of the game. Don Swanson attempted a pass, which Gingrass intercepted and returned 18 yards to the Gophers' 32.

Wisconsin didn't cash in on that opportunity, but it forced Minnesota to punt on the next series, then drove 70 yards on 12 plays for the Badgers' first touchdown, with Miller running the final four yards for the TD. Buzz Wilson got the extra point on a high, wobbly kick to give Wisconsin a 7-0 lead.

Minnesota brought the kickoff to its 24, but was pushed back to the Gophers' 13-yard line by a savage Wisconsin defensive line. Dale Quist's punt was fielded at the Wisconsin 47 and returned 24 yards to the Gophers' 29.

Miller got loose on a buck-lateral for 28 yards. Two plays later, Ameche bulled over the final yard for the TD and a 13-0 lead. Paul Shwalko's extra-point kick was wide.

The Gophers returned the next kickoff to their 27. On the first play, Wells Gray dropped Minnesota's Dick McNamara for a nine-yard loss. Bob McNamara smashed for a 1-yard gain, then John Dittrich and Ameche broke through to drop Quist for an 8-yard loss to the Gophers' 11.

On fourth down, Messner stormed through and pressured Quist's punt, which Norm Amundsen returned to the Gophers' 3-yard line.

Miller then called Ameche's number and the big fullback sliced through left tackle for the touchdown. Shwalko's extra-point kick was good this time and the Badgers' lead was increased to 20-0.

Wisconsin's last touchdown came after Ameche's third-quarter injury forced him to the sidelines.

After Gingrass' punt went out of bounds on Minnesota's 12-yard line, the Gophers ran for six yards on two attempts. On the next play, Bratt intercepted a Minnesota pass at the Gophers' 25 and returned it nine yards to the 16.

Wisconsin acted like a team in a hurry at this point and scored in three plays. Bratt ran over right tackle for seven yards, Gingrass hit the middle for five yards, then Bratt splintered right tackle for a touchdown. Shwalko's point-after kick gave the Badgers a 27-0 victory.

A third-quarter ankle injury forced Ameche to the sidelines for the rest of the game.

Wisconsin's Iron Horse Hits His Heisman Stride

By Robert McG. Thomas Jr.

Lee-no. Lee-no. Lee-no-Lee-no-*Lee-no*. For a nation whose immigrants are greeted by a Statue of Liberty offering succor to the outcasts of the world, America can be strangely cruel to its recent arrivals. Even those who are born here to old-world parents sometimes feel the sting of being different.

For Lino Dante Ameche, who was born in Kenosha, Wis., on June 1, 1933, the difference was even more pronounced and so was the sting. Taken abroad when he was a toddler, he spent part of his pre-school years in Italy. When he returned to the land of his birth to start school he spoke no English.

That, coupled with his funny, foreign name made him an instant object of riducule among some of his schoolmates. It didn't help in a blue collar factory town that Lino, whose father, Augusto, worked at the local Simmons bed factory, grew up not so much on the wrong side of the tracks as practically on the tracks, near a freight yard, a junk yard and a coal yard.

For all of his childhood poverty and the ridicule, Lino had a couple of things going for him. One was America, itself, despite its occasional cruelties, a land of real opportunity. Another was his adored brother, Lindo, five years older and five years wiser, who found the immediate solutions to Lino's problems.

Rigging up makeshift barbells from paint cans filled with concrete, Lindo encouraged Lino to build up his body as armor against the schoolyard taunts. As a diversion, Lindo also intro-duced him to classical music, which became a lifelong passion. Then, to remove the immediate object of the teasing, he took Lino to the Kenosha Federal Courthouse, where for 50 cents apiece they exercised their common law right to choose their own names.

Lindo became Lynn, and Lino Dante Ameche became Alan Ameche — a man, it became increasingly clear over the next four decades, who would bring honor to any name he was known by.

For the boy who became Alan (the Horse) Ameche, setting collegiate rushing records as a pile-driving Wisconsin fullback and winning the 1954 Heisman Memorial Trophy, not only went on to an acclaimed, six-year professional career with the Baltimore Colts, he followed that with a highly successful business career.

Then after retiring a wealthy man, he shifted his attention to philanthropy and community service, touching everyone he met with a special light.

When he died after undergoing heart surgery in August 1988, at the age of 55, it would be hard to deny that Lino had done himself and his nation proud.

No wonder. More than four decades earlier, his brother's body-building strategy had worked. By the time Ameche was a high school junior, his classmates were still chanting his name, but no longer in derision. For Lino had grown into a star athlete — a 10.2 sprinter in the 100-yard dash, a champion shot-putter (50 feet 2.375 inches) and, quite possibly, the greatest high school football player the state of Wisconsin has ever known.

As a junior, Ameche led his high school conference in scoring. As a senior in 1950, he became the state's most famous athlete, leading his team to an undefeated season, while averaging 8.1 yards a carry and scoring a conference record 108 points.

More than 40 years later, in August 1993, a panel of coaches polled by The Milwaukee Journal selected Ameche as the state's all-time high school player.

After that sensational season, the only question was which college to pick, a choice that was quickly narrowed to Notre Dame and the University of Wisconsin. In a visit to Kenosha, Notre Dame coach Frank Leahy won over Ameche's mother, and even persuaded the youth's second cousin, the actor Don Ameche, to call him on behalf of Notre Dame, even though the actor, a Kenosha native, had attended law school at the University of Wisconsin.

Ameche's girlfriend, Yvonne Molinaro, also favored Notre Dame because, as she candidly explained in an interview in the spring of 1994, "There weren't any girls at Notre Dame."

Notre Dame, which even agreed to accept two of Ameche's high school teammates, never had a chance — and not because Wisconsin had agreed to take seven of his Kenosha teammates. The decision had been made two years earlier when Ameche spent a weekend with his brother at Wisconsin and came home raving about the beauty of the Wisconsin

Alan Ameche, a three-time all-America fullback for the Badgers, won both the Heisman Trophy and the Chicago Tribune's Silver Football Award in 1954. He was later drafted by the NFL's Baltimore Colts.

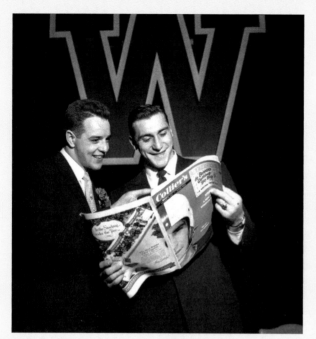

ABOVE LEFT: Ameche and teammate Gary Messer get a look at the Dec. 12, 1954 issue of *Collier's*, which featured Ameche on the front cover. ABOVE RIGHT: Ameche and his wife, Yvonne, teach their first son, Brian, to eat spaghetti.

campus, about the Wisconsin fight song and especially about the Wisconsin music room. As Yvonne later recalled it, "He said they had every phonograph record in the world there and you could play them as loud as you wanted to."

On Wisconsin.

Arriving in Madison in 1951, Ameche, showed immediate promise. When the freshman coach, George Lanphear, saw his hard-charging, knees high, running style, he said he ran like a horse. It was then that a nickname and a legend was born.

Although freshmen were then eligible for varsity football in the Big Ten, Ameche was assigned to the junior varsity. But not for long. After hammering the line and making several long gains in the J.V. opener against Iowa, he was yanked from the game and told to report to the varsity.

The next day, in the varsity opener, against Marquette, he didn't get in until the next to last play, gaining one yard on a single carry.

Two games later, he was the staring fullback, displacing the team captain, John Hammond, who played out his senior season on defense.

Over the next four years, Ameche ran roughshod over all opposition, setting school, conference and collegiate records and winning accolades.

Ameche, who led Wisconsin to a 26-8-3 record, never missed a game in his four seasons, often playing hurt, but never complaining. When new restrictions on substitutions forced him to become a two-way player his junior year, he made the difficult adjustment, becoming a competant line-

backer, an experience he said made him a better runner. Ameche, who regularly played almost 60 minutes a game, was soon known as the Iron Horse.

Ameche, whose amiability and sensitivity made him one of the most popular figures on campus, was far more than a football hero, although he was surely that. So much so that when Yvonne visited him during his freshman year, she was said to be miffed at all of the adoring attention her boyfriend received from Wisconsin coeds — 11 of whom, it was once reported, called for him while she was waiting for him in his boarding house parlor.

Yvonne doesn't remember it that way. "I'd like to think it was the other way around," she said. Whoever was receiving what attention from whom, the matter was settled on Thanksgiving Day in Ameche's sophomore year when he and Yvonne were married. By the time he was a senior they had two children.

Ameche, who had worked hard building up his body with his brother's barbells, continued working at Wisconsin, spending hours lifting weights and running in soft sand.

A slow reader from the days he first entered an American classroom speaking no English, Ameche also spent hours on his studies, earning high enough grades to win him recognition as an academic all-American. The early handicap, he said, was an advantage since he had to work harder.

Ameche, whose best game netted 205 yards, never had one of those really big, "Heisman" games, but he had sixteen 100-yard games and under his sure, steady running, the yards piled up until his career output, 3,212 yards, established a new collegiate rushing record.

Modest about his accomplishments, he said he hadn't even known that as a junior he'd finished in the top five in the Heisman voting. When he won in 1954 he said the honor meant a lot because he would finally get to meet his idol, Doc Blanchard, the 1945 winner from Army.

Passed over by his home-state Green Bay Packers because he was judged too slow to run off tackle in the pros, Ameche was drafted in the first round by the Baltimore Colts. On his first play from scrimmage, against the Chicago Bears, he ran 79 yards for a touchdown and went on to lead the league in rushing as a rookie. Over the next six seasons he gained a total of 4,045 yards, scored 40 touchdowns, was named All-Pro four times and provided an important counterpunch to quarterback John Unitas' acclaimed passing game.

For all of that, he is perhaps best known for a footnote to football history, his one-yard touchdown run on Dec. 28, 1958, that secured the Colts' overtime championship victory over the New York Giants in what has been called the greatest pro football game ever played.

"It's probably the shortest run I ever made," he said later, "and yet it's the most remembered."

Ameche, whose career ended when he injured an Archilles tendon in Dec. 1959, never looked back. He and some associates started a series of Baltimore restaurants known as Ameche's, which later became Gino's, a chain of 550 fast-food restaurants named for Ameche's teammate, Gino Marchetti.

Even before the chain was sold to the Marriott Corporation in 1982, Ameche had gone on to other things, opening a series of indoor tennis clubs in the Philadelphia area, and even, at one point, becoming a sports agent.

The endeavor lasted only six months, when Ameche, whose initial Colts' contract had been for $15,000, became disillusioned.

"I was trying to play by the rules," he said, "but I was working against guys who break all the rules."

Ameche, who was inducted into the National Football Foundation's College Football Hall of Fame in 1975, donated his Heisman Trophy to the University of Wisconsin in 1984. In his last years, he broadened his philanthropic and civic work, serving, among other things, as a director of the Philadelphia Orchestra and Corporations Chairman of the United Negro College Fund.

After college, his family continued to grow with a total of six children.

Following Ameche's death in 1988, his friends created a memorial, the Alan Ameche Foundation, which is devoted to two of Ameche's major interests, children and education. It provides to more than 30 children in the Philadelphia area, not for athletic ability or academic achievement, but on the sole basis of need, the kind Lino felt as a boy, when his brother provided the help that Lino, through his family and friends, continues to provide to other Linos of the world.

Ameche powers through the Marquette defense for a touchdown in the Badgers' 13-11 in 1953.

Iowa Defeats Buckeyes, Earn Rose Bowl Bid

By Bert McGrane

The Des Moines Register

Iowa City, Iowa | November 17, 1956

Ohio State	0	0	0	0	—	0
Iowa	0	0	6	0	—	6

Meet the champ. That's Iowa.

The dead-game Hawkeyes precipitated the wildest scene within memory here today when they beat Ohio State, 6-0, clinched the Rose Bowl assignment, grabbed a share of the Big Ten championship, broke the longest string of victories in the conference record books and charged ahead into history as one of the greatest Iowa teams of all.

Step aside, Ironmen. Move back, you stars of 1921 and '22.

Great as you are, your deeds were no more heroic than the devasting all-season show of these unheralded Hawks of 1956.

None can doubt that this was the greatest victory of all. It meant more than any game ever played in Iowa Stadium.

Both teams were involved. Ohio State was fighting for a third straight league championship, something that had never been recorded in the Big Ten. It was also fighting to extend a string of 17 straight victories in the conference.

Iowa's one big touchdown came immediately after the second-half kickoff, which the Hawks returned to their 37. Quarterback Ken Ploen's 17-yard pass to end Jim Gibbons produced the score.

And with the victory went tremendous spoils.

Iowa will win the Big Ten title outright if Michigan beats Ohio State next Saturday.

The Hawkeye opponent in their first Rose bowl assignment will be Oregon State, which assured the New Year's Day classic of its first rematch with a 14-10 squeaker today over Idaho. Iowa defeated the Beavers, 14-13, in the Hawks' second game at Iowa City, on Oct. 6.

But a snap of the fingers to official announcements. Iowa's Big Ten season is over. The Hawks are in.

But at halftime, they were all tied up, 0-0.

And then they came out for the third quarter. There was no hint of a complete change in the game, but it was developed nevertheless.

Iowa became the ruthless attacking force. Its defense was even stronger than ever but now it went on the prowl.

It smashed Ohio State, modestly perhaps, but to a degree that Iowa supremacy broke the Buckeyes' poise, sent them into retreat and finally left them on its verge of panic.

Who knows what pointed up the cold, unyielding fury with which the Hawkeyes played the second half?

Truly it was the most remarkable spectacle ever seen in Iowa Stadium.

Mass confusion reigned at the finish.

Ohio State got the ball with 2 minutes 30 seconds to play. The Bucks were back on their own 20. Only passes could do it.

They tried to buy their efforts — but this appeared a shade amateurish in the face of the poised operations of the Hawks.

A pass fell incomplete. Another picked up a mere six yards, an insignificant advance considering that Ohio State needed 80 in a hurry.

Finally they got a first down. Less than a minute and a half remained. In their desperation the Bucks called on Don Sutherin to pass. Iowa's Frank Gilliam smashed him down for a 15-yard loss and the clock kept running.

1:10 left. This time it was Jim Roseboro trying for the desperation pass and he was back on his own 12-yard line.

Alex Karras of Iowa stormed through. He smashed down Roseboro away back on the Buckeyes' 3-yard line. And Iowa took the ball there on downs.

Iowa might have won by a larger score, but nobody seems to know exactly what happened. The Hawks attempted one play. Time ran out and the horn signaled the end of the game.

A crowd broke through all restraining lines and swarmed onto the field.

The all but helpless officials tried to get the crowd off the field. They had called a penalty of some sort, although nobody seemed to know what it was.

Finally the crowd cleared the field. By this time the Hawks and Bucks were in conference on the field.

It was disclosed after the game that a roughing penalty had been called against Ohio State. The Hawkeyes conferred with

Ken Ploen's 17-yard game-winning TD pass to Jim Gibbons (88) earned the Hawkeyes a trip to the Rose Bowl.

the officials, declined the penalty and began jumping ecstatically.

The game was over, Iowa had won. There was no replay of that final effort, although if there had been the Hawks conceivably could have scored.

But what was the need of more points? The Buckeyes had none at all.

The announcement that Minnesota had squeezed out a one-point victory over favored Michigan State brought only grins from the Iowa crowd.

So what? That about covered the situation.

Ohio State's second half kickoff was a low, spiral boot down the middle and Ploen, in the middle of line of Iowa's receivers, picked it off the ground on Iowa's 26 and ran it to the 37.

From there the Hawks went 63 yards in nine plays.

As they reached the Ohio State 36 Don Clark, the Buckeye defensive back, smashed into Iowa's Don Dombrino on the 20-yard line before he had a chance to nail a pass from Ploen.

The officials ruled pass interference and Iowa had a first down on the Buckeyes' 20.

Two more plays sufficed. Bill Happel, the hustling, hard-hitting little Hawkeye halfback, hit through for three yards. On second down, Ploen saw Gibbons run past two Buckeyes and into the end zone.

As Gibbons crossed the OSU goal line, Ploen let fly a lazy lob pass, which cleared the heads of all defenders and into Gibbons' arms.

Iowa had a touchdown after 4 minutes 19 seconds of the third quarter. In came Bob Prescott, the point-getting specialist who had kicked 13 in a row.

Maybe that's Prescott's unlucky number. His fourteenth try sliced off to the right and the referee stopped to give that negative, cross-arm signal. In the end, it didn't matter.

Ohio State was no great threat after that. The Buckeyes, in fact, got across midfield only once and that venture ended 43 yards short of the Iowa goal line.

You can find scads of heroes — Happel, who outgained all of the famous Buckeye backs, and Ploen, who ran the team like the strategist and stylist that he is.

But save a spot for fullback Fred Harris, who really ripped the heart of the Buckeyes with his clutch drives near the finish.

Fifteen yards once, 13 the next, he headed the advance that kept the ball in Iowa's possession through the last fateful minutes until the Hawks finally drove within 23 yards of the Ohio State goal line. From there, the Iowa defense took charge.

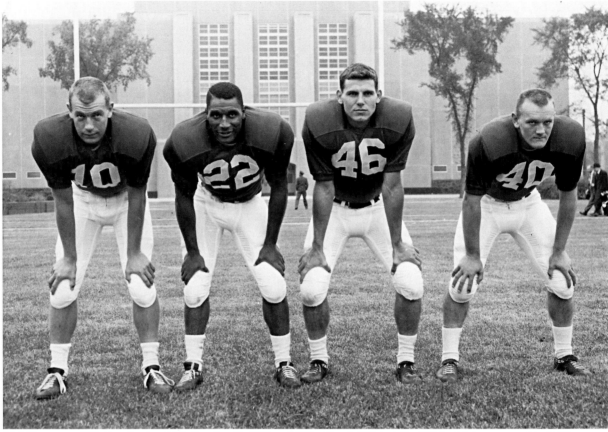

Dick Thornton (10), Ron Burton (22), Ray Purdin (46) and Mike Stock (48) led the Wildcats' turnaround in 1958.

Wildcats Roar in Romp Over Mighty Michigan

By Howard Barry
Chicago Tribune

It was Fantastic! The upsurge of Northwestern's Wildcats from the 1957 football disasters attained an undreamed apex as they beat Michigan's once mighty Wolverines, 55-24, today in Dyche Stadium. The win gave the Wildcats an unblemished record of 4-0 this season.

The crowd of 41,345 volleyed cheers of mixed amazement and jubilation through an afternoon of stunning developments.

When Dick Thornton, the Wildcats quarterback, passed down the middle to Ron Burton for 34 yards and a touchdown less than five minutes into the game, Northwestern fans were electrified at this excellent start.

Evanston, Ill. | October 18, 1958

Michigan	0	0	8	16	—	24
Northwestern	9	34	6	6	—	55

The gathering expected Michigan to strike back quickly, but the Wolverines failed to respond. Instead, there was a whirlwind of Northwestern touchdowns.

At one stage of the second quarter, Northwestern scored four touchdowns in a space of 7 minutes and 9 seconds. It was 43-0 at halftime.

At that point, the regulars went out and the reserves came in — and still the Wildcats scored.

Never before had a Northwestern team scored so many points in a conference game. The Wildcats' previous high had been 53-6 in a victory over Illinois in 1943.

It was also the most points ever scored on Michigan. The Wolverines had lost, 40-0, to Minnesota in 1935 and 46-0 to Yale in 1883.

The Wildcats showed their spirit in the way they fought for extra yardage when tackled. On one occasion, Al Kimbrough seemed hopelessly trapped at the line of scrimmage. But he kept his feet with tacklers hanging on him and went 5 yards before he was downed. That was the way the Wildcats battled all afternoon.

Wilmer Fowler carried the ball 14 times for 70 yards and scored two touchdowns. Sam Johnson added 46 yards on five carries and Mike Stock rushed for 34 yards on eight attempts.

Thornton finished with five completions on nine passes for 106 yards and one touchdown. Chip Holcomb completed two of his passes, including one for a touchdown.

Michigan was backed against its goal line on a fumble after the opening kickoff. Brad Myers punted out to the Wolverines' 43 and Burton returned it to the 26. After two plays had lost 8 yards, Thornton threw down the middle to Burton, who caught it at the 5 and stumbled into the end zone. Thornton's extra-point kick made it 7-0.

Later in the first quarter, a Northwestern punt was downed at the Michigan 5-yard line. Two plays later, Fowler tackled Fred Julian in the end zone for a safety to give the Wildcats a 9-0 lead.

After receiving Michigan's free kick, the Wildcats drove 72 yards for a touchdown. It was sparked by Thornton's 25-yard pass to Fred Williamson to reach the Michigan 14 and an 11-yard pass from Thornton to Williamson that went to the Michigan 1. Burton then dove over the middle for the touchdown. Thornton added two points with his pass to Elbert Kimbrough to give Northwestern a 17-0 lead.

Minutes later, Williamson recovered Darrell Harper's fumble on the Michigan 34. Thornton's 18-yard pass to Elbert Kimbrough moved the ball to the Wolverines' 14. The Wildcats' quick-strike advance was finished with Fowler's 1-yard run to give Northwestern a 23-0 lead. Thornton's extra-point kick, however, was wide.

A few minutes later, Thornton intercepted John Spidel's pass and ran 37 yards for a touchdown and a 29-0 lead. Thornton's 2-point pass fell incomplete.

Ray Purdin, the Northwestern halfback, recovered Brad Myers' fumble on the Michigan 39. After Al Kimbrough ran for 5 yards, Johnson got loose and ran 34 yards for a touchdown to increase the Northwestern lead to 35-0. Holcomb's 2-point pass failed.

Michigan's woes continued when Paul Yanke, the

Northwestern coach Ara Parseghian (left), athletic director Stu Holcomb (right) and William Rohr — the trio who guided Northwestern in the late 1950's.

Northwestern end, recovered Spidel's fumble on the Michigan 13-yard line. Three plays later, Elbert Kimbrough was interfered with while reaching for a Holcomb pass in the end zone. The penalty moved the ball to the Michigan 1-yard line. Burton then plunged over for the touchdown. Holcomb's pass to Yanke made it 43-0.

Early in the third quarter, Thornton's attempted lateral was intercepted by Michigan's Gary Prahst, who flashed in from left end and grabbed the ball and raced 33 yards for a TD. Tony Rio dove over for two points, but his fumble was recovered by teammate Gary McNitt in the end zone to cut Northwestern's lead to 43-8.

Late in the third quarter, Thornton recovered a fumble on the Michigan 46 and drove his squad for another touchdown. His 18-yard pass to Elbert Kimbrough reached the Michigan 6-yard line. Fowler's 2-yard run made it 49-8, but Thornton's pass fell incomplete.

The Wolverines scored on the next series, which was highlighted by Darrell Harper's 42-yard run to the Wildcats' 14 and his 8-yard TD romp. Harper added two points on a dive that cut Northwestern's lead to 49-16.

The Wildcats then drove 84 yards for their final touchdown, with Holcomb connecting on a 13-yard pass to Yanke and a 19-yarder to Purdin for the TD. Holcomb's extra-point pass failed.

Michigan wrapped up the scoring on a 16-yard run by Jared Bushong. Bushong added the two points on a dive to make it 55-24.

Wisconsin Soars Past No. 1 Northwestern

By Monte McCormick
Wisconsin State Journal

Madison, Wisc. | November 10, 1962						
Northwestern	0	0	0	6	—	6
Wisconsin	7	3	21	7	—	38

Wisconsin exploded the rocket that was heard around the world today before it went into orbit. The explosion rocked the Northwestern football team, 37-6, and turned the Big 10 race into a three-way tie with Wisconsin, Northwestern and Minnesota sharing the deadlock.

The defeat was the first of the season for the Wildcats and put a crimp in their plans for an undisputed conference title. The Badgers and Northwestern now sport 4-1 Big 10 records and are 6-1 this season.

Among the 65,501 Homecoming fans who jammed every cranny of Camp Randall Stadium for a new all-time record, were 12 members of Wisconsin's undefeated 1912 champions, who tamed the Wildcats, 56-0. Wisconsin has won 11 of the last 13 games with the Wildcats.

The Badgers posted one touchdown in the first quarter and a field goal in the second for a 10-0 lead, then they put the contest out of reach in the third quarter with three touchdowns to reach 31-0.

Northwestern then scored its touchdown on a long pass. The Badgers responded by marching for its final score.

Today's game was billed as a passing duel between Northwestern's Tom Myers and Ron Vander Kelen.

Myers completed 16 of 27 passes, including one that went for a touchdown — a 39-yard toss to fullback Steve Murphy, who only had to elude one Badger defender.

Vander Kelen lived up to his billing by completing 12 of 22 passes for 181 yards and 3 TD's.

Gary Kroner, completely healed after a hip pointer injury kept him out of several games, led the Badgers in scoring by collecting Wisconsin's first 17 points and a total of 19 for the game.

The other 18 points were amassed by Louie Holland, who scored three touchdowns.

Kroner scored in the first quarter on an 11-yard pass from Vander Kelen. He booted a 38-yard field goal in the second quarter and opened the flood gates in the third quarter when he broke through a would-be tackler at the Wildcats' 5-yard line and danced into the end zone on a 23-yard pass from Vander Kelen.

When he kicked his second extra point, it gave Wisconsin a 17-0 lead. Less than six minutes later, the Badgers were in front, 31-0.

Vander Kelen was the engineer of the Badgers' offense, but Holland was the locomotive as he circled end for nine yards and slashed off tackle for four more to score a pair of TD's.

After Northwestern got on the scoreboard, Holland took an 11-yard pass from Vander Kelen, dodged a tackler on the five and raced into the end zone with 12 seconds left.

Wisconsin got its first score on a 77-yard drive with five first downs before Vander Kelen hitting Kroner with an 11-yard pass.

The next time Wisconsin had the ball, it marched 45 yards to Northwestern's 18, with Kroner kicking the field goal for a 10-0 lead.

Kroner started the Badgers' third-quarter explosion with a 45-yard kickoff return. He later scored on a 23-yard strike from Vander Kelen.

Shortly after the Badgers' touchdown, Ron Carlson batted a Myers pass and Roger Pillath caught it and ran to the Northwestern 21. This set up Holland's first touchdown — a 9-yard run that boosted the Badgers' lead to 24-0.

Merritt Norvell recovered a Wildcats' fumble on the Northwestern 27 to set up Wisconsin's third touchdown in the third quarter — a 4-yard run by Holland — and for all practical purposes the lights went out for Northwestern.

The Wildcats' lone score came when Myers threw a 39-yard pass to Murphy, who made a move on Norvell, then raced into the Wisconsin end zone.

In the final minutes of the game, Wisconsin marched 75 yards, with the big play being a 34-yard pass from Vander Kelen to Pat Richter. Vander Kelen connected with Holland for an 11-yard pass for the games' final touchdown with only 12 seconds left to play.

Richter caught a total of five passes for 77 yards.

Wisconsin's Gary Kroner (47) scored on an 11-yard TD pass in the first quarter. He scored 19 of the Badgers' points.

Michigan Snaps Spartans' Nine-Year Win Streak

By Tom Rowland
The Michigan Daily

East Lansing, Mich. | October 10, 1964						
Michigan	0	3	0	14	—	17
Michigan State	7	0	0	3	—	10

Michigan's offensive machine sputtered, coughed and waited until late in the fourth quarter to roar with two touchdowns that whipped Michigan State here this afternoon, 17-10, ending a nine-year winless string against the Spartans.

It was also the first time since 1955 that the Woverines have won their first three games of the season.

A stadium-record crowd of 78,234 watched sub halfback Rick Sygar haul in a five-yard pass from quarterback Bob Timberlake for one touchdown and then throw one himself to end John Henderson from 31 yards out for another TD as the Wolverines erased a 10-3 deficit late in the game.

In a do-or-die effort midway though the final quarter, the Michigan offense finally got rolling after a series of fumbles and a rugged Spartan defense almost completely stymied the Blue attack.

Timberlake keyed the Wolverines to midfield with a pair of 11- and eight-yard passes to Sygar and then let loose with a 29-yard bomb to Henderson as Michigan created its first major offensive threat.

Henderson was finally stopped at the Michigan State 21, and on the next play it was Sygar again getting the pitch from Timberlake on the often-used option. He dashed to the nine-yard line before being forced out of bounds.

Two plays later, Timberlake hit Sygar on a swing pass, and the Niles, Ohio, sophomore neatly dodged a Spartan defender and jumped into the end zone. The first Wolverine touchdown of the day pushed the score to 10-9, with the Spartans on top with just seven minutes to play.

Michigan coach Bump Elliott had the choice to either pass or run for two points or stick with a one-point kick that would tie it up. Elliott took one look at the clock and made up his mind — go for broke.

"We went for two after the first touchdown because we wanted to win it right here and then."

With all of jammed Spartan Stadium in a single, held breath, Timberlake rolled to the left on the option and pitched to fullback Mel Anthony going around the end. Anthony cut in, twisted, dove and ended up only millimeters away from the goal stripe.

Taking Timberlake's kickoff, the Spartans had only to hang on to the football for six minutes to take the one-point victory.

But a fired-up Michigan defense, paced by big tackle Bill Yearby, stopped State in its tracks on three downs, and on the fourth Dick Rinduss returned the Spartans' punt to the Michigan State 41.

Carl Ward hit left tackle for four yards, Timberlake pitched to Sygar, who lofted the winning pass to Henderson, who was clear in the MSU secondary, and Henderson romped into the end zone for a 15-10 lead.

Timberlake put on the finishing touches, firing to end Steve Smith for the two-point conversion.

Earlier in the game it was a different story.

Michigan received the opening kickoff and immediately fumbled the football. On the second play from scrimmage, Anthony fumbled a Timberlake pitchout and the Spartans' Ed Macuga pounced on the loose ball at the Michigan 17.

It was only a matter of minutes before State made the most of the break. A key pass from quarterback Steve Juday to quarterback-playing-flanker Dave McCormick put the ball at the Michigan 4, and Juday followed two plays later with a one-yard quarterback sneak for the touchdown.

Michigan halfback Jim Detwiler fumbled the kickoff following State's touchdown, but Ward recovered. Then on the first play, Ward fumbled and recovered the ball again.

Timberlake passed 29 yards to Smith for a first down, but after the Wolverine drive moved the ball to the Michigan State 18, Detwiler fumbled again and the ever-wary Spartans jumped on the ball.

State showed off its new spectacular pass-catching end Gene Washington, a glue-fingered sophomore, on the next series as Washington outstretched Rindfuss on a 43-yard pass play that sent the Spartans to the Michigan 5-yard line.

The fumbles weren't all Michigan's, though, as Juday, hit

John Henderson (81) grabs a pass from halfback Rick Sygar to score the Wolverines' winning touchdown.

hard by red-dogging linebacker Tom Cecchini, fumbled on the next play and Yearby recovered for Michigan.

The Wolverines got their first big chance to get some points on the scoreboard in the middle of the second quarter when a 16-yard dash around right end by Anthony and a pass interference call pushed the Wolverines to the State 14 and a first down. When three plays fizzled, Timberlake's 22-yard field goal attempt sailed wide to the right.

Returning to the Spartans' territory just before halftime, Timberlake's pass for Ward went incomplete, but a second pass interference call gave the Wolverines the ball at State's 35. The veteran quarterback again went to the air lanes, and with just seconds to go before intermission hit Henderson, who stepped out bounds at the 13.

Timberlake then swung his foot through a 29-yard field goal and three points on the last play of the half to cut the Spartans' lead to 7-3.

The intermission wasn't rest enough on the kickoff. Ward lost the ball on a hard tackle and once again the Spartans

recovered, gaining possession at the Michigan 18.

This time the Wolverine defense held and on fourth down from the 14 State's barefoot kicker, Dick Kenney, misfired on the first of two attempts.

The second one came half a period later when the Hawaiian import's boot went wide to the left on a kick from the 34.

State knocked on the Michigan end zone door at the beginning of the fourth period when McCormick engineered a drive that was halted at the Michigan 9-yard line. It was two strikes and you're out for Kenney. On fourth down and 5, Spartans coach Duffy Daugherty sent in sophomore Larry Lukasik to boot the field goal that gave the Spartans a 10-3 lead.

The Wolverines held State's leading ground-gainer, Clinton Jones, to a minus two yards rushing and allowed the Spartans only four completions in 12 pass attempts. Timberlake hit home on nine of 18 pass attempts through the air, while Anthony was Michigan's big man on the ground with 70 yards on 21 carries.

Phipps & Co. Rout Ohio State in Columbus

By George Bolinger
The Journal and Courier

Columbus, Ohio | October 15, 1967						
Purdue	14	21	6	0	—	41
Ohio State	0	0	0	6	—	6

Purdue's Boilermakers, winners of nine in a row and firmly entrenched as the No. 2 team in the nation, got one of its most impressive and most satisfying victories in school history today with its 41-6 pounding of Woody Hayes' Ohio State Buckeyes before an over-capacity crowd of 84,069 at Ohio Stadium — most of whom were just as shocked as Hayes.

Purdue took the lead with less than a minute into the game, had a 14-0 lead after the first quarter and was up, 35-0, at halftime and quite a few of the 84,069 were thinking about heading for the exits.

The Buckeyes, who didn't get untracked for 59 minutes, finally scored in the final half-minute.

Dennis Cirbes, a Purdue senior, scored the first touchdown of his career on the fourth play of the game, intercepted a pass from Buckeyes quarterback Gerry Ehrsam and raced to the

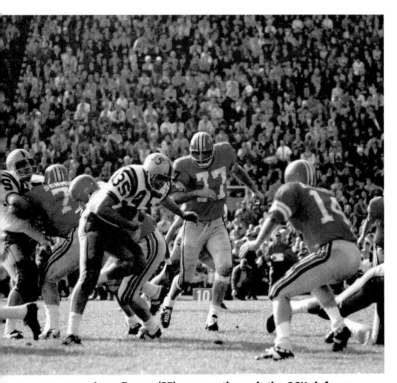

Leon Troyer (35) powers through the OSU defense.

Ohio State end zone.

On Purdue's first drive, Mike Phipps drove the Boilermakers 67 yards in 14 plays for a 14-0 lead, with Perry Williams diving over for three straight plays until he crossed the Ohio State goal line.

In the second quarter, Phipps threw 9 straight completions as he marched Purdue 70 yards for its third touchdown, with Phipps connecting on a 5-yard pass to Marion Griffin in the end zone for the score. With four minutes left in the half, the Boilermakers led, 21-0.

Following a Buckeyes punt that went out of bounds at the OSU 45, Phipps threw two straight passes to Leroy Keyes to reach the OSU 22. Two plays later, Jim Beime flew from left end and into the end zone, raced past five Buckeye defenders, looked up and the ball was arriving in his arms for another TD. With 1:51 left before halftime, Purdue was up, 28-0.

On the Buckeyes' second offensive play, Don Webster forced a fumble and Cirbes recovered the ball on the OSU 27.

Three plays later, Keyes showed the crowd of 84,069 why he is gaining so many headlines, by racing 21 yards into the Ohio State end zone. With 1:11 remaining in the second quarter, Purdue was on top, 35-0.

Phipps & Co. continued their memorable performance in the third quarter by taking the second half kickoff and driving 73 yards in 10 plays with Phipps running and passing to the OSU 7-yard line. Williams then bulled his way over for the touchdown, taking a couple of Buckeyes with him the last few yards. Bob Baltzell, who been successful on his extra-point kicks all afternoon, finally missed one, leaving the score at 41-0.

Afterward, the Purdue reserves took over.

Ohio State's lone score came on a 10-yard pass from backup quarterback Kevin Rusnak to Bill Anders to cap a 67-yard, 13-play drive.

Phipps finished with 210 yards passing and 49 running, Williams had 47 yards on the ground and Keyes had 39 rushing and 64 yards on four catches.

Ohio State defender Ted Provost (46) intercepts a pass intended for Purdue's Lee Ryan in the Buckeyes' end zone.

Indiana fans celebrated the school's biggest win, which gave them the Big Ten title and trip to the Rose Bowl.

Hoosiers Win Big Ten Title, Rose Bowl Next

By Bob Hammel
Sunday Herald-Times

Bloomington, Ind. | November 25, 1967						
Purdue	7	0	7	0	—	14
Indiana	7	12	0	0	—	19

The Miracle of Indiana, college football's most thrilling and captivating story in a generation, came to pass with simple figures late this afternoon: Indiana 19, Purdue 14.

Indiana, the Big Ten's synonym for loser in football ... Indiana, a 51-6 victim of arch-rival Purdue one year before ... Indiana, with that 19-14 conquest of the team ranked No. 3 in the nation and rated as Purdue's best ever, suddenly stood as the tri-champion of the Big Ten and the legitimate, credentialed representative of the nation's most prestigious conference in the nation's most prestigious game — the Rose Bowl.

John Pont's Hoosiers will go to Pasadena to meet No. 1-ranked Southern California on New Year's Day as the last Big ten team ever to make the trip ... but the first from

Hoosierland ever to go as a champion.

The 9-1 record, second-best in Indiana's 80 football seasons, also made the Hoosiers — scoffed all year by non-believers — the fourth-glossiest Big Ten representative in the 22 years the league has been sending teams to Pasadena. Only unbeaten Michigan in 1947, Illinois in 1951 and Michigan State in 1965 topped the Hoosiers' mark. When Purdue went last year, the Boilermakers were 8-3 and runnerup in the Big Ten.

The fantastic Hoosiers closed with typical 1967 Indiana drama, with Purdue on the Indiana 23 and struggling to get a play off when the gun sounded.

It closed the biggest Hoosier victory in the most climactic game ever played in the bitter 77-year Indiana-Purdue series.

With the final gun, red-capped faithful among the record 52,770 crowd at IU Stadium spilled onto the field and mobbed their heroes.

It was Indiana's first victory over Purdue at Bloomington in a dismal 20 years, and only the second anywhere in that period, during which Purdue won 17 times and tied once.

Indiana never trailed in a game which it entered as a 14-point underdog.

The Hoosiers took the lead with a play that typified the season as sophomore quarterback Harry Gonso fired a short yardage touchdown pass to sophomore flanker Jade Butcher, who entered the end zone with the ball held high in the cocky, uninhibited style that transformed a perennial loser into a champion.

The Hoosiers had all 19 of their points posted by halftime, and the defensive unit made those stand up by containing the most powerful offense in Big Ten history.

Purdue came close to spoiling the Hoosiers' plans.

The Boilermakers methodically cut a 19-7 hole to 19-14 with a ground-bound third quarter touchdown march, and in the fourth period they marched goalward again.

But linebacker Ken Kaczmarek, a senior who was trampled in the 51-6 massacre last year, saved the Hoosiers' season by smashing into Purdue fullback Perry Williams at the Indiana 3-yard line, jarring the ball loose.

Sophomore Mike Baughman pounced on the ball at the Hoosier 1, and Purdue never got that far again.

There were other "Rose Bowl" plays that will live in Indiana football history:

Sophomore John Isenbarger's 63-yard pressure punt that pushed the Boilermakers deep into their own territory with 5 minutes left to play.

Junior defensive end Cal Snowden's pell-mell rush through a touted Purdue passing pocket to down passer Mike Phipps on a fourth-and-8 play at Indiana's 45, with 2:42 left to play.

Senior fullback Terry Cole's lightning, 63-yard thrust up the middle for the touchdown that proved to be the game-winner. For Cole, whose labors in this, his senior season, had been primarily spent in unglamorous blocking that made all-America nominees out of sophomores Gonso and Isenbarger, the run highlighted a 155-yard rushing day that represented an IU record for a Big Ten game.

Gonso's gambling, bullseye fourth-down-and-2 pass to the reliable Butcher for a 9-yard gain that kept the Hoosiers going toward their second touchdown, which ultimately was gained by senior Mike Krivoshia's 2-yard line buck ... a "Second-effort" play on which he was stopped inside the one, but lunged on forward to get the score.

The hard-hitting game included five fumbles — all by Purdue, and four of them were recovered by Indiana.

Gonso put the Hoosiers ahead with a four-play, 51-yard surge in the first period that was launched by another long Cole dash — 42 yards — to Purdue's 9. On third down, Gonso hit Butcher slanting through the middle of the Purdue defense to get the touchdown, at 7:44 of the first quarter.

Purdue drove right back for the tying score with an 80-yard march. Williams got the touchdown from the 9, tying the game at 7-7 with 3:42 left in the first period.

The decisive second quarter fireworks started with Snowden's recovery of a Leroy Keyes fumble at the Indiana 37. Gonso hit 3-for-3 on passes — to three different sophomores, Eric Stolberg, Isenbarger and Butcher — for 58 of the yards and Krivoshia got the final 2 yards with 11:06 left in the half.

Cole's 63-yard touchdown bolt came on the third play after sophomore Harold Dunn had recovered a Bob Dillingham fumble at Indiana's 29.

"It was third-and-2 and we were over on the sidelines screaming, "get the first down ... get the first down," said Indiana defensive coordinator Ernie Plank. It was the best first down of the year."

Plank's crew held Purdue'a all-America ball carrier, Leroy Keyes, to his least-impressive marks of a fabulous season. He carried 20 times for 114 yards — spectacular for anyone but Leroy — and he caught two passes for 34 yards. He missed most of the last quarter with rib injuries.

Keyes' rushing total left him only 4 yards short of the Purdue single-season record set by Harry Szulborski in 1948. Keyes, however, did lead both the nation and the Big Ten in scoring.

Phipps, the Purdue sophomore quarterback, did set a new Boilermakers' single-season passing record with 1,993 yards — 29 more than Bob Griese' mark which was set last season.

But Phipps hit only 11 of 28 tosses and averaged just 5 yards per pass. For the year, the Columbus, Ind., passer, who had been the Big Ten passing leader, had been averaging 8 yards per toss.

For Indiana, besides Cole's spectacular day, Isenbarger ran for 61 yards to set a Hoosier sophomore record with 579 yards. Gonso completed a sensational regular season by throwing for 111 yards and his 9th touchdown, and Butcher equaled the Hoosier record by scoring his 10th TD.

But it was a day for team achievements, not individual. And, never, ever did an Indiana team achieve more in one sunshiny, crisp, memorable, historic afternoon.

Buckeyes Romp Over U-M

By Lou Smith

The Cincinnati Enquirer

Columbus, Ohio	November 23, 1968					
Michigan	7	7	0	0	—	14
Ohio State	7	14	6	23	—	50

Ohio State's all-winning football team, nifty as an army tank, squashed the highly-touted Michigan attack like a bug today and ground to a Big Ten championship and a 50-14 victory — a score so fictitious before a record-breaking Ohio Stadium crowd of 85,371.

The Ohio State defense stopped Michigan's fine running backs and held the Wolverines' rushing attack to only 140 yards and allowed only 171 via the air. The Buckeyes pounded out 421 yards on the ground and 146 by passing.

The defeat was the worst suffered by Michigan in the long and colorful series, dating back to 1902. The worst previous setback was a 50-20 pasting by the Buckeyes in 1961.

No match for the hard-hitting Buckeyes offensively, the Wolverines did what they could to check Woody Hayes' squad and put them under extreme pressure for the best part of two quarters and held Ohio State, 21-14, at the half.

Coming to the last 10 minutes of the third quarter, Michigan was still very alive when Ohio State halfback Larry Zelina led his beleaguered cohorts out of the woods with a six-yard touchdown dash to climax a 72-yard drive.

In the end it was a rout as Ohio State, showing no mercy to its nearest conference foe, ran up four touchdowns and Jim Roman booted a 22-yard field goal.

Finishing a nine-game schedule without a defeat while running its victory total to an impressive 13 over a two-season period, Ohio State not only wrapped up its 12th Big Ten championship, but also the right to clash with Southern California in the historic Rose Bowl on New Year's Day.

In the closing minutes, the record-breaking crowd was chanting the inevitable "We're No. 1."

And it's a valid claim that the Buckeyes are the nations' best.

Ohio State, like in most of the previous games, was alert and aggressive as it played heads-up ball to swarm the Wolverines off their feet, grabbing the halftime lead with a touchdown in the final 36 seconds.

The Wolverines, who reeled off eight straight victories after dropping their season opener to California, scored first in the contest. They swept 80 yards in eight plays, with all-American halfback Ron Johnson turning in a dazzling 39-yard run and a two-yard plunge for the score.

The Buckeyes had no standout performers, but there were heroes all over the place.

After spotting the Wolverines the lead, the Buckeyes came right back to make it 7-7 with 2:04 left to play in the first quarter. They sped 45 yards in 10 plays, with fullback Jim Otis scoring the first of his four touchdowns on a plunge from the Michigan 5-yard line.

Ohio State moved out front early in the second quarter, with Kern scoring on a 5-yard run.

Michigan made it 14-14 with 7:12 left to play in the half with Johnson's 1-yard TD run.

Undaunted, and with the clock ticking off the final seconds of the first half, Ohio State moved back in front to stay, with Otis finishing a 17-play, 86-yard drive by hurtling over from the Michigan 1-yard line.

The second half was a nightmare for the thousands of Michigan fans as the Buckeyes ran through, over and around the bewildered and out-manned Wolverines.

Zelina ran wild for a touchdown in the third quarter, Roman connected on a 22-yard field goal, Otis muscled his way into the Michigan end zone twice and Kern added another on a 3-yard run.

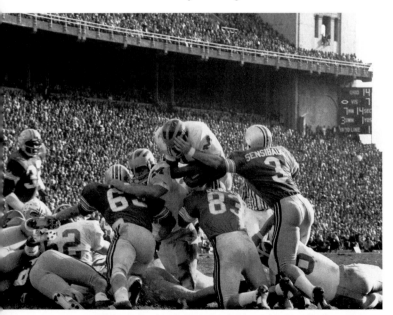

OSU's defense slammed Michigan backs all afternoon.

Quarterback Rex Kern (10) ran for 2 TD's against Michigan. The OSU offense piled up 567 yards of total offense.

Purdue halfback Leroy Keyes, a two-time all-American, won the Big Ten's Silver Football Award in 1968.

Catch Him If You Can

BY MIKE BYNUM

For three seasons, the frequent battle cry of Purdue football fans at Ross-Ade Stadium and other Big Ten gridiron palaces was "Give the ball to Leroy!"

And for three seasons, he delivered as a triple-threat runner, passer and as a defensive back.

Leroy Keyes was the greatest player in Purdue football history and his performance on the gridiron was unforgettable.

As a sophomore, he played mostly on defense and part-time in the backfield with Bob Griese and Perry Williams on the Boilermaker squad that won the 1967 Rose Bowl, 14-13, in a fierce battle with Southern Cal.

As a junior in 1967, while playing on defense he held Notre Dame's all-America receiver, Jim Seymour, to just one reception. Playing on offense, he ran for 27 yards on eight carries and caught nine passes for 108 yards and one touchdown.

In 1968, Notre Dame students plastered campus billboards with "Most Wanted" signs bearing Keyes' face on them. Instead of scaring him, the ploy only got him more fired up.

On gameday, Keyes was a one-man wrecking crew. He ran for 90 yards and two touchdowns on 15 carries. He also had three pass receptions for 33 yards and completed a TD pass for 17 yards. On defense, while playing part-time in the secondary, Keyes helped keep Irish receiver Seymour out of the end zone for the second straight year.

His biggest game in his senior season was against Indiana. In that contest, he ripped off four touchdowns, including a 56-yard pass reception and a 1-yard run for the game-winning TD in a memorable 38-35 win.

Keyes was picked to both the All-Big Ten and all-America teams in 1967 and 1968. He finished third in the balloting in the Heisman Trophy voting in 1967 and was the runnerup in 1968.

He later played in the pros for the Philadelphia Eagles and the Kansas City Chiefs and was inducted into the College Football Hall of Fame in 1990.

In 1987, Keyes was voted the greatest player in the first 100 years of Purdue football.

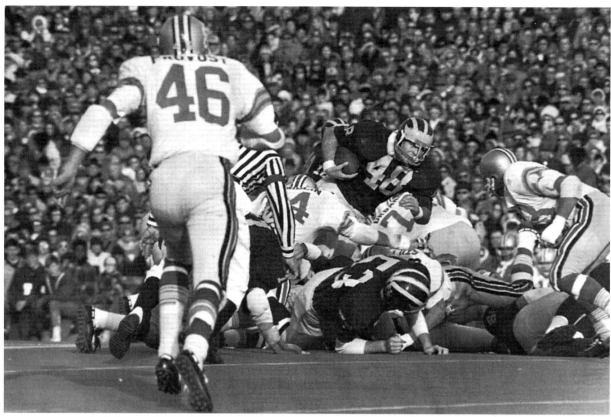

Michigan halfback Garvie Craw (48), who scored 2 TD's, pounds through the middle of the Buckeyes' defense.

103,588 Watch as U-M Humbles the Buckeyes

By Joe Falls
Detroit Free Press

Ann Arbor, Mich.	November 22, 1969						
Ohio State	6	6	0	0	—	12
Michigan	7	17	0	0	—	24

Garvie Craw, the hard-working football player, stood in the middle of the Michigan dressing room after today's stunning 24-12 victory over the Ohio State Buckeyes and he said it all.

"Unbelieveable ... fantastic ... the greatest victory in the history of the world!" he bellowed.

Craw, like his teammates, couldn't hide his elation.

"I think," the young man said with a smile, "Bo has Woody's number. They didn't do a thing our coach hadn't told us they would do. Bo's got to be Coach of the Year, and if they don't give him a million awards, it'll be a sin."

It was a mad, mad scene in the Michigan locker room. The players thundered up the tunnel, shouting and screaming and belting each other on the back.

"We're No. 1. We're No. 1!" They kept yelling.

The walls of their locker room shook and the tremor probably could be felt all the way to Columbus, Ohio.

"Bring on the Vikings!" someone shouted. "Yeah!" answered another group of players. "Bring on the Vikings!"

The boss, Bo Schembechler, had that wild look of victory on his face.

"We're going to the Rose Bowl as the co-champions and

don't forget that," he said almost defiantly. "You know what they are saying out on the West Coast — that they don't even want us."

"I wouldn't even have wanted to go if we didn't win today, but now we're going and we're going as champs."

Quarterback Don Moorhead, who outplayed the celebrated Rex Kern all the way, spoke easily, confidently about the stirring triumph.

"We felt we could do it all along," he said. "All that business about them being supermen was such a bunch of bull. We knew they could be had.

"We didn't do anything differently," Moorhead went on. "We just went out there and punched it to them. We thought they'd be weak off the tackles and so that's the way we went."

Moorhead had a much better afternoon than Kern, who was eventually removed from the game.

"Yeah, I feel good about getting the best of him," said Moorhead. "That's what our coach told us at the start of the week — that we all had to beat the man across the way from us. Kern happened to be the guy I had to play against."

Moorhead couldn't keep the smile off his boyish face.

"It made us sick all that stuff we were reading about Ohio State," he said. "You know that petition they got up out on the West Coast about them wanting Ohio State in the Rose Bowl.

"It just made us to want it all the more."

Michigan's plan was simple, according to Bo Schembechler.

"We just decided to run at them," he said. "We watched all of their game films and we saw that whenever anyone made a mistake against Ohio State, they got behind and could never catch up.

"We were determined not to make those mistakes. We knew (Jim) Otis would get his yardage, but we knew we had to stop Kern."

Henry Hill, Michigan's middle guard and a key man in the defensive alignment, said the plan was to keep Kern hemmed in.

"The (game) films showed us that every big play he made, he made to the outside," said Hill. "We just tried to keep him from going wide."

Barry Pierson, the Wolverines' defensive back who played so superbly picking off three of Kerns' passes and setting up a touchdown with a magnificent punt return, spoke as if he knew the Wolverines were going to win all of the time.

"Yeah!" he said. "We knew it — we knew it last Monday. In fact we knew it all season. You could just feel it in the guys.

"You could tell right after the first series of downs. The guys up front could feel it, and Ohio State felt it. They moved on

us, but we adjusted and stopped them."

Michigan captain Jim Mandich sat quietly in front of his locker, accepting the congratulations of well-wishers. He said, "When they put those first six points up there, I had visions of last year.

"But our confidence came right back. I think when we came back and scored so quickly, it demoralized them a little."

Mandich said that the Wolverines put in no new plays for the game.

"Oh!" he corrected himself. "We had one new one but never used it."

Craw, who scored the Wolverines' first two touchdowns — the ones which put Michigan ahead each time, kept shaking his head in astonishment.

"That's just got to be the best victory this school has ever had," he said. "It's unbelievable, that's all. I still can't wait until I read the newspapers. Then maybe I'll believe it."

Craw broke into a laugh.

"You know," he said. "I get those four touchdowns at Illinois, but I gained only 18 yards all day and I felt little guilty. But, man, I don't feel guilty today."

As Schembechler walked off the field, he was met by Woody Hayes. Woody offered him one word: "Congratulations."

"I didn't say anything," Bo said. "I just shook his hand."

One game statistic stunned Schembechler, who was an Ohio State assistant for six seasons.

"You mean we intercepted six passes against Ohio State? I can't believe it," he said.

Tight end Jim Mandich cuts upfield against the Buckeyes.

It's Official ... Spartans Defeat No. 1 Ohio State

BY CHARLIE VINCENT
Detroit Free Press

East Lansing, Mich.	November 9, 1974					
Ohio State	3	0	3	7	—	13
Michigan State	0	3	0	13	—	16

It was like a Cecil B. DeMille movie.

The cast of thousands sprawled in cinemascopic grandeur from one end of Spartan Stadium to the other, milling about aimlessly, or casually lounging around in groups of twos or threes while the Michigan State band entertained during the 46-minute wait between the end of today's MSU-Ohio State game and the official announcement of its outcome.

"The final score," a voice finally boomed over the public address system, "...Michigan State 16, Ohio State 13."

And what remained of the crowd of 78,533 broke into a thunderous cheer, then filed orderly out of the stadium for the delayed "happy hour."

It was Michigan State's biggest win in years, one deserving of the pandemonium caused by its many odd turns, topped by the indecision at the final gun that led to the long delay in making the Spartans' victory over the No. 1 in the nation official.

Twice during the Buckeyes' final ill-fated drive, one of the officials overruled another and the last mix-up came on the final play and caused Big Ten commissioner Wayne Duke — who viewed the game from the press box — to go pale, then race to the officals' dressing room for an explanation.

Ohio State had marched 70 yards — to MSU's 1-yard line — and appeared on the verge of snatching the victory away from Michigan State.

With 29 seconds left to play, Champ Henson smashed into the middle of the line.

Thud ... nothing. Nothing but a mass of green-shirted bodies lying on top of him and refused to allow him to get off the ground and back into the OSU lineup.

Eventually, he did make his way out of the tangle of arms and legs and took his place in the Ohio State backfield. And the Buckeyes did run off a play — a play that resulted in one official signaling "touchdown" and two others waving it off, indicating time had run out before the play was run.

Thousands of fans mobbed the field immediately while players and coaches from both teams were trying to get an explanation of what had happened.

As Duke left the press box, he said: "Don't announce a thing until I return from the officials' dressing room."

And so everybody hung by their fingernails for three-quarters of an hour.

On the first play of that drive — which started with three minutes and 11 seconds remaining — Michigan State linebacker Terry McClowry came up with what, for a moment, appeared to be a game saver.

He dived in front of a Cornelius Greene pass at OSU's 37-yard line and head linesman Ed Scheck ruled it an interception but umpire Frank Stocchia waved that one off, contending McClowry had dropped the ball.

It had been that kind of game from the very start. A game of great individual efforts, mixed with bungled opportunities, hyperboles and contradictions.

Mike Hurd, one of the most reliable Spartans receivers, was all alone, with no one within 10 yards of him, when he dropped a Charlie Baggett pass on OSU's 20 during the Spartans' first possession.

He dropped another on the Buckeyes' 30 late in the first half, too. But he caught an 18-yarder from Baggett that ended with Hans Nielsen's 39-yard field goal that allowed the Spartans to go into the dressing room tied, 3-3, at halftime.

The Spartan defense gave up 19 first downs ... and 377 yards total offense. But they frustrated the Buckeyes time after time inside the 10.

The No. 1-ranked Buckeyes had to abandon its thunderous running game and resort to field goals not once, not twice, but three times — as Michigan State stopped them at the five, three and eight.

Tom Klaban kicked the first two field goals — from 22 and 20 yards, but missed the third, leaving the Buckeyes with a 6-3 lead going into the final quarter.

A fumble by Baggett led to Ohio State's only touchdown, with 5:57 left in the fourth period, and it appeared the

Michigan State's Mike Jones (84) scores on a 50-yard, fourth-quarter pass that narrowed Ohio State's lead to 13-9.

Spartans' magnificent bid to an upset was doomed.

Steve Luke got the Buckeyes started, falling on Baggetts' bobble at MSU's 44, and Henson ended the drive eight plays later by smashing in from the 1-yard line.

Then Michigan State struck with amazing quickness and authority.

Baggett began passing. He hit fullback Levi Jackson for 17 yards, Mike Jones for six, then found Jones all alone behind Ohio State safety Tom Fox and threw the 50-yard bomb that pulled the Spartans to within four, 13-9. Baggett passed to Jackson on the two-point attempt, but the Spartans fullback fell to the turf short of the end zone.

The Michigan State defense, however, made the Buckeyes give the ball back four plays later. Ohio State's Tom Skladeny punted all the way to the 12 and the Spartans found them 88 yards away from the end zone.

And with the No. 1 team in the nation staring them in the face, few in the overflow crowd expected what would happen next.

Jackson, a 215-pounder from Detroit Kettering, slammed into the middle of the Buckeye line, found himself wide open, gave linebacker Arnold Jones a little fake, headed for the sidelines and outran everybody in his 88-yard journey to the Ohio State end zone as the crowd went wild and Woody Hayes went livid.

Neilsen converted and that set the stage for the fantastic finish.

And in the excitement, no one even seemed to notice Archie Griffin went over the 100-yard mark for the 19th straight game, rushing for 140.

Twice as Spectacular

BY ED SHERMAN

There were players who ran for more yards. There were players who instilled deeper memories of their spectacular dashes to glory.

There definitely were players who went on to have much better pro careers. There also were players whose national fame endured long after their last run.

And yet of all the college football players, all the great stars and legends, there's only one Archie Griffin. What separated Griffin from the rest was the number two. Two as in two Heisman Trophies.

In the first 70 years of the award, Griffin has been the only player to be honored twice by The Downtown Athletic Club. Not Matt Leinhart, not Roger Staubach, not Tony Dorsett, not Paul Hornung: the list goes on.

Not one of those icons in the game was able to accomplish what Ohio State's Archie Mason Griffin did. For that achievement, Griffin will always hold a unique and treasured place in college football history.

In 1974, Griffin's junior year, he rushed for 1,620 yards, averaging 6.9 yards per carry. When it came time for the Heisman balloting, Griffin easily outdistanced Southern Cal's Anthony Davis.

The next year the big question was whether Griffin would do it again. He went in as a marked man. Griffin took so much punishment in 1975 he rarely was able to practice before Wednesday after Saturday's games. Nevertheless, Griffin shined again, rushing for 1,357 yards in leading the Buckeyes to an 11-0 regular-season mark. Over a remarkable three-year stretch, Griffin had an NCAA-record 31 games where he rushed for more than 100 yards.

California's Chuck Muncie had better numbers in 1975, but the voters went in for Griffin, giving him an unprecedented second Heisman Memorial Trophy. Practice obviously makes perfect, because after being overcome by emotions in his first ceremony, Griffin was much more composed the second time around.

"Winning the Heisman is a dream I first had when I was 9 years old," Griffin said. "To have it happen once is great. Then to go back again ... it's a great feeling. It amazes me. I say to myself, 'I did that?' "

Griffin was an unlikely candidate. The press guides listed him at between 5-foot-9-inches and 5-11, but in reality Griffin was just under 5-foot-8 and weighed only 182 pounds. His first pro coach, Cincinnati's Bill Johnson said of him, "When you first look at him, you say, 'My God, look how little he is.' "

But his college coach and biggest fan, Woody Hayes, used to say, "It's not how big the dog is, but how much fight is in the dog."

Griffin clearly was a fighter. He always talked of "the three D's: Determination, dedication and desire."

For Griffin, it wasn't always a corny slogan, it was a way of life. It's what set him apart on the football field.

Hayes called Griffin the greatest runner he ever saw, which takes in quite a few runners. What impressed tough-nosed Hayes the most was Griffin's ability to block.

Hayes used to go on and on about Griffin. And on and on, and on and on.

"Archie Griffin is the greatest back I've ever seen or coached," Hayes said. "He's also the most popular player we've ever had, by far. In fact, we value Archie's attitude more than his football ability. Which is saying something, because he can do everything. He's a great blocker, a great faker and a great broken-field runner, one of those rare backs who can run over you or around you. It's like Rommel's wide-front attack or Sherman maneuvering through Georgia. No one ever knew which way he was going either, and from there on it was strictly option football."

Hayes' monologue went on to include that Griffin should go into politics because "he's a middle-of-the-roader, and that's what our country needs today."

Get the idea that Hayes liked the guy?

Ohio State's opponents didn't feel the same way.

Former Indiana coach Lee Corso said of Griffin: "He has unbelievable peripheral vision. I saw him go through a hole in our line that wasn't there. It was off-tackle to the left. You could see the hole develop, but then three of our men played it perfectly and closed it up. Griffin suddenly got through for 12 yards. It was one of the greatest runs I've ever seen."

After a game against Minnesota, the Gophers coaches were scratching their heads over how Buckeye quarterback Cornelius Greene shook loose for 57 yards and a touchdown.

"We thought that our safety, Doug Beaudoin, could make that tackle, and he seldom misses," said Minnesota assistant coach Dick Moseley. "Until we saw the films, we didn't realize Griffin had put a block on Doug and just plain knocked him down."

Griffin was the complete player for Ohio State. His roots with the school went extremely deep. How could Griffin not

Ohio State's Archie Griffin (right) joins his coach, Woody Hayes, at New York City's Downtown Athletic Club to accept his second Heisman Trophy in 1975. Griffin also won the Heisman in 1974.

Griffin (45) led Ohio State to three straight meetings with Southern Cal in the Rose Bowl in 1974, 1975 and 1976.

be a Buckeye after being born in Ohio State's campus hospital in 1954?

Griffin was the fourth of eight children born to James and Margaret Griffin. His father used to work several jobs to support the family. Archie called him, "The hardest-working man there ever was."

His father's goal was to send all of his children to college. He met that goal. Besides Archie, two of his brothers, Ray and Keith, also went on to have careers in the National Football League.

The Griffins instilled the value of education into Archie. James Retter, one of his junior high teachers, called him a "model student."

Indeed, it was hard to find a flaw in Griffin. When *Sports Illustrated* asked his girlfriend, Loretta Laffitte, who eventually became his wife, if there were any chinks in the armor, the best she could come up with was, "He's late picking me up sometimes."

When it came time to pick a college, Griffin almost chose

Northwestern. He liked the academics and he thought he was too small to play at Ohio State. Hayes, though, had different thoughts. He put a full-court press on both Griffin and his family. Hayes' wife, Anne, even took Mrs. Griffin to launch. Hayes always said afterward that had sealed the deal.

Griffin's college career would have an unimpressive start. In his first game against Iowa, he bobbled a pitchout for a five-yard loss. Officially, he carried the ball in 90 seconds of action.

The next game, though, was a different story. Griffin didn't even expect to get in the game, but Rudy Hubbard, one of Hayes' assistants, implored the coach to use Griffin. Hayes would never again think twice about using Griffin.

Griffin had runs of 32, 22 and 55 yards. When it was over, he had rushed for 239 yards in a 29-14 win over North Carolina. A stunned Tar Heel coach Bill Dooley said, "We came here not even knowing Archie Griffin existed, and now you tell me he's (just) a freshman."

A legend was born in Columbus on that day.

Griffin finished his freshman year rushing for 772 yards and 3 touchdowns. As a sophomore, he emerged as a bonafide star, rushing for 1,428 yards, and averaged 6.3 yards per carry. He finished fifth in the Heisman balloting; teammate John Hicks, an offensive tackle, placed second. In that year's Rose Bowl, Griffin ran for 149 yards in the Buckeyes' 42-21 win over USC.

There was no stopping Griffin during his junior year. He ripped through the Big Ten, with hated rival Michigan looming in the season finale. Griffin's presence only fueled the passion between Hayes and his protégé, Bo Schembechler. Before the game, a Wolverine player said, "if Archie Griffin gains 100 yards, it will be over my dead body."

Griffin wasn't bothered by the remark, but it fired up the Buckeyes' offensive line. Griffin rushed for 111 yards in Ohio State's 12-10 win, which sent them to another Rose Bowl.

A few weeks later, Griffin won his first Heisman, prompting a popular car sticker in Columbus: "Thank you, Mrs. Griffin."

During his emotional speech, Griffin said, "To me, football represents the good things in life. I'll do everything in my power to set the greatest example. If today's young people look up to the Heisman winners and other stars the way I did, they'll do as I did."

The only dark spot for Griffin occurred in the ensuing Rose Bowl. The Buckeyes blew a shot at the national championship, suffering a heartbreaking 18-17 loss to USC.

All eyes were focused on Griffin the following year. Could he repeat his Heisman performance? His mother had a premonition about her son achieving such a feat.

"When he was in high school, I saw it all in a dream," Margaret Griffin said. "I saw Archie standing with the Heisman Trophy. I saw us standing beside him and all the people gathered around. Well, I had that dream more than once."

Griffin, though, knew it would be tough. It's one thing for a defensive player to apply a solid hit on an ordinary running back. It's quite another to cream a Heisman Trophy winner.

"Arch gets hit almost every play, and when he has the ball, he gets hit about four times," Hayes said.

Hayes had Griffin use lineman's thigh pads to soften the blows, but they did little good. He went through the entire season bruised and battered.

"Being tagged the Heisman winner, naturally guys on other teams were after me more," Griffin said. "They all tackled me clean, but hard. They might say a few things like, 'Get up Heisman winner.' "

Griffin, though, prevailed. He was the dominant force on a Buckeye team that went through the regular season undefeat-ed. The Wolverines limited Griffin to 46 yards, breaking his 100-yard streak, but the Buckeyes still won the game, 21-14.

When it came time for the 1975 Heisman vote, there was some sentiment for Muncie, who had out-rushed Griffin by 103 yards that season and had a 6.4 yards per carry average, compared to Griffin's 5.5. Nevertheless, the award went to Griffin.

"(The Heisman criticism) didn't bother me a bit," Griffin said. "But if it meant giving the trophy back, I wasn't going to give it back. If Muncie had gotten it, people would have said, 'Dorsett deserved it.' There will always be comment and criticism. You can't satisfy everyone."

Griffin would travel to New York in December to pick up his second Heisman. Unfortunately, his career ended on a sour note when UCLA upset the No. 1 Buckeyes in the Rose Bowl, 23-10. Griffin called it, "the biggest disappointment in his career."

Griffin quickly got it over, graduating ahead of his class. He then went out and gave motivational talks to youngsters, spreading his motto of "Desire, dedication and determination."

Griffin's pro career was largely average. The Cincinnati Bengals picked him in the first round of the 1976 draft. He finished his rookie year rushing for 625 yards, and in 1979 he ran for 688 yards (a 4.9 average) and 43 pass receptions. Unfortunately, Griffin never got to carry the full load for the Bengals. When Cincinnati earned a trip to Super Bowl XVI in 1981. Griffin had only one carry for four yards. The Bengals didn't offer him a contract after the 1983 season, thus ending his football career with the NFL. The next season, he would have a brief fling with Jacksonville in the USFL.

Bengals owner Paul Brown called Griffin "a class person," stating Griffin should be proud of his years in Cincinnati. Griffin agreed.

After football, there was one logical place for Griffin to land: Ohio State. He eventually landed in the athletic department, where he rose to become the Buckeyes' Assistant Athletic Director and now leads the OSU Alumni Association and serves as one of the school's top ambassadors.

"College, in general, was the greatest time of my life — the people I know, the people who have helped me, the education I received. Those things will be with me forever. The Heisman is a part of all this."

Actually, two parts of it. Obviously there's more to Griffin than the Heisman Trophy. But the memories always will remain.

For two glorious autumns in Columbus, Griffin stood on top of the college football world. And when it comes to future Heisman winners, Griffin will continue to be the measuring stick.

Boilermakers Defeat No. 1-Ranked Michigan

BY JEFF WASHBURN AND BOB SCOTT
The Journal and Courier

West Lafayette, Ind.	November 6, 1976						
Michigan	7	0	7	0	—	14
Purdue	7	6	0	3	—	16

Purdue shook down the thunder from the college football skies today, pulling the rug out from under the nation's No. 1-rated Michigan Wolverines, 16-14, before 57,205 unsuspecting fans in Ross-Ade Stadium.

Exploiting the old "take it to 'em" theory, Purdue pulled the upset behind a bristling defense, the bullseye passing of Mark Vitali and the battering rushing of Scott Dierking and John Skibinski.

Purdue's offense elected to meet the vaunted Michigan defense head-on up the middle and Vitali's passing in clutch situations kept the Wolverines off balance all afternoon. The Purdue defenders more than made up for last week's collapse at Michigan State by limiting the top-rated Michigan rushing attack to only 256 yards.

The loss was Michigan's first of the season and it marked the first time Purdue had been able to whip the Wolverines since 1966. In fact, it was Michigan's first loss to a Big Ten team, other than Ohio State, since Michigan State in 1969.

Purdue's Dierking once again proved he deserves national recognition as he stole the show from Michigan's Rob Lytle, depsite the fact that Lytle went over the 1,000-yard mark of the season on his first carry of the game.

Dierking set both Purdue and stadium records in hauling the football 38 times. His workhorse performance topped the old Purdue standard of 36 by Tony Butkovich against Ohio State in 1943 and the Ross-Ade Stadium mark of 37 by Southern Cal's Ricky Bell earlier this year.

For the game, Dierking rushed for 162 yards while Lytle, who spent some time on the sidelines with a bruised right hip, finished with 153 yards on 21 attempts. Skibinski, whose 17 trips bullied the Wolverines for 81 yards, while Vitali pinpointed six different receivers for 10 completions on 14 tosses for 109 yards.

True, you have to get a lift from Lady Luck occasionally to win one like this. Purdue, which ended a three-game losing streak and hiked their record to 4-5 overall and 3-3 in the Big Ten, got theirs in the fourth quarter during a menacing Wolverine drive.

With just 4:31 remaining in the game, Purdue's Rock Supan had booted a 23-yard field goal to put the Boilermakers in front, 16-14.

Michigan then launched a 12-play drive with the following kickoff that was finally ended when Bob Wood, who had converted on six of eight field goal tries this season, misfired with just 14 seconds left from the Purdue 37.

However, in between Purdue got a break when Jim Smith dropped a "sure" touchdown pass from Rick Leach on the Purdue 6-yard line.

Then Purdue's Mark Travline batted another TD strike away from Jim Smith at the goal line and the Boilermakers line did the rest on five rushing plays to force the last gasp field goal attempt.

Michigan started out living up to its press clippings as it scored on its first possession of the game after a fumble stopped a promising Boilermaker offense at the Michigan 42.

The Wolverines went 58 yards in only six plays with Lytle and Harlan Huckleby doing the work before Leach swung left and went in from eight yards out. Wood's conversion was good and with 9:38 left in the first period the No. 1 Wolverines appeared awesome.

Purdue, however, wasn't shaken by the turn of events. The Boilermakers' Fred Arrington recovered a Michigan fumble by Russ Davis on the Wolverines' 48 and Purdue needed only four plays to cash in and tie things up with 37 seconds remaining in the first quarter.

Vitali, who got Michigan's attention by throwing on Purdue's first offensive play of the day, opened the march by hitting Ray Smith for 20 yards. Dierking gained five yards and Skibinski made a great run up the middle for 19 yards to the Michigan 4-yard line. Dierking then rammed the ball over for the TD and Supan booted the extra point.

The Boilermakers stopped the Michigan offense cold on its next series and opened the door for Purdue to take the lead.

Taking possession of John Anderson's punt on the Purdue

Purdue's Mike Northington pressures Michigan kicker Bob Wood to miss a field goal in the game's final minutes.

46 after Jerome King's 16-yard return, Purdue needed only nine plays to go the route on a heady mixture of rushing and passing plays that kept the Wolverines guessing.

Dierking also capped this march with his longest dash of the day — a 25-yard scoring burst on a cutback — but with 9:57 to go in the half Supan's extra-point kick was blocked by Michigan's Mike Jolly to give Purdue a shaky 13-7 lead that was to stand up the rest of the half.

The Boilermakers threatened to expand that margin by driving from their own 24 to the Michigan 40, converting a pair of fourth-and-one situations in the process, before a Vitali pass was intercepted by Jerry Zuver.

Michigan couldn't move very far, however, and left the field for the first time this season trailing at the end of the first half.

The handwriting began to appear on the stadium turf right at the start of the third period as Purdue's confidence was ballooned by a gutty goal line stand that all but put out the Michigan fire.

The Wolverines hammered the kickoff from their own 29 to a first down on the Purdue 4-yard line with Lytle's runs of 20 and 34 yards highlighting the march. Three plays netted the Wolverines just nine yards and on fourth-and-one Huckleby fumbled a Leach pitchout with the play resulting in a 15-yard loss and Purdue taking over on downs.

As most of those in attendance feared, the six-point margin didn't hold up as Michigan wrested the lead away at 14-13, when Leach hooked up with Smith for his first completion of the day — a 64-yard scoring bomb — following Purdue's only punt of the game. Wood converted at the 5:34 mark of the third period.

Zuver's second pass theft stalled the next Purdue bid, but Lytle fumbled the ball away to Blane Smith and the Boilermakers then launched the parade that led to Supan's game-winning kick.

Purdue strung together four first downs with the last one coming at the Wolverines' 11. Dierking, Vitali and Skibinski punched to the Michigan 6-yard line, and on fourth-and-five, Supan made good and Michigan's banners were drooping in the fading dusk.

Minnesota's Mark Carlson (12) celebrates with teammate Marion Barber (41) after his first-quarter touchdown.

Gophers Stun No. 1 U-M, Return Little Brown Jug

BY JON ROE
Minneapolis Tribune

Minneapolis, Minn.	October 22, 1977						
Michigan	0	0	0	0	—	0
Minnesota	10	3	0	3	—	16

A week of introspection and hard work, a speech that took about as much time to deliver as the Gettysburg Address and 60 minutes of frenzy were the mortar in the University of Minnesota's 16-0 victory today over No. 1-ranked Michigan at Memorial Stadium.

When the Gophers joyfully charged across the never-so-green turf of the place they've renamed Brick House to carry off the Little Brown Jug, a crowd of 44,165 stood in celebration. But that was nothing compared with the caphony that followed in the Minnesota locker room as the Gophers tried to comprehend just what they had accomplished — so thoroughly and convincingly.

"It is the greatest victory I have ever experienced," said Cal Stoll, the Gophers coach.

The win over Michigan also returned the Little Brown Jug to Minnesota for the first time since 1967.

What the Gophers did today may have been ignited by a rigorous week of practice, or maybe the victory was born when assistant coach Butch Nash delivered a short but dramatic talk on Friday night about what the Minnesota-Michigan series and the Little Brown Jug are all about. The speech didn't last five minutes, but every Gophers player said that its message will remain for the rest of their lives.

This afternoon, the Wolverines never seriously threatened to score. Michigan never got inside the Minnesota 18-yard line and only had four first downs rushing all day. They finished with only 202 yards of offense — which was below its average of 400 yards a game.

The Gophers defense not only stymied the Wolverines, it created plays that allowed the Gophers' offense to enjoy good field position. The Gophers recovered three Michigan fumbles and picked off 2 passes.

Gopher linebackers Michael Hunt and Steve Stewart combined for 24 tackles.

And the elusive Harlan Huckleby, who led the Big Ten in rushing with 112 yards per game, could only muster 52 yards on 13 carries.

After stopping Michigan's first drive and forcing a punt, the Gophers took over at the Minnesota 43. Mark Carlson completed a 23-yard pass to Jeff Anhorn, then 2 plays later hit halfback Steve Breault for 10 yards to reach the Michigan 24. After losing 7 yards on three plays, Paul Rogind booted a 41-yard field goal to give Minnesota a 3-0 lead.

On Michigan's first play after the field goal, Michigan quarterback Rick Leach's pitchout to Huckleby resulted in a fumble that Gopher defender Keith Brown recovered at the Wolverines' 12-yard line. Carlson picked up six yards on a run off a pass play.

Marion Barber, a freshman halfback from Detroit, then took special glee in scoring the game's only touchdown of the day — plunging in from 3 yards on fourth down for a 10-0 lead midway through the first quarter.

In the second quarter, Rogind added a 37-yard field goal with 57 seconds left before halftime to boost Minnesota's lead to 13-0.

Rogind added another field goal late in the fourth quarter — a 31-yarder — to seal Minnesota's 16-0 upset.

A pair of Gopher fullbacks led the game in rushing. Kent Kitzmann churned for 71 yards in 17 attempts, while freshman Gary White rushed for 66 yards in 15 tries.

Steve Stewart (97) shows off the Little Brown Jug, which Minnesota had won for the first time in 10 years.

Badgers tailback Chucky Davis powers through a pair of Michigan defenders for a 1-yard TD in the second quarter.

No. 1 Michigan Stunned in Season Opener by Badgers

By Tom Butler
Wisconsin State Journal

Madison, Wisc. | September 12, 1981						
Michigan	0	7	7	0	—	14
Wisconsin	0	14	7	0	—	21

A mostly delirious crowd of 68,733 witnessed history this afternoon at Camp Randall Stadium.

Those who don't fit the above description were stunned Michigan fans who watched Wisconsin dismantle the No. 1-ranked Wolverines, 21-14, with a devasting offense and pulverizing defense.

Actually, the final score doesn't reveal the domination exhibited by the Badgers in their first victory against Michigan since 1962, which broke a 14-game losing string at the hands of the Wolverines.

Wisconsin executed 78 offensive plays to Michigan's 53, rolled up a first-down advantage of 23-8 and outgained the Wolverines in total yards, 439 to 229.

It was also only Wisconsin's second victory over Michigan in Madison. The other win being a 16-13 decision in Camp Randall Stadium 21 years earlier.

And it was Michigan's first loss in an opening game on the road since a 4-0 loss to Harvard one hundred years ago, in 1881.

"It's a great, great feeling to start your season by beating

the No. 1-ranked team in the country and it's something the Wisconsin football program needs," Badgers coach Dave McClain said.

Take away an 89-yard touchdown run by Butch Wookfolk in the third quarter and the Wolverines' offense shows only 140 total yards. That electrifying dash down the east sidelines, coupled with Ali Haji-Sheik's extra-point kick, tied the game at 14-all with nine minutes, 16 seconds left in the period.

It was one of the few defense breakdowns of the afternoon for the Badgers, spearheaded once again by nose guard Tim Kumrie, who had 13 tackles, and ball-hawking safety Matt Vanden Boom, who had three pass interceptions.

Following Woolfolk's touchdown, Wisconsin's sophomore quarterback, Jess Cole, guided the Badgers 81 yards for the winning score. Seventy-one of that total came on Cole's screen pass from a shotgun formation to tailback John Williams, who outran the Michigan defense after getting a crunching block from flanker Marvin Neal for the game-winning TD.

Michigan scored first after recovering Dave Keeling's punt on Wisconsin's 33 with 12:06 left in the second quarter. Quarterback Steve Smith guided the Wolverines to the end zone in six plays, including all-America Anthony Carter's only reception of the game, an 11-yard pass on the first play.

Smith scored on a keeper around right end and Haji-Sheik booted the first of two extra-point kicks.

After Brian Carpenter returned a David Greenwood punt 48 yards to the Wisconsin 24, the Badgers defense then stiffened and Kumrie sacked Smith for a 7-yard loss on third down, which forced a Haji-Sheik field goal from the 37, which failed. He also missed a 41-yard attempt during the scoreless first quarter.

Cole then led the Badgers 71 yards in seven plays, including his scrambling pass out of another shotgun formation to tailback Chucky Davis, who wasn't corralled until reaching Michigan's 41.

An interference penalty gave Wisconsin a first down on Michigan's 28. Three plays later, Cole sailed a 17-yard picture pass to Neal in the southeast corner of the end zone for a touchdown. It marked the first score for Wisconsin against Michigan since 1976. During this five-year stretch, the Wolverines outscored the Badgers, 176-0.

The first of Mark Dorian's three extra-point kicks tied the game at 7-7 with 3:47 left in the first half. Incredibly, Cole engineered a go-ahead touchdown before halftime with Davis lunging over from the Michigan 1-yard run with two seconds left on the clock.

Davis, who was voted the outstanding player of the game by members of the media, accounted for 29 of the drive's 55 yards on four carries, and Cole's 14-yard pass to freshman split end Michael Jones put the Badgers in scoring position on the Michigan 3-yard line with 26 seconds left before intermission.

There was some concern that time would out after two runs failed, but Cole remained cool, regrouped his team without a huddle and sent Davis over the right side of the line for the TD.

Dorian's extra-point kick sent the Badgers into halftime with a 14-7 lead and left Wisconsin fans drained of emotion.

Davis finished with 69 yards rushing on 15 carries along with two pass receptions for an additional 48 yards. Badgers fullback Dave Mohapp was the team's leading rusher with 87 yards on 19 carries.

Besides being intercepted three times, Smith completed only three of 18 passes for 39 yards. Woolfolk finished with 119 yards rushing.

Following the game, Wisconsin fans rushed onto the field to celebrate their win over the No. 1-ranked Wolverines.

Illini receiver David Williams (1) had six receptions for 127 yards and 1 TD against the Wolverines.

Illini Defeat Michigan, Rose Bowl Berth Nears

BY MIKE CONKLIN
Chicago Tribune

Champaign, Ill.	October 29, 1983					
Michigan	3	0	3	0	—	6
Illinois	0	7	0	9	—	16

Illinois football fans had the most beautiful sight in 20 years unfold before them today. When the afternoon was over, they were staring directly at the Rose Bowl.

The Fighting Illini, who earlier had beaten Big Ten contenders Iowa and Ohio State, swept aside Michigan, 16-6, to clear the last major obstacle to their first trip to Pasadena since 1964.

"We got the job done," Illini coach Mike White said after the victory over their most disliked opponent and No. 1 bowl

rival gave the Illini rose-colored thoughts.

"This thing right here is a pretty good deal," he added, holding up a rose for everyone to see. "We want it badly. But we better play them all."

There was no restraining the championship-starved fans in a record Memorial Stadium crowd of 76,127, thousands of whom spilled onto the field with eight seconds remaining to tear down the goal posts for the third time this season.

"Rose Bowl! Rose Bowl!" was the growing chant, once Joe Miles sealed the verdict by nailing Michigan punt returner Evan Cooper for a safety and the final 16-6 score with 1:22 remaining.

The cry grew with each ticking second and, after the final gun, White and his players, who needed nearly 10 minutes to battle their way to the locker room, were hoisted on the shoulders of their jubilant followers.

Players had bouquets of roses waiting for them in their dressing quarters, a bottle of champagne was popped, and quarterback Jack Trudeau, as brilliant this day as the blue skies, already was wearing a shirt with an emblem of a rose sewed on the collar.

Only Minnesota, Indiana and Northwestern, three of the poorest teams in the Big Ten, remain for an Illinois team that is 6-0 in the conference for its best league start since 1914. The Illini's 7-1 overall record includes seven consecutive victories for their longest streak since 1951.

Six different teams have represented the Big 10 in the Rose Bowl since Illinois last appeared, in 1964. No conference rival has dominated the Illini like Michigan, which hadn't lost a game in memorial Stadium since 1957.

That's what made today's triumph so sweet. The Wolverines were 14-0 against Illinois under their coach, Bo Schembechler. The only thing more enjoyable than victory for many Illini faithful was seeing their chief antagonist rant at officials late in the game, when the momentum had turned in favor of the home team.

Adding to Schembechler's discomfort was the way White's sophisticated passing attack made Bo's conservative ground game look like a Model-T Ford. Illinois players all were surprised that the Wolverines made such little use of their dangerous option play with quarterback Steve Smith.

"I've always believed in the pass, and I can honestly say it bailed us out against Ohio State and today," said White. "The pass gives us confidence. It's our trump card."

Trudeau played it 31 times and completed 21 for 271 yards and two touchdowns to go with Illinois' 107 yards on the ground. While Michigan's more methodical approach gave the visitors nearly a 10-minute advantage in possession time, the more streamlined Illini still outgained Schembechler's team 378 yards to 246.

David Williams was Trudeau's most lethal target. The sophomore snared six passes for 127 yards, including a 47-yard TD on the first play of the fourth quarter. Tim Brewster also caught six passes for 68 yards as Trudeau confidently picked apart Michigan's defense with medium-range passes.

Trudeau's split-second timing was as admirable as his confident recovery from two fumbles he lost to Michigan. The first came at the Wolverines' 26 and took his team out of a good drive when it trailed, 3-0, on a 38-yard field goal by Bob Bergeron in the first quarter.

However, a punt by Michigan's Don Bracken, who was harassed all day by Illinois' special teams, was partially deflected by Luke Sewell and gave the Illini the ball back at Michigan's 49 early in the second period. Trudeau quickly drove his team to its first touchdown on a 9-yard pass to running back Thomas Rooks.

Still leading, 7-6, following another Bergeron field goal in the third quarter, Illinois drove all the way to Michigan's 1-yard line before Trudeau fumbled a snap. It was recovered by the Wolverines' Carl Rose, who killed an Illini chance for victory last year with a goal-line tackle.

Again, Michigan had to punt, and Illinois quickly struck on Trudeau's 46-yarder to Williams to make the score 14-6.

Michigan was left in the hole much of the second half, thanks to Chris Sigourney's punting and good special-teams coverage, and that helped the Illini defense from scoring a touchdown for the first time in 20 games.

"Their defense was able to control the line of scrimmage to win," said Schembechler. "And horrendous punting absolutely ruined our field position. Defense is the key. They're good."

Good enough for the Rose Bowl.

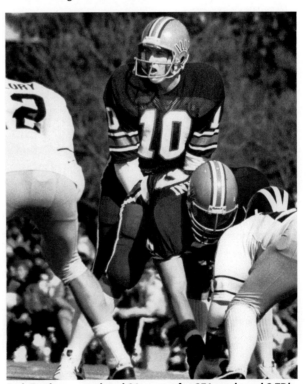

Jack Trudeau completed 21 passes for 271 yards and 2 TD's.

Purdue Stuns No. 2 Bucks, Take Big Ten Lead

BY JEFF WASHBURN
The Journal and Courier

West Lafayette, Ind.	October 6, 1984					
Ohio State	7	3	7	7	—	23
Purdue	7	0	7	14	—	28

Quarterback Jim Everett and free safety Rod Woodson shocked No. 2-ranked Ohio State with big plays this afternoon, leading Purdue to a 28-23 Big Ten Conference football upset at Ross-Ade Stadium.

The victory, coupled with Michigan State's 19-7 upset of Michigan, left the Boilermakers all alone in first place. Purdue, 4-1 overall and 3-0 in the Big Ten, is off to its best start since 1979. Ohio State is 4-1 overall and 2-1 in the Big Ten.

The last time Ohio State and Michigan lost a conference game on the same day was Oct. 14, 1978. Ironically, Purdue defeated Ohio State, 27-16, and Michigan State defeated the Wolverines, 24-15.

Although outgained by 194 yards, 570-376, Purdue used Everett's 65-yard touchdown pass to Steve Griffin, and Woodson's 55-yard pass interception return for another score to erase a 17-7 Ohio State lead in the second half.

"We're an improving football team, but we're still so young that our real future is ahead od us," Leon Burnett, the Purdue coach, said. "We've done what it takes to win. That's why we're in first place."

Boilermaker fans spent this afternoon waving gold towels, encouraging the defense, which had to contain Ohio State's massive tailback Keith Byars, who rushed for 191 yards and caught 9 passes for 102 yards.

Byars rushed for two touchdowns and Rich Spangler added a 34-yard field goal to give the Buckeyes a 17-7 lead midway through the third quarter.

Everett, who completed 17 of 23 passes for 257 yards and three TD's, then connected on the bomb to Griffin with 5:26 left in the quarter, pulling Purdue to within three points.

The Boilermakers drove 79 yards in eight plays on their next possession, taking a 21-17 lead with 14:03 left on a 4-yard TD pass from Everett to fullback Bruce King.

Four minutes later, Woodson intercepted a Mike Tomczak pass and sprinted 55 yards down the sideline, giving Purdue a 28-17 cushion.

Ohio State scored with 2:38 left on a 5-yard pass from Tomczak to Chris Carter, capping a 5-play, 48-yard drive, but failed on a two-point conversion try.

The Buckeyes got the ball one more time, but the drive ended on the Purdue 34 with five seconds to play when Tomczak threw a fourth-down pass out of bounds, losing track of the down.

Fans sitting in the Purdue student section swarmed the field as the final gun sounded, temporarily detaining an ambulance, which was attempting to rush Boilermaker defensive back Tommy Lee Myers to the University Hospital.

Myers injured his back in the final minute when he crashed into the Ohio State bench. Denny Miller, the Purdue trainer, said Myers was taken to the hospital for precautionary X-rays, and was released.

Rod Woodson's fourth-quarter interception for a TD proved to be the game-winner.

Kevin Sumlin (44) and Rod Woodson (26) corral Buckeyes halfback John Wooldridge in the first half.

No. 2 Michigan Upset by Houghtlin's Kicks

By Ron Maly
The Des Moines Register

Iowa City, Iowa | October 19, 1985						
Michigan	0	7	0	3	—	10
Iowa	0	6	0	6	—	12

Rob Houghtlin kicked a dramatic 29-yard field goal as the final 2 seconds kicked off the clock today, lifting No. 1-ranked Iowa to a 12-10 victory over No. 2 Michigan in one of the most suspenseful football games in Hawkeye history.

"I knew when I hit the ball it was good," said Houghtlin, who accounted for all of the Hawkeyes' points and tied a school record with his four field goals.

Houghtlin, a sophomore from Glenview, Ill., who enrolled at Iowa without a football scholarship after feeling unwanted at Miami of Ohio, also booted field goals of 35, 27 and 36 yards.

"I had a feeling the outcome would come down to a field goal, but I also thought we might score a touchdown on the final drive," Houghtlin said.

Michigan hadn't allowed a point in the fourth quarter all season until Houghtlin kicked his field goals today.

His four field goals matched the total by Dave Horsclaw against Minnesota in 1977.

Asked what he was thinking about during the two timeouts before the final kick — one called by Iowa, one by Michigan — Houghtlin said, "I wasn't thinking, I was praying, asking the Lord for strength — and direction."

The victory sent Iowa's season record soaring to 6-0 and its Big Ten mark to 3-0 before a record crowd of 66,350 in Kinnick Stadium.

Representatives of the Sugar, Orange, Cotton, Fiesta, Independence, Cherry and Florida Citrus bowls were among those who watched on a rainy, gray day.

It was left to Houghtlin to insert a huge ray of sunshine into the happenings for Iowa fans when he booted his winning three-pointer.

Ecstatic Hawkeye followers stormed the field after officials signaled the kick good. The goalpost at the north end of the field tumbled in the celebration, but the other one survived.

In addition to keeping Iowa No. 1 in The Associated Press rankings, Houghtlin's kick enabled the Hawkeyes to take a sizeable step toward the conference championship and a berth in the Rose Bowl.

There are still conference games remaining against Northwestern, Ohio State, Illinois, Purdue and Minnesota, but winning this one was important to Coach Hayden Fry and his players.

"There's no doubt this was my biggest win at Iowa," said Fry. I'm even going to vote us No. 1 in the UPI poll."

Fry is on the UPI panel of coaches and he hasn't voted the Hawkeyes No. 1 previously this season.

"We did what we had to do to win," said Fry. "All great teams do that."

Michigan coach Bo Schembechler said, "The reason Iowa won the game was its offense. With Chuck Long and Ronnie Harmon on the same team, it makes it extremely difficult to shut them down."

Long completed 26 of 39 passes for 297 yards, and Harmon ran 32 times for 120 yards and caught six passes for 72.

Long probably enhanced his Heisman Trophy chances with his strong performance, but he said he was "very critical of myself."

"I thought I had an average game. I missed a few opportunities to score."

Iowa dominated the statistics, rolling up 422 yards to 182 for Michigan, which now stands 5-1 for the season and 2-1 in the Big Ten.

Another set of figures found Iowa controlling the ball for 38 minutes 5 seconds to Michigan's 21:55.

"I can't believe we had 64 plays to their 41," said Fry.

Yet, so outstanding was Michigan's defense that the Hawkeyes had to take a game televised to 80 percent of the nation down to the very end before pulling it out.

Houghtlin had seen a streak of 10 straight field goal successes end when his 44-yard attempt was short and wide to the right with 7:38 left to play.

But nothing negative was going through the soccer-style kicker's mind when he prepared for the winner.

Because of a strained muscle in his kicking leg, Houghtlin

Ron Houghtlin booted 4 field goals to defeat Michigan. Afterward, the Hawkeye fans brought down the goalposts.

hasn't been practicing in the last couple of weeks.

"The leg doesn't bother me on Saturdays," he said.

The game wasn't without some controversy. Iowa had an apparent 18-yard touchdown pass from Long to Scott Helverson was nullified when officials ruled Helverson was out of the end zone.

But television replays showed he appeared to be inbounds, and Fry said three of his receivers told him Helverson's catch should have been worth six points.

"We used that call to motivate our players," Fry said. "We should have been ahead, 10-7, at halftime instead of being behind, 7-6."

The Hawkeyes had to settle for Houghtlin's 35-yard field goal with 9:05 left in the first half after Helverson's catch was wiped out. This gave the Hawkeyes a 3-0 lead.

The fans and Michigan quarterback Jim Harbaugh were key participants in the game's only touchdown.

After Jamie Morris returned the kickoff 60 yards to the Iowa 31 following Houghtlin's first field goal, Michigan scored on an ad lib play after Harbaugh had retreated three times from the center snap because of crowd noise.

Fry disagreed.

"It was obvious Harbaugh could hear," said the Iowa coach. "He was standing there, reading our goal-line defense. He

was audibilizing at the line.

"There was nothing the referee could do because of the new rule the NCAA recently passed.

"Harbaugh took advantage of not having a penalty rule."

Asked if Harbaugh's actions were done deliberately to quiet the crowd, Schembechler said, "Of course not."

Once Michigan did snap the ball, Harbaugh flipped an impromptu shovel pass to fullback Gerald White, who stretched far enough to get into the end zone with 6:06 left in the first half.

Mike Gillette was razor-sharp with the extra-point kick, just as he was on his 40-yard field goal with 10:55 remaining in the game to give Michigan a temporary 10-9 lead.

Houghtlin's 27-yard field goal as time expired in the first half made the score 7-6. His 36-yarder with 14:20 remaining in the game pushed Iowa in front, 9-7.

But Michigan then stormed back, getting a 17-yard run from No. 2 fullback Bob Perryman and a 24-yarder from Morris before bogging down.

On first down at the Iowa 17, Michigan was called for illegal procedure, then Nate Creer nailed Morris for a 5-yard loss. Gillette's 40-yard field goal followed.

Houghtlin's field goal with 2 seconds left to play gave the win to the Hawkeyes.

Ohio State Shocks No. 1 Iowa Hawkeyes

By Cindy Starr
The Cincinnati Enquirer

Columbus, Ohio | November 2, 1985

Iowa	0	7	0	6	—	13
Ohio State	5	10	0	7	—	22

The storm came first, before the drizzle, before the downpour, before Ohio State's stunning 22-13 victory over No. 1-ranked Iowa today at soggy Ohio Stadium. The storm came in the form of the words and emotions of Keith Byars, the Buckeyes' wounded tailback.

After breakfast today, in a pre-game meeting with his teammates, the normally soft-spoken Byars did a worthy impersonation of Knute Rockne. He stood up. He shouted. He slammed his fist against a tray and knocked it over. He yanked a tablecloth, sending glasses rolling. "This is Iowa," Byars exhorted. "We can't lose. No one, no one, should be able to beat us at home."

Byars told his teammates that he would be with them, spiritually, on every play. But he said he would only enter the game if he were "totally needed." Said Pepper Johnson, "Keith has never done that before."

Said Mike Lanese, "I hadn't seen Keith so emotional since I've known him."

The Buckeyes, moved by Byars' plea, played with such spirit and precision that they never trailed the undefeated Hawkeyes and never needed their trump card, who stood on the sidelines in uniform, with a badly injured foot.

The Buckeyes' stellar defense caused five turnovers — intercepting four of Chuck Long's passes — and blocked a punt in the end zone for a safety. Quarterback Jim Karsatos threw for 151 yards, injured tailback John Wooldridge, wearing a flak jacket, gained 89 yards on nine carries and scored on a 57-yard run. And sophomore George Cooper gained 104 yards, becoming the first OSU fullback to gain 100 yards in a game since 1979. The offense also played its eighth straight game without losing a fumble.

"This is one of the greatest victories I've been associated with as a coach," said Earle Bruce, after his first upset of a No. 1-ranked team at OSU. "We weren't going to be denied today."

The Buckeyes, tied for the Big Ten lead with Iowa at 4-1, will go to the Rose Bowl if they win their three remaining games against Northwestern, Wisconsin and Michigan. If OSU loses one of those games and Iowa wins its three remaining games (against Illinois, Purdue and Minnesota), Iowa will go to the Rose Bowl.

But Bruce looked ready to kiss someone when he learned of the 3-3 deadlock, which prevented a three-way tie for the conference lead and which put OSU in a position to determine its own fate. The Buckeyes, which came into the game 6-1 overall and ranked No. 8 nationally, are destined to rise in the ratings. "In our minds, we're No. 1," said OSU receiver Mike Lanese. "We're the best in the country. I don't think you can be No. 1 unless you think you're No. 1."

Iowa coach Hayden Fry praised the Buckeyes for its execution and said his team was hampered by the rain and the crowd noise. Asked if anything surprised him, he said, "I was surprised that I didn't see Byars until after the game."

Bruce, when asked about Byars' status, said, "There was no way Keith could have played today."

Bruce apparently was not even sure Wooldridge could play. Wooldridge was in the game on a few first-quarter plays, but he did not carry the ball until the second quarter, when Bruce asked him whether he felt up to it. "I said I could run the ball," Wooldridge said. And run he did. On his first carry, he used a perfect block from Cooper and ran 57 yards for an OSU touchdown and a 12-0 Buckeye lead.

The Buckeyes, playing before a record crowd of 90,467, opened fast. They forced Iowa to punt on fourth down and then exploded from the starting block.

On their first offensive play, Karsatos hit Lanese for 21 yards. Then he hit Cris Carter for 17. The drive stalled at the Iowa 9-yard line but Rich Spangler kicked a 28-yard field goal to give Ohio State a 3-0 lead.

Spangler missed a 31-yard field goal on OSU's next drive, but the Buckeyes increased their lead to 5-0 shortly thereafter when defensive back Sonny Gordon blocked a punt in the end zone. What was OSU's mood early in the game?"

"It's a feeling you can't describe," said linebacker Chris

Ohio State's John Wooldridge (25) breaks lose for a 57-yard touchdown run in the second quarter.

Spielman, who had two interceptions and 19 tackles. It's like a dream come true. You're here and you float to the other end of the field."

Woodridge gave OSU a 12-0 lead with 9:06 remaining in the first half, and Spangler nailed a 26-yarder with five minutes left to make it 15-0.

Iowa's Long, the nation's top-rated passer coming into the game, had completed only six of 12 passes for 37 yards — with three interceptions — up to this point.

"It was a matter of changing up all of our defensive coverages," Bruce said. "We had to disguise it. He couldn't read where to throw the football."

Long rallied, however, and led Iowa to its first touchdown with 28 seconds left in the first half. Tailback Ronnie Harmon, who gained 120 yards in the game, scored from three yards out on a sweep, and Iowa pulled to within 15-7.

"We thought we'd win the game at halftime," Fry said.

"We had all of the momentum. We should have been down at least two more touchdowns."

When Spangler missed a 29-yard field goal on OSU's first drive of the second half and when Karsatos was intercepted deep in his own territory, the Buckeyes looked fragile. But the defense came up with a pivotal series, and Speilman stopped Harmon on fourth down and 2 at Ohio State's 10-yard line with 3:07 remaining in the third quarter. The Buckeyes increased its lead to 22-7 on a 4-yard run by freshman tailback Vince Workman, and then Long brought Iowa to within 22-13, with the help of two pass interference penalties.

The two-point conversion failed.

Iowa held firm on defense and then drove again, this time missing a 42-yard field goal attempt with less than four minutes left in the game. The Hawkeyes' final drive ended with Spielman's second interception.

Hoosiers Shatter OSU 36-Year Win Streak

By Bob Hammel
Sunday Herald-Times

Columbus, Ohio | October 10, 1987						
Indiana	7	3	7	14	—	31
Ohio State	0	10	0	0	—	10

The longest, most humiliating streak in Indiana football history was snapped with 31-10 finality today against the Ohio State Buckeyes.

A 36-year streak that had been kept alive by scores such as 56-0, 46-8, 44-7, 49-9, 47-7, 56-17 and — on the last two Indiana trips into Ohio Stadium — 50-7 and 48-7, ended by a score that screamed of a gray, drizzly day's great ironies.

When first-year coach Woody Hayes lost to Indiana at Columbus in 1951, the score was 32-10 and legend was that Hayes vowed Indiana would never beat him again.

"He did vow that," said Paul Hornung, who covered the Ohio State beat for The Columbus Dispatch through the Hayes years and, though retired, watched the game from the pressbox today. "I remember him saying that."

Hayes was absolutely right. His teams went 22-0-1 against the Hoosiers in the last 27 years of his Hall of Fame career. The tie was 0-0 in 1959, and it was accepted bitterly in Indiana, where Hoosiers felt a line plunge by fullback Vic Jones was well over the goal line before Jones was thrown back, but the score stood ever after as 0-0 and the streak rolled on.

More irony: Hayes' last coaching victory was over Indiana, 21-18, at IU's Memorial Stadium in 1978 — the closest Indiana came to him after the vow.

Earle Bruce, an assistant coach along with Indiana coach Bill Mallory under Hayes in the late 1960's, picked up the dominance when he became coach in 1979. Bruce's teams averaged 41.3 points per game in winning eight straight from Indiana — a 23-game winning streak against the Hoosiers overall, the longest ever by one Big Ten over another, and a 31-game unbeaten streak that was only three games short of the NCAA record.

Today's win came with big play after big play, by offensive players and defensive in a second half that Indiana thoroughly dominated against an OSU team that went into the game 3-0-1 and ranked No. 9 in the country.

The halftime score was 10-10, and that was still the score in the third quarter when Tony Buford's 40-yard punt return carried to the Ohio State 19.

In four plays — all of them on the ground against a defensive unit that hadn't allowed a touchdown by a running play in its four games — Indiana drove to the tie-breaking touchdown. Senior fullback Tom Pulce caught the Buckeyes rushing to cover sophomore tailback Anthony Thompson and burst through the middle untouched from there.

That was with 2:09 to go in the quarter, but the quarter ended with Indiana in trouble. Punter Tom Tupa's fourth-down kick sailed to the Indiana 2. Three plays later, not quite a minute into the fourth quarter, Indiana punter Dan Stryzinski had to kick from his end zone and the Buckeyes' offense went to work at the Indiana 40.

On second down, Brian Dewitz — a high school teammate and best buddy of Buckeye all-America teammate Chris Spielman at Massillon, Ohio — cut in front of tight end Alex Higdon for an interception, the first college interception for Dewitz, who started last year's Ohio State game at quarterback for Indiana.

Indiana compounded the jolt for the Buckeyes and the 90,032 drenched fans by driving from the 46 — Dewitz's stopping point after the interception — to a margin-doubling touchdown. The passing combination that has been redoubtable for the Hoosiers this year — "the Elkhart Connection," Dave Schnell to crosstown high school rival Ernie Jones — got the touchdown on third-and-8 from the Buckeye 15 with 8:47 to go.

One minute later, Ohio State was at the Indiana 21 after two straight strikes from Tupa to wide receiver Everett Ross. The Buckeye quarterback missed on his next three throws, and Ohio State turned the ball over on downs at the 20.

The Buckeyes got the football back with 5:18 to go. They had moved to the Indiana 46 when Dewitz made his second interception — at the Indiana 31, with 4:26 to go.

Indiana ran the ball through the gambling Buckeyes to reach the OSU 7. From there, Schnell faked a run and lofted a pass

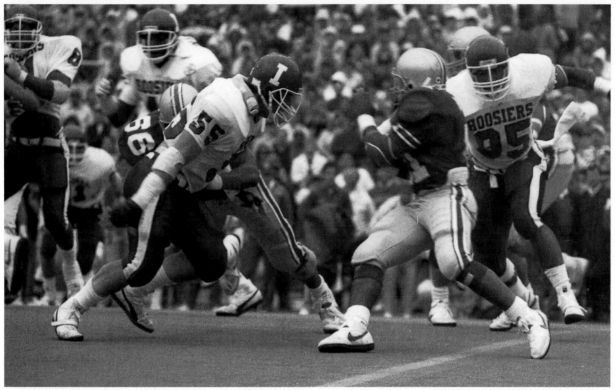

Indiana defenders such as Dan Bauer (55) and Walt Harris (95) held Ohio State to only 85 yards in the second half.

to Polce for the touchdown that — with 1:05 to play — made victory absolutely sure.

Schnell called a timeout just ahead of the pass. The timeout and the throw represented respect for the Buckeyes, not an attempt to pile on embarrassment.

Indiana got its victory with a 405-yard attack: 205 yards rushing (120 by Thompson), 200 passing (15-for-23 by Schnell, five of the completions to Jones for 89 yards and their eighth touchdown connection of the season).

The 10-10 halftime score represented disappointment for the Hoosiers, who took a 10-0 lead and watched the last of it vanish on a career-record 51-yard field goal by Ohio State's Matt Frantz on the last play of the half.

Indiana went ahead with a 10-play, 63-yard touchdown drive on its second possession of the game. Thompson swept the left side of the Buckeye line to score — the first ground touchdown allowed by the Bucks.

"Ernie (Jones) and Tony Buford got the key blocks," Thompson said, "I saw the daylight there and it felt great."

The Hoosiers drove from their 18 to the Ohio State 27 before Pete Stoyanovich widened the lead to 10-0 with a 44-yard field goal — his 24th as a Hoosier, tying the Indiana career record (set by Chris Gardner in 1970-72).

Ohio State's only touchdown came on an odd drive that was kept alive by two long runs by Tupa on plays intended to

be passes. With his receivers covered, he pulled the football down and ran 21 yards to the Indiana 27, then 13 yards (on third-and-5) to the OSU 9. On second down from the 8, sophomore tailback Jaymes Bryant drove to the touchdown.

The tying field goal came after Ohio State took possession at its 20 with 46 seconds to go in the half. On second down from the 27, Tupa passed 24 yards to Ross, and 15 more yards went onto the play when linebacker Van Waiters was called for a personal foul — for hitting Tupa in the head with an all-out rush that just missed catching him before the pass was launched.

With five seconds to go, Ohio State took timeout and brought Frantz on for the field goal that tied the Ohio Stadium record — set by Buckeye Rich Spangler in 1982 against Indiana.

The Waiters penalty was as close to an error as the Hoosiers came on a day when they had no turnovers to three by Ohio State, who was the No. 1 team in the Big Ten in that category going into the game. In the second half, Indiana outgained the Buckeyes, 237 to 85, had an 11-4 edge in first downs, and controlled the football so totally that the Hoosiers wound up with almost 37 minutes of possession to just over 23 minutes for Ohio State.

The victory popped Indiana into a first place tie with Minnesota and Michigan State.

Hoosiers Lead Big Ten After Tripping Michigan

BY BOB HAMMEL
Sunday Herald-Times

Bloomington, Ind.	October 24, 1987					
Michigan	0	10	0	0	—	10
Indiana	7	0	7	0	—	14

Indiana turned to its defense today for another second-half turn-around that snapped one more longtime Hoosier hex — Michigan — into the victim on the soggiest and happiest Homecoming in at least 20 years, 14-10.

The first Memorial sellout in more than a year, 51,240, saw Indiana trail, 10-7, at halftime, and it could have been worse. A blocked punt let the Hoosiers jump ahead with just an 11-yard drive in the first quarter. From there until halftime, Michigan monopolized the football with strong line play that whipped the Hoosiers on both offense and defense.

In the second half, though, the Wolverines gained just 88 yards and never got closer to the goal line than the Indiana 24. In the last three games, successive wins over contenders Ohio State, Minnesota and Michigan, Indiana now has trailed at halftime twice and stood even once, then outscored the three by a combined score of 34-3 in the second half.

Michigan had beaten the Hoosiers 15 straight times since a 27-20 Homecoming loss at Ann Arbor. Bo Schembechler, who took over at Michigan in 1969, coached his team to 14 of those victories over Indiana.

The victory gave Indiana a 4-0 Big Ten record and a half-game lead over Michigan State.

Indiana took the lead on a 3-yard option run by quarterback Dave Schnell with 2:38 to go in the third quarter. It came at the end of a 65-yard drive that included two third-down pass interference penalties against Michigan — both called when Indiana's all-America candidate at flanker, Ernie Jones, went up to try to catch a pass.

The second of those was in the end zone, giving Indiana a first down at the Michigan 15. The Hoosiers ran the ball three straight times — fullback Tom Polce for a yard and tailback Anthony Thompson for two 4-yard gains — to face fourth and 1 at the Michigan 5.

Schnell dived ahead on a quarterback sneak for a first down at the 4. After Thompson dove to the Michigan 3, Schnell started left on an option play, saw an opening almost immediately and powered through it for the score that stood up as the game winner.

Michigan had the ball three times after that. The Wolverines:

■ Put together two first downs to move from their 14 to the 43 before two straight incompletions forced a punt.

■ Took over a Thompson fumble, and managed two first downs again before incompletions on third and fourth downs gave Indiana the ball at the Hoosier 31 with 7:40 to go.

■ Took possession at the Michigan 32 on an interception of a deflected Schnell pass, running three plays to to get one first down (as the clock moved under 4 minutes) before turning the ball back when a fourth-and-10 pass to star tailback Jamie Morris produced just six yards before defenders Jim Sams, Willie Bates and Eric Hickerson threw him down.

Only 3:03 was left then, and Indiana had possession at the Michigan 49. The Hoosiers gave the ball to Thompson for gains of 2, 6 and 1. On fourth down, with a foot to go and 1:20 left to play, Schnell called a quarterback sneak.

No measurement was needed. The first-down signal was given, the clock restarted at 1:18. Indiana ran it out with two plays and a defensive off-side call against Michigan.

A Hoosier walk-on, junior Bill Reisert of Jeffersonville, dashed in from the outside to block the first Michigan punt of the day and give Indiana its opening break — the first block of a Michigan punt in 41 games, three years and 159 punts.

The ball bounced behind punter Monte Robbins and Indiana took possession at the Michigan 11. On second down, Schnell hit flanker Ernie Jones knifing across the middle. Jones caught the ball at about the 5, "made a little dip inside and got in," Schnell said. Jones cut around a defender who, he said, "thought I was going to head right up for the end zone." His fake in that direction ran two Wolverines into each other and he crossed the goal line untouched — the ninth TD reception of the year for Jones, one short of the Indiana record.

Indiana had a chance to widen its 7-0 lead minutes after the touchdown when Michigan passer Demetrius Brown's throw

The Hoosiers celebrated ending their 14-game losing streak to Michigan by tearing down the goalposts.

was intercepted by Indiana free safety Brian Dewitz at the Wolverines' 28.

A first down holding call backed Indiana to the 38. Schnell completed a pass to Jones for 15 yards, but Schnell was sacked on third down. Pete Stoyanovich's 44-yard field-goal attempt was tipped at the line by Michigan's Allen Bishop and the kick fell well short of the goalpost.

Michigan took solid command for the next 15 minutes. The Wolverines tied the game with a 74-yard drive that brought the day's first controversy.

With Michigan facing third-and-7 at the Indiana 8, the Hoosier crowd roared for the defense and Brown backed away from center, saying he couldn't communicate his plays. He stepped over center again; the crowd noise rose again; he backed off. For almost five minutes, Brown stood away from center, referee Tom Quinn made no move to restart the clock, and the noise continued.

The Wolverines backed away from the line, went to it again, and Brown finally started play, lofting a pass to John Kolesar for the touchdown to touch off an angry reaction of boos.

Kolesar's 22-yard return of Indiana punter Dan Stryzinski's longest kick of the year — 56 yards — gave Michigan

possession at the Michigan 42 to start Michigan's tie-breaking drive. The Wolverines reached the Indiana 24 before a fumbled pitchout on third down made them settle for Mike Gillette's 44-yard field goal. It came with 7:02 to go in the half and made the score 10-7.

Just before halftime, Indiana moved to a first down at the Michigan 47, but Schnell's sideline pass was intercepted by Michigan's Doug Mallory, the Indiana coach's son's first of three big plays. The recovery on the Thompson fumble in the fourth quarter and the pass deflection that brought an interception were both by Mallory, a Wolverine captain and safety.

After the last play of the half, Indiana was called for a personal foul, with the 15-yard penalty assessed against the Hoosiers on the kickoff opening the second half. That forced Indiana to kick from the 20, and Michigan's Morris returned the ball to the Michigan 47. Another personal foul call against Indiana gave Michigan a first down at the Hoosier 39, and Michigan moved to another at the Indiana 26. However, a second-down holding call against Michigan left the Wolverines at the 35 on fourth down, and Gillette's 52-yard field goal try was short.

From there, Indiana drove to the winning touchdown.

The Greatest Hoosier

By Bill Benner

T he time was August 1986. The place was the north end zone of Indiana University's Memorial Stadium. The occasion was media day, the opportunity for sportswriters and sportscasters from around the state to meet and interview the coaching staff and players who would comprise the Hoosier football team for the upcoming season.

This particular media turnout was larger than usual. For starters, there was a sense that coach Bill Mallory — even though his first two IU teams had gone 0–11 and 4–7 — had nonetheless established a firm foundation on which he could build a successful program.

Furthering the budding optimism, however, was the presence of a freshman running back from Terre Haute North High School. To land this particular recruit, Mallory had gone against Bobby Bowden at Florida State, Bo Schembechler at Michigan, and Earle Bruce at Ohio State.

The recruit's name? Anthony Thompson.

Thompson was a blue-chip recruit for a program better known for gathering the cast-offs the "name" football schools didn't want. So without yet winning a game, Thompson already constituted a significant victory for IU, Mallory, and the long-suffering Indiana football faithful.

Thus, when Thompson appeared in that end zone, the media quickly moved in on their prey. As the pack grew larger, the circle around the stout, young lad grew tighter and tighter.

What the mini-cams and tape recorders picked up was, well, barely audible. Thompson hemmed. He hawed. He mumbled. His voice barely above a whisper, he grasped both for words and, it seemed, for air, clearly uncomfortable with the attention from the media. The questions came in rapid fire, from all angles. The responses were half-utterances, incomplete sentences, and unfinished thoughts.

The media members were disappointed. This Thompson kid better be a great running back because he's sure one lousy interview. Some openly expressed the thought that Hoosier fans better enjoy Thompson in the fall, because he'd be academically ineligible by spring.

Fast forward to a scene 3-plus years later. The time is December 1989. The place is the posh Downtown Athletic Club of New York, in the middle of Manhattan. The occasion is the nationally televised Heisman Trophy Award Ceremony.

There, in the front row, is that same young man who first cowered in front of the media in Memorial Stadium. Anthony

Anthony Thompson won both the Big Ten's Silver Football Award and all-America honors in 1988 and 1989.

Thompson is seated in that front row, because he has become that most rare of Indiana University football species: A Heisman Trophy finalist — eventually, the runner-up.

It has been quite a journey, and Thompson has gone much further than the 5,299 yards he gained rushing during his IU career, including the record-setting 377 he amassed on one incredibly memorable afternoon in Wisconsin's Camp Randall Stadium.

And he has achieved much more than the honors he has gained, even though the accolades are many: the Walter Camp Foundation Player of the Year; the Chicago Tribune Silver Football Big Ten MVP (at that time, only the third player in the 66-year history of the award to win it twice); consensus first-team All-American; and the first Hoosier athlete in any sport to have his number (32) retired.

More importantly, the Anthony Thompson at the Heisman ceremony is poised. He is polished. He is articulate. He deals easily with the national media. And he is comfortably on his way to earning his IU degree, even though it took several more years to complete it.

In other words, he represents the educational opportunities that participation in intercollegiate athletics can provide. As IU had invested its football future in Anthony Thompson, Thompson had invested his energy in an Indiana University education.

Kit Klingelhoffer, now an assistant athletics director at IU but then the school's sports information director, recalls those New York moments with the Hoosier simply known as A.T.

"I've been here 36 years, and of all the championships we've won, the big games we've won, the bowl games we've won, the Bucket games we've won, whatever, the thing I've been most proud of is being at the Heisman ceremony with Anthony," Klingelhoffer says. "That was when I was most proud to be a member of IU athletics. The atmosphere in that room before the cameras went on, surrounded by the pictures of all those Heisman winners, well, it was pretty special, because I kept thinking about how far Anthony had come."

Bill Mallory remembers, too.

"I'll never forget how well he stood up and expressed himself," Mallory says. "It was like day and night [from when he arrived at IU]. You just saw this kind of maturity, dealing with people, dealing with the public. He had come into his own."

If it ended right there, it would be a great story, no doubt about it. A backwards, shy, introverted youngster from a single-parent home in a poor section of Terre Haute goes to the state university, gains miles of yards, scores loads of touchdowns, helps his team win many games and his program earn respect, garners national attention, comes out of his shell, eventually earns his degree, and makes everyone proud.

Yes, darn good story, right there.

Only this one, to this day, just keeps getting better. And better. And better.

It's because Anthony Thompson never lost sight of who he is. And who he is, foremost, is a child of God, a servant to his Lord, and now, a minister to his flock at the Light House Community Church on Bloomington's south side.

It's because Thompson never forgot the best way to be a good teammate is to be a good person — selfless, dedicated to helping others, ministering to their needs, offering inspiration and salvation.

And it's because Thompson has come full circle, back to his beloved IU, first as an assistant coach on the football team during the Cam Cameron era and now, where the passion he once had as a running back is the passion he has in promoting Hoosier athletics through his work with the Varsity Club, as an assistant director for development.

Perfect fit, really, because who knows better the value of supporting intercollegiate athletics than one who so benefited from that support.

"I always tell people IU has done a lot more for me than I've done for the university," says Thompson. "It took me out of Terre Haute, Indiana, and gave me a world view of things. It gave me great knowledge. It enabled me to communicate with people, to come out of my shyness and articulate myself."

Thompson's early reticence in the public spotlight needs to be placed in the perspective of his upbringing. He is one of Helen Thompson's seven children. He never knew his father. Times were difficult.

"We didn't have much growing up," A.T. recalls. "We didn't have nice clothes. We hated when the holidays came around, like Christmas, Halloween, or Valentine's Day, because we didn't have the money to buy costumes or cards. We didn't have anything to bring to the table."

Poverty, however, didn't mean there wasn't richness in other ways. A trio of uncles — Hubert, Squire, and Denny Thompson — along with family friends Jeff Lough and Danny Tanoos took young Anthony under their collective and protective wing.

"Those guys showed me how a young man should conduct himself," Thompson says. "I bless God for putting those guys in my life, and each had an intricate part in shaping me and molding my character."

Helen Thompson took care of the rest.

"Mom instilled in us the value that you are somebody," Thompson says. "I also tell people I've been on 'drugs' since I was 8 or 9, because my Mom 'drug' us to church every Sunday. It gave me a foundation, a base, as to what life is really all about. Another thing that kept us out of trouble was that she had a rule: When the street lights came on, we were supposed to be home. And football, being an athlete, having a purpose, kept me off the streets."

It was in eighth grade, at Chauncey Rose Junior High, that the light turned on for A.T.

"That's when I began to realize that football could be my meal ticket out of that environment," he says. "But my Mom told me, 'If it's no grades, it's no football.' I was never the biggest, never the strongest, never the smartest kid, but I had a burning desire to be somebody. I didn't know what at the time, but I knew if I worked hard, I could achieve my dream."

An extraordinary career at Terre Haute North set the table. The recruiters came calling. Bowden, Schembechler, Bruce … and Mallory.

"I was never into that 'blue chip' stuff, but if ever there was a blue chip, Anthony was it," Mallory says. "[Assistant coach] Steve Stripling put a lot of time and effort into recruiting him, and I did, too. And all the people in Terre Haute were in our corner. I think he realized he could come in here and help get this program turned around and there's no questioning the great impact he had."

For a meat-and-potatoes coach like Mallory, Thompson was the full-meal deal, an ideal fit for a coach who demanded harder noses on his team than you'll find on Mount Rushmore. Both Mallory and Thompson shared the same ethic: Whatever it took to win, which at IU meant doing more than the opposition.

"He was a young man who always did the extra," Mallory says. "We worked our kids hard, ran them hard. But if we asked the running back to run 25 yards (after a carry) in practice, Anthony would run 45 or 50. At the end of practice, we would run 40's (sprints). And then Anthony would go run the stadium steps.

"I never, ever, had to address him for having a big head. Each year he got better, each year he took himself to the next plateau because of his focus and commitment to excel and do well."

As Thompson went, so went the Hoosiers. Four years, three bowl games. A narrow miss at a Big Ten championship in 1987. Victories over Ohio State and Michigan in the same season.

In the meantime, Thompson emerged in other ways. In the early days, he would hide from the media or dash out of Memorial Stadium before they could get to him.

"'Introvert' wasn't the word for it," Thompson says. "I was backwards, shy … I didn't like all the attention. Coach Mallory finally sat me down one day and said, 'Look, you're not doing this for yourself. You're doing it for the team, for the program.'"

Thompson's exploits led him to the NFL, but a holdout slowed his start, and a wrist injury hastened his retirement after four seasons, two with the Phoenix Cardinals and two with the Los Angeles Rams.

Thompson had no regrets. For one thing, he had found the lady of his life, Lori Russell, also a native of Terre Haute. A friendship turned into romance, romance turned into marriage. They've now been wed 14 years and have three children: Anthony, 12; Ciara, 10; and Jacob, 6. Lori Thompson, MD'93, has a family practice in Bloomington.

As his NFL days waned, Thompson also was hearing a higher calling.

"The Lord had begun to show me that football was just a platform for where he wanted to take me," Thompson says. "Football became less important, and my passion to serve the Lord became more important. Football had been my god, my life, and I thought that's who I was.

"I also found out that even though I climbed the ladder of

Thompson was the first Indiana player, in any sport, to have his number retired after playing for the Hoosiers.

success, my ladder was leaning against the wrong building. In football, I felt like I'd achieved my goals. But spiritually I asked myself, 'Is this what it's all about?' I had money, cars … all the temptations, but I was empty. A lot of people think you have to be down and out to come to the Lord. I was up and out. I had everything at the age of 25, but I was miserable. I had a bunch of friends, but I was lonely."

So Thompson said so long to the NFL. He and Lori moved back to Terre Haute. He invested in rental properties and began to move into the next phase of his life.

It began with a ministry to prisoners at the federal penitentiary in Terre Haute. His faith journey began to accelerate. It hit full speed when a bad thing happened: IU fired Bill Mallory. But it was followed by a good thing — Mallory's successor, Cam Cameron, hired Thompson to become the Hoosiers' running backs coach.

"And now that I look back, as I was coaching, God was preparing me to be a minister," Thompson recalls. "I started a Bible study on Thursday nights. It began with about with five in attendance and grew to about 50 or 60. We had athletes, and we had people just coming in off the streets."

It was during that time that Thompson decided to make a full commitment to serving the Lord.

"But I found out you can't make a deal with God," Thompson says. "God says, 'This is the deal.' "

The deal for A.T. was that he would become pastor of the

Thompson splits his time between working for the Varsity Club and preaching at Bloomington's Light House Church.

Light House Church. The previous pastor, and Anthony's close friend, the Rev. Charles Finnell, was called to take over the Christ Temple Church in Indianapolis. Thompson ministers in the time after his full-time commitment to the IU Varsity Club. Friends fill in for him at church when business prevents him from attending services.

Thompson had always been a guy looking to run through holes. Now he was going to fill one. He's been pastor for four years. He finds there are many similarities with football.

"I look at my congregation as a team," he says. "Now I'm just an assistant coach. We've got a Head Coach. Every Wednesday and Sunday, I get the playbook — the Bible — and I get the game plan, and I go and talk to the team. In my prayer time, and in my devotional time, I'm listening to the Lord for what to tell the team. I inspire the team, I encourage the team, I motivate the team, and sometimes I discipline the team.

"I preach like I coach football, and I minister like I played ... all out, with passion, no straddling the fence."

He brings that same energy to preaching the gospel of Indiana University athletics.

Scott Dolson, the executive director of the Varsity Club, told Thompson when he hired him that he would have to prove to donors that he was more than just a football player. That hasn't been a problem.

"He has personality, he has passion, and he connects with people," Dolson says. "He would be an effective fundraiser even if he had never played football. That he did only enhances his abilities.

"And he's living proof of why we're asking for money. Here's a guy who benefited from an athletics scholarship."

With his work at the Varsity Club, with his ministry at the Light House Church, with three busy children, and a wife engaged in an active medical practice, it's just as difficult to tackle Anthony Thompson these days as it was in Memorial Stadium.

Priority one is growing his church. They've moved into a new facility but want to expand. Fundraising has begun. The campaign got a kick start recently from former IU great and Pittsburgh Steelers Super Bowl champion Antwaan Randle El, BS'01. He addressed A.T.'s congregation and quietly slipped Thompson a check. Thompson couldn't believe his eyes: the check was for $50,000.

"We didn't want his money, just his blessing," says Thompson. "But we were rejoicing."

Light House has more than 100 members. A.T. says he wants quadruple that number. And he doesn't want it to be a "black" church.

"We need to be more of a diverse congregation," he says. "Whites, blacks, Hispanics, Asians. I told the congregation, 'We need to look like what heaven's going to look like. There's not going to be a black section over here or a white section over there. It's going to be the body of Christ.' "

Exhibit A is that Thompson's best friend, Terry Modisett, is a white attorney from Terre Haute. They met at health club shortly after A.T. came back to Indiana after playing in the NFL. Casual conversation led to a shared commitment to the Lord. They hold each other "accountable" through nearly daily phone conversations and prayer.

"We talk about trying to have a ministry together someday that would overcome some of the racial barriers," Modisett says. "We're best friends, and we don't look at any of that [racial] stuff. The community needs to know that. The world needs to know that. The last thing we think of is being a different color. We see each other as great friends."

Anthony Thompson is too busy to think about his end game. All he thinks about is improving his church, improving his university, improving himself. It's the same kind of drive that has carried him through life.

"I want to be a better father, husband, pastor, employee, and friend tomorrow than I was yesterday," he says. "I know the church will be filled to capacity one day. I hope and dream our kids will go to IU one day. Right now, my wife and I, we're living our dream, being married 14 years, having three wonderful kids, being productive in the community.

"I'm living my purpose."

Iowa halfback David Hudson (20) attempts to break through the grasp of a Buckeyes defender.

Hartlieb, Cook & Co. End Ohio Stadium Jinx

By RON MALY
The Des Moines Register

Columbus, Ohio	November 14, 1987					
Iowa	3	12	0	14	—	29
Ohio State	7	7	7	6	—	27

There have been some dramatic victories in the history of University of Iowa football, but none had a more rousing finish than the one the Hawkeyes seized here today.

Quarterback Chuck Hartlieb and tight end Marv Cook combined on a 28-yard touchdown pass with 6 seconds remaining that produced a 29-27 decision over Ohio State.

Maybe it wasn't a hopeless situation for the Hawkeyes. But on fourth and 23, it certainly couldn't be labeled as promising.

Cook was a driven man after catching the pass at the 9-yard line. The 232-pounder from West Branch, Iowa — a junior all

too familiar with Iowa's past frustrations in Ohio Stadium — refused to be tackled as he barreled toward the end zone with Ohio State defenders clinging to him and seconds expiring from the clock.

"I think I made it by an inch," Cook said as he reviewed tha play that caused celebration on the Hawkeye bench and had Coach Hayden Fry giddy long after the game had ended.

This was Iowa's first victory in Columbus since 1959. Ohio Stadium with its roaring thousands, had been the only place

118

in the Big Ten Fry hadn't won.

He brought the No. 1-ranked team here two year's ago and went home a 22-13 loser.

Today's courageous effort gave Iowa an 8-3 record heading into its regular-season finale next Saturday against Minnesota in Iowa City. The Hawkeyes are 5-2 in the Big Ten and very much alive in the bowl picture.

After the game, Iowa was still under consideration by such bowls as the Hall of Fame, Holiday, Freedom, Liberty and Peach.

Fry wanted this victory badly. And when he got it, he didn't attempt to mask his feelings.

"Oh, boy!" Fry shouted. "I hugged everyone in that dressing room.

"What a game. I've been associated with some great ones in 36 years of coaching, but I've never had one that was more meaningful to a group of players.

The decisive scoring pass was the first against a proud Ohio State defense, which hadn't allowed a touchdown through the air in 13 quarters.

And it came after Fry second-guessed himself on the sideline before a crowd of 90,090.

Had Fry gone with his first impulse, Cook wouldn't even have been in the game on the big play.

"Mike Flagg (another tight end) had gone on the field," Fry said, "but something told me to call him back.

"I did, and sent Cook in. Flagg would have caught the ball and made a great effort for the goal line, but he's not quite the runner Marv is."

Hartlieb, who finished with 20 completions in 37 pass attempts for 333 yards, said the winning play was put into Iowa's game plan last week.

"After Cook caught the ball, I wasn't sure he was in the end zone," Hartleib said. "I was a long way away, so I hustled back down there in the event we needed another play."

Hartlieb said Iowa wanted to win the game as much as any he's been connected with in his four years as a Hawkeye.

"We almost dedicated spring practice to winning the Ohio State game," place-kicker Rob Houghtlin said after becoming the school's all-time scoring leader with 278 points.

Houghtlin kicked field goals of 39, 41 and 22 yards, and added two extra points. The 22-yarder came as time was expiring in the second quarter, and gave Iowa a 15-14 halftime lead.

Kevin Harmon, looking like the runner he was early in the season, scored on a 50-yard dash with 9 minutes 10 seconds left in the second quarter, and finished with 151 yards.

The Hawkeyes' other touchdown came on a 1-yard dive by

fullback David Hudson with 9:11 left in the game. That score, plus Houghtlin's conversion, sent Iowa in front, 22-21.

But Ohio State came back to take a 27-22 lead when freshman Carlos Snow dashed 14 yards for a touchdown with 2:45 left to play.

Harmon returned the kickoff 35 yards to the 36, and here came the Hawkeyes.

Hartlieb hit Rick Bayless with a 5-yard pass, then found Flagg for a 14-yarder. Another 15 yards were tacked on because Ohio State had too many men on the field, giving Iowa a first down at the Buckeye 30.

But Iowa was guilty of holding on the next play, and was penalized 10 yards. Then Hartlieb was sacked and fumbled. But Hudson recovered for an 11-yard loss.

Now it was second-and-31 at the Iowa 49. It was time for Cook to go to work. He teamed with Hartlieb for a 27-yard pass with 1:24 to play.

Hudson gained 2 yards and Hartlieb hit Cook with an 8-yard pass to the 15. Eric Kumerow sacked Hartlieb on a play that cost Iowa 8 yards to the 23.

Harmon slipped going wide right and lost 5. On third and 23, Hartlieb passed too low to Travis Watkins, but then he and Cook pulled their magic out of a hat for the win.

Marv Cook snags an 8-yard pass in the fourth quarter.

Spartans halfback Hyland Hickson (30), who rushed for 92 yards on 20 carries, sweeps outside the Michigan defense.

Perles' Fiesty Spartans Upset No. 1 Wolverines

BY JACK BERRY
The Detroit News

Ann Arbor, Mich. | October 13, 1990

Michigan State	7	0	7	14	—	28
Michigan	7	0	7	13	—	27

Finally, in a rivalry so long devoid of really big plays and down-to-the-wire thrills, there were plenty of big plays and key plays today. But the biggest came with only six seconds left: Michigan's two-point attempt.

Wolverines quarterback Elvis Grbac, who had completed 17 of 32 passes for 213 yards, two touchdowns and two interceptions, had marched U-M 71 yards for the touchdown, which set the stage for the dramatic finish.

But the two-point attempt failed, although if the Big Ten had pro football's replay review, Michigan might still be No. 1 and Michigan State again would be the frustrated loser.

Instead, State knocked off No. 1 Michigan, 28-27, when Desmond Howard didn't hang onto Grbac's pass into the north end zone of Michigan Stadium.

Michigan (3-2 overall, 1-1 in the Big Ten) felt Howard first was interfered with and second that he had possession long enough to count. The officials didn't.

"I felt myself being tackled through the whole route," said Howard, who hadn't had a finger laid on him earlier in the game when he answered a Spartans touchdown with a 95-yard kickoff return, the second-longest in Wolverines history.

"The (game) film will show it (interference)," Howard said. "The film doesn't lie."

Michigan State defensive back Eddie Brown said: "When he

came off the line he kind of ran into me and grabbed me. He turned me so he could get inside of me and when he did that, I gave him a push. That's when he stumbled. He fell and the ball bounced off him."

Brown admitted he looked for a yellow flag and, relieved when he didn't see one, ran off the field.

"Eddie Brown was cocked to my inside and I gave him a fake," Howard said. "The only contact I gave him was a swim (move) because he tried to jam me. When I got past him, he did the only thing a DB could — try to grab me because it was do or die. I'd do the same thing if I was in his position."

As I looked up when the ball popped out when I hit the ground, the first thing I saw was the referee's face and I was looking for him to raise his arms (to signal a touchdown). He didn't and he didn't say anything to me, so I thought it was an incomplete pass.

"After the play, when they were celebrating, I was looking for a flag but there were only yellow pom-poms on the field. I couldn't believe it."

Referee John Nealon permitted only Michigan sports information director Bruce Madej to quiz the officials.

"The covering official didn't see the interference," Nealon said. "To have possession you have to be able to run with it, hold it or kick it and he didn't have control of the ball. As far as I could see, he never had possession of the ball."

TOP: Desmond Howard (21) was unable to pull down an Elvis Grbac pass in the game's final minutes. ABOVE: Spartans quarterback Dan Enos (4) ran for 1 TD and passed for another.

Hawkeyes' Upset of Michigan: Fry's Biggest

By Buck Turnbull
The Des Moines Register

Ann Arbor, Mich. | October 20, 1990

Iowa	0	7	3	14	—	24
Michigan	7	7	6	3	—	23

Iowa coach Hayden Fry couldn't have contained his elation today if he had tried. And he didn't.

He called his team's 24-23 upset of No. 10-ranked Michigan the biggest victory of his career — and that covers about 30 years.

"Can you believe this? Whoo-ee!" Fry yelled. "Two times in the state of Michigan in the same year — the first time Iowa has ever defeated Michigan and Michigan State on the road in the same year.

"I'm happier that if we won the Big Ten championship or a big bowl game."

The Hawkeyes, 13-point underdogs against Michigan's defending Big Ten Conference champions, followed the accurate right arm of quarterback Matt Rodgers to their thrilling come-from-behind victory.

It put them among the leading contenders in the race for the conference championship and the automatic Rose Bowl berth. But not exactly in the drivers's seat, Fry said.

"We're in the rumble seat," he said with a grin. "We're in the caboose, but at least we're on the train."

Amazing Iowa improved its record to 5-1 and stayed unbeaten in the conference with a 3-0 record, pinning the first Homecoming loss on Michigan in 23 years in front of a crowd of 105,517.

"Coach Fry is like a little kid in the candy store," Rodgers said. "He smells the Rose Bowl now, and it carries over to the rest of us. He's got us all excited."

Rodgers played an almost flawless game, connecting on 27 of 37 passes for 278 yards and one touchdown. He also scored on a quarterback sneak.

On Iowa's winning drive, he hit five of six passes to put the ball in position for sophomore fullback Paul Kijawa's 1-yard touchdown plunge with 1 minute 9 seconds remaining.

That tied the score, 23-23. Jeff Skillett, who kicked a 32-yard field goal in the third quarter, came on to deliver the extra point that produced pandemonium on Iowa's sideline.

Two plays after the nect kickoff, victory was assured when Hawkeye linebacker John Derby intercepted a pass, dooming the Wolverines to their third loss of the season. Just two weeks ago, they were ranked No. 1.

Michigan, which had been favored to become the first team in Big Ten history to win three straight conference outright championships, fell to 3-3 for the season and 1-2 in the league.

The Wolverines built a 14-7 halftime lead on the running of Jon Vaughn, the nation's No. 1 rusher, and built the margin to 20-10 late in the third quarter.

But once again, Iowa's defense was superb down the stretch, choking off almost everything Michigan tried to do in the second half.

The Wolverines, who entered the game leading the nation in total offense, couldn't get a first down in the third quarter. They were limited to three first downs and 66 yards in the last half.

Michigan's only touchdown in the second half came on a blocked punt. Dave Ritter raced in to smother Jim Hujsak's punt, and Dwayne Ware picked up the ball and ran 7 yards into the end zone.

After that score, the Wolverines decided to go for two points on a fake conversion attempt, but fullback Jarrod Bunch was stopped short.

The lost point came back to haunt the Wolverines. Had they made the extra-point kick, they would have forced Iowa into a late-game decision of whether to go for a tie or a victory.

Michigan coach Garry Moeller said he instructed his place-kick holder to call for the two-point run if he saw the right opening.

"It had been there before," Moeller said. "It wasn't there this time, but he went for it anyway."

The leading tacklers for the Hawks were Matt Ruhland and Leroy Smith with seven apiece, but none of the contenders played a better game than cornerback Merton Hanks.

In addition to making six unassisted tackles, Hanks blocked a Michigan field-goal attempt in the first half. It was the

Iowa coach Hayden Fry (left) and Michigan's Gary Moeller visit before the game.

seventh blocked kick of his career, an Iowa record, and his third this season.

Rodgers took the Hawks on a 67-yard, 10-play drive to a touchdown that he scored on a quarterback sneak play early in the fourth quarter, cutting the deficit to 20-17.

Vaughn was out of the game by this time after re-injuring an ankle. He totaled 86 yards, about half of his average in the first five games.

His replacement, Allen Jefferson, was stopped by Iowa cornerback Eddie Polly for no gain on a key third-and-2 situation with more than 4 minutes left. The Wolverines had to settle for J.D. Carlson's 47-yard field goal and a 23-17 lead.

Rodgers then piloted the Hawks downfield on five completions to different receivers — Kujawa, Sean Smith, Jon Filloon, Nick Bell and Tony Stewart. Kujawa finished with six catches and Danan Hughes had five.

The Hawks had trouble with their running game, netting only 91 yards, but they did get one key gain on the ground late in their winning drive — a 15-yard burst by Stewart on a draw play.

That put the ball on Michigan's 15, and two plays later, Rodgers rifled a pass to Stewart just short of the goal line. Kujawa then banged across for the TD.

Hawkeyes quarterback Matt Rodgers (7) dives over the Michigan defense for a 1-yard TD in the fourth quarter.

Paterno's Lions Roar Into Big Ten With Air Show

By Randy Johnson
Centre Daily Times

State College, Pa.	September 3, 1993					
Minnesota	7	6	7	0	—	20
Penn State	21	10	0	7	—	38

Folks in Ann Arbor and Columbus and Iowa City must be scratching their heads over this one. Penn State became a full-fledged member of the Big Ten this afternoon, a seemingly perfect match between a conference of run-oriented teams and a program that has traditionally adhered to a similar philosophy.

So what happened at Beaver Stadium?

Penn State, with a big assist from Minnesota, turned that Big Ten image on its ear.

Behind John Sacca's four touchdown passes to Bobby Engram, the 17th-ranked Nittany Lions ushered in their Big Ten existence by outgunning the Golden Gophers, 38-20, before a crowd of 95,387.

The Penn State victory wasn't unexpected, but the method was.

"How many passes?" Penn State coach Joe Paterno asked afterward. "Sixfty-five? Do you mean combined?"

No coach, 65 passes didn't even cover Minnesota's total — the Gophers had 66. Add in Penn State's 34 aerials and the game featured an even 100 — a number that had Paterno rubbing the back of his neck and looking down in disbelief.

Still the veteran coach didn't care how his team won for the first time as a Big Ten conference member. He was just relieved they had won.

"If feels pretty good. I'd be dishonest if I told you otherwise," said Paterno, Division I's winningest active coach with 248 victories. "I went into the game with some anxiety."

The game went well from the start for Penn State and poorly for Minnesota.

Consider these tidbits:

■ The Lions scored on their first play from scrimmage — a 29-yard screen pass from Sacca to Engram — and had 28 points on the scoreboard before the game was 16 minutes old.

■ Sacca finished the afternoon 18 for 32 for 274 yards, four touchdowns and no interceptions.

■ The Penn State running game racked up 230 yards —

including 120 yards on 15 carries for Ki-Jana Carter, the most effective of the rotating trio of redshirt sophomores.

■ And Engram, the sophomore who missed last season for disciplinary reasons, set a school record with his four TD catches and eight receptions for 165 yards on the afternoon.

"Penn State played unbelievable," Minnesota coach Jim Wacker exclaimed. "we weren't just flopping around, they were good."

Penn State's quick-strike offense was at its best in the first quarter.

The first Lions touchdown was set up when cornerback Derek Bochna read the eyes of Gophers quarterback Tim Schade, stepped in front of a Gopher receiver and picked off the pass at the Gopher 29-yard line. From there, Sacca and Engram paired up on the scoring play.

"The opening play was just a flanker screen," Paterno said. "We were just looking for 8 or 10 yards."

Penn State put up its second touchdown in a more conventional manner.

After taking over at Minnesota's 11, the Lions rode the running of Carter and Stephen Pitts on a 10-play march. After Sacca hit wide receiver Justin Williams for a 14-yard gain to the Gopher 31, Engram made the most spectacular play of the day.

With Minnesota's Juan Hunter in single coverage, Engram broke for the right corner of the end zone, got past Hunter and made a diving catch for the 14-0 lead.

"John just made a great throw," said Engram, whose four touchdowns eclipsed the PSU record of two that had been set 30 times.

The Sacca-to-Engram combination worked again later in the first quarter after Shelly Hammonds gave Penn State excellent field position with a 67-yard kickoff return. Facing third-and-4 from the Gopher 20, Engram worked his way free in the end zone and Sacca delivered the TD pass.

"They were single-covering Bobby a lot and we took

Sophomore halfback Ki-Jana Carter (32) ran for 120 yards on 15 carries against Minnesota.

advantage," explained Sacca. "There's not many people in the country who can single-cover Bobby."

Wacker was just as impressed with Sacca, who won the starting job over Kerry Collins and Wally Richardson.

"I don't know how they had any trouble picking him for the starting quarterback," Wacker said. "I like him. He made some outstanding throws."

And Penn State's defense made some outstanding plays, which led to a 28-7 lead in the second quarter.

Following Engram's third touchdown, Gophers running back Chris Darkins fumbled after a heavy hit from Lions linebacker Terry Killens. Defensive tackle Tyoka Jackson recovered at the Minnesota 17 and Carter scored six plays later. Minnesota could've held the Lions to a field goal, but an offsides call on fourth-and-2 kept the PSU mini-drive alive.

As impressive as Penn State's offensive performance was, so was the sheer firepower Minnesota displayed.

Under Wacker's run-and-shoot offense, Schade and receiver Omar Douglas made life tough on the Lions defense. A

transfer from Texas Christian in his first game as a Gopher, Schade completed 34 of 66 passes — both PSU opponent records — for 478 yards. He also kept the Lions off balance with a nifty quarterback draw play, which resulted in a 13-yard touchdown run that trimmed Penn State's lead to 14-7 in the first quarter.

"That's a very complicated offense," Paterno offered. "Most of those guys are back from last year and their only question mark was their quarterback. He looked pretty darn good."

However, Penn State's defense stiffened. Minnesota tried a fake punt on fourth-and-10 from its own 28 late in the third quarter, but the Lions stuffed the up-back, Justin Conzemius for a 3-yard gain.

From there, the Lions defense had its way with a fatigued Minnesota offense. In the fourth quarter, Penn State limited Schade to 9 completions in 28 attempts.

"The game started to get long at the end," Sacca said. "But I wouldn't mind throwing the ball 65 times, too."

In this new-look Big Ten, maybe he'll get his chance.

Paterno's Lions Get Biggest Big Ten Win

By Randy Johnson
Centre Daily Times

Ann Arbor, Mich.	October 15, 1994					
Penn State	10	6	8	7	—	31
Michigan	0	3	14	7	—	24

As Joe Paterno responded to the myriad of questions, he spotted someone among the mass of personnel in the Michigan Stadium visitor's media room he just needed to acknowledge. It was his wife, Sue, and the Penn State football coach greeted her by blowing her a little kiss.

Nothing seemed more appropriate and telling at the time. Because what Paterno had just witnessed before 106,832 — the third-largest crowd in football history — is surely something he'll savor forever. Paterno's Nittany Lions had just completed a stirring, 31-24 victory over Michigan in a game featuring as many twists and turns as a Formula One race.

"If that game goes another quarter," Paterno decided, "who knows who's gonna win it?"

On this picture-perfect fall day, third-ranked Penn State won it. The Lions won it by building an early lead, seeing it evaporate in mere minutes, regaining the lead, seeing Michigan come back and tie it, and finally winning the thing with an offense that delivered in the clutch and a defense that ultimately denied Michigan.

"We came up with the big plays when we had to," Paterno said. "Even though they might have been a little bit tired, they sucked it up when they had to."

Such an effort kept Penn State's Big Ten and national title hopes alive.

The Nittany Lions (6-0 overall, 3-0 Big Ten) will likely do some poll-vaulting when the rankings come out. Top-ranked Florida lost, 36-33, to Auburn, while No. 2 Nebraska downed Kansas State, 17-6. Penn State is a lock to be ranked at least No. 2, which would be its highest ranking since winning the national title with a 14-10 victory over Miami in the 1987 Fiesta Bowl.

"For me, the is the biggest game of my life," said Lion tailback Ki-Jana Carter, who rushed 26 times for 165 yards in his duel with Michigan's Tyrone Wheatley, who carried 19 times for 144 yards and a pair of scores. "It was a big game for Penn State football history, too. The so-called powerhouse of the Big Ten is Michigan."

That could change. The Lions are 3-0 in the conference and alone atop the standings since Purdue and Wisconsin tied 27-27. Penn State controls its own Rose Bowl destiny and five more wins will put the squad in Pasadena.

That the Lions have such control can be credited to how they played in the fourth quarter, especially during the game's final six minutes. Michigan tailback Tshimanga Biakabutuka knotted the game at 24 with his 1-yard touchdown run with 11:37 remaining.

After the two teams traded possessions, Michigan got the ball at its own 21 with 6:20 left.

A pair of Wheatley runs netted 7 yards and the Wolverines faced third-and-3 from the 28. When quarterback Todd Collins dropped back to pass, Lions linebacker Willie Smith came on a blitz and nailed Collins, who fumbled. Although fullback Che

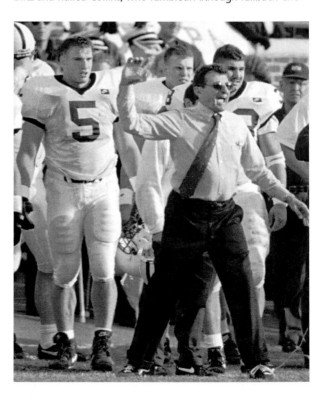

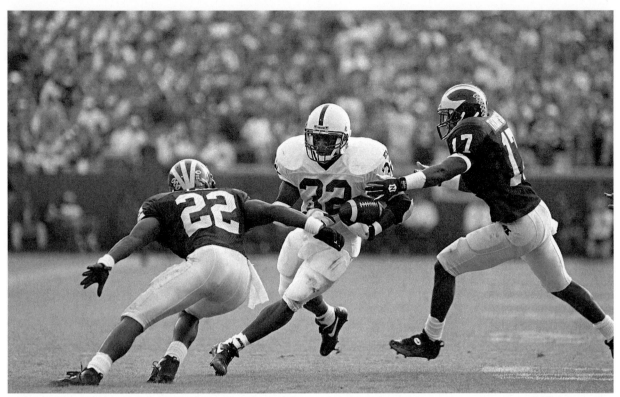

ABOVE: Ki-Jana Carter (32) ran for 165 yards against Michigan. OPPOSITE PAGE: Joe Paterno gives the officials an earful.

Foster recovered, the Wolverines were forced to punt and the Lions took over at their own 45 with 4:46 left.

"My feeling was, 'If we get the ball back, we're gonna score,' " Paterno said.

Penn State quarterback Kerry Collins, who completed 20 of 32 passes for 231 yards and three touchdowns, hit split end Bobby Engram for a 16-yard gain on first down. Then came Carter, who rambled 26 yards on a delay to the Michigan 15.

Two plays later, Collins found Engram on a slant pattern for a 16-yard touchdown pass and a 31-24 lead with 2:53 left.

"You can't allow them to score on a swing pass," said Michigan coach Gary Moeller, who's seen his team drop late-game heartbreakers to both Colorado and the Lions this season at Michigan Stadium. "They may have surprised us on that play, but you can't throw that pass and score."

But they did. "It was just unbelievable," said Engram, who had two of his three catches on the winning drive. "I saw the ball in the air and I knew I had to make the big catch."

While Penn State's offense produced the go-ahead points, its maligned defense had to stop a Michigan attack that produced big play after big play all afternoon.

When the Wolverines took over at the 20 with 2:53 remaining, the result of their first play didn't bode well for the Lions. Wheatley, who scorched the Lions for touchdown runs of 69 and 21 yards in the third quarter, ripped off a 30-yard gain to midfield.

"After the first run when Tyrone got to the 50-yard line, it was starting to worry me a little," Lions defensive tackle Eric Clair said. "I don't know how many games I've been in where a team has gone down the field in the final minutes, like Notre Dame did a couple of years ago." Wheatley's run, however, proved to be Michigan's final kick.

On first down from the 50, Todd Collins threw a bomb for wideout Amani Toomer, who already had seven catches for 154 yards. Toomer got behind the Lions secondary inside the 20, but the ball was overthrown and fell harmlessly to the ground.

"I think I just misjudged it," Toomer said. "I was going one way and the ball drifted the other."

A 9-yard gain by Biakabutuka left Michigan with third-and-1 from the Lions' 41. But Smith stuffed the tailback for no gain and cornerback Brian Miller picked off Todd Collins' fourth-and-1 pass with 1:26 left.

"We all just gathered together and said, 'We're not going to let them get a yard,' " Miller said. "We knew that we would come through in the end."

So did Bucky Greeley, Penn State's starting center. "After we scored that last touchdown, I just had this feeling that our defense was going to stop them," he said. "Call me psychic or whatever."

Northwestern's Gamble Upsets No. 7 Michigan

By Bill Jauss
Chicago Tribune

Ann Arbor, Mich. | October 7, 1995						
Northwestern	0	6	3	10	—	19
Michigan	3	3	7	0	—	13

Michigan's proud, talented, unbeaten Wolverines had plenty of time left to move 33 yards for the touchdown and extra point that would beat Northwestern.

Everybody — the roaring crowd of 104,642 fans, band members from both schools, and the 11 Wildcat defenders and 11 Wolverine attackers in the light mist falling today at Michigan Stadium — knew it.

But as the huge crowd gaped in amazement, NU's stonewall defense came up with the last ditch stand to hold off the No. 7-ranked Wolverines, 19-13.

By upsetting 16-point Michigan (5-1, 1-1 in the Big Ten), the No. 25-ranked Wildcats snapped a run of 19 straight Wolverines victories in the series and turned the Big Ten football world topsy-turvey.

Northwestern (4-1, 2-0 in the Big Ten), which has not won a Big Ten title since 1936, now leads the Big Ten. The Wildcats vaulted to the top on the strength of their gambling defense and an offense that scored after three Michigan turnovers, squeezing out 19 points on Sam Valenzisi's four field goals and Steve Schnur's 2-yard touchdown pass to Matt Hartl.

"Our defense was relentless," said Northwestern coach Gary Barnett. "We had just enough offense to take advantage of their turnovers. You're not going to make long marches against Michigan. They're too good."

Michigan fans had one last hope when the Wolverines had first down on the NU 33 with 2 minutes 15 seconds remaining. Sophomore quarterback Brian Griese, whose Hall of Famer father, Bob, used to engineer come-from-behind victories for Purdue and the Miami Dolphins, looked on first down to his brilliant receiver, Amani Toomer.

NU defensive coordinator Ron Vanderlinden put in a new blitz at halftime, and the blitz was on as Griese overthrew Toomer.

On second down, Tim Biakabutuka, who riddled the Wildcats for 205 rushing yards, fumbled, and teammate Joe Runyan recovered for a 5-yard loss on the 38.

"When the ball was loose, and Michigan recovered it," said

NU offensive guard Ryan Padgett, watching helplessly from the sideline. I almost swallowed my tongue."

Valenzisi, whose field goals of 29, 28, 32 and 22 yards ran his school record run to 11 in a row, kept control of his tongue and his emotions.

"I was thinking ahead that, if they scored and went ahead, 20-19, we'd have time to get into position for another kick to try to win it, said Valenzisi.

Valenzisi did not have to kick again, thanks to the special blitz designed by Vanderlinden and executed successfully by Pat Fitzgerald and William Bennett.

On third down, the blitzers roared in on Griese. Fitzgerald's arm struck Griese's as he threw incomplete. Fourth down.

"The blitz was designed for either Fitz or me to get to Griese," said Hudhaifa Ishmaeli, who stripped a fumble from Griese to set up the fourth of Valenzisi's field goals, from 22 yards. "Fitz got there first."

"Our hair was on fire in that last series," said defender Matt Rice. "Michigan had the best offensive line I'd ever faced. But we went after them. When Fitz deflected the ball, I was jubilant."

Griese had one more chance. Fitzgerald and Ishmaeli blitzed again. Fitzgerald again knocked Griese's arm. William Bennett made a diving interception on the NU 21.

"The blitz is a gamble," said Bennett. "It leaves us (defensive backs) one-on-one. But it hurries the quarterback."

"Both times I came in untouched," said Fitzgerald. "I felt I had to do something to make up for the (interception) I didn't get."

The Wildcats had an earlier interception, by Eric Collier, who returned it 4 yards to the Michigan 31 to set up NU's only TD. It vaulted the Wildcats from a 13-9 deficit to a 16-13 fourth-quarter lead. Toomer's fumbled punt set up a field goal for a 6-6 halftime tie.

"The turnovers gave us the opportunities," said Johnson. "We wouldn't have won without them."

D'Wayne Bracy pulls in a pass from Steve Schnur, which set up one of Sam Valenzisi's four field goals.

No. 2 Lions Rally to Defeat No. 7 Ohio State

BY KIMBERLY JONES
Centre Daily Times

State College, Pa. | October 11, 1997

Ohio State	3	10	14	0	—	27
Penn State	10	7	7	7	—	31

Jim Nelson raised his helmet. Brandon Short blew kisses to the crowd. Mike McQueary pumped his fists. And Curtis Enis cried.

No. 2 Penn State rallied from 10 points down to defeat No. 7-ranked Ohio State, 31-27, today before a record Beaver Stadium crowd of 97,282.

Many of those fans — rambunctious throughout and downright deafening in the fourth quarter — hung around after the final gun sounded.

They saluted their Nittany Lions. And the Lions responded with high-fives and wide smiles and shouts of thanks.

"I don't think anyone went to the bathroom the entire game. I never saw an empty seat," said Nelson, who had a game-high 11 tackles. "The crowd won the game."

"They were the 12th man," added Short. "I don't think they know how important they are."

The Nittany Lions broke a two-game losing streak to the Buckeyes. In the process they likely recaptured the nation's No. 1 ranking. Top-ranked Florida lost to No. 14 Louisiana State, 28-21, tonight.

"I think we're pretty good, obviously," Joe Paterno said. "But we've got a long way to go."

On the game's final play, with the Nittany Lions threatening at the Buckeye 5, Paterno directed McQueary to drop to his knee. It was an act of remarkable class.

"I thought Penn State had a great football team," Ohio State coach John Cooper said. "I told Coach Paterno after the game they're going to get my vote for No. 1 this week."

"They put together an excellent offensive football team," added Buckeyes linebacker Andy Katzenmoyer. "I don't expect them to lose a ballgame."

For a while, it looked like the Nittany Lions would lose today.

When the Buckeyes took a 27-17 lead on tailback Pepe Pearson's 8-yard run, the Nittany Lions' hopes dimmed.

"I said to myself," Paterno said, " 'We'll find out what kind of a team we are right now.' "

Just 1:42 remained in the third quarter and McQueary, sharp as a tack through four games, was struggling. He was only 7 for 15 for 68 yards at halftime.

Perhaps it took 10 unanswered points by the Buckeyes to get him in gear.

"Another guy may fold in that situation," McQueary said. "I'm not gonna be the guy who costs this team a game."

He wasn't, of course, finishing 14 for 30 for 129 yards and one touchdown. But it was fullback Aaron Harris who might've won it.

Harris, a bruiser who bounces off tacklers like a high-energy pinball, sloughed off a quartet of Buckeyes and rumbled 51 yards into the end zone to cut Ohio State's lead to 27-24 with 20 seconds remaining in the third quarter.

Harris rejuvenated his teammates — and the crowd. Even the Penn State defense was energized: Ohio State ventured into Lions territory once thereafter, and safety Shawn Lee responded by intercepting a Joe Germaine pass.

The Lions offense, a high-octane running machine that generated 316 rushing yards, spread the ball around throughout the day. Harris scored the game's first touchdown on a 5-yard run.

Travis Forney added a 23-yard field goal which Ohio State's Dan Stultz answered from 27, and the first quarter ended with Penn State leading, 10-3.

The Lions took a 17-13 lead into intermission. Penn State's touchdown, sandwiched between two Ohio State scores, came on a 6-yard McQueary pass to an uncovered Joe Nastasi. "That," Nastasi said, "should never happen."

In the third quarter, Ohio State rallied with a pair of touchdowns. The first came on a 1-yard Germaine pass to David Boston, set up by a 30-yard halfback option pass from Michael Wiley to Steve Wisniewski. The second was Pearson's 8-yard run.

Four plays later, Harris trucked into the end zone to bring Penn State within a score.

The game-winning drive started with 13:16 remaining in the fourth quarter.

Lions tailback Curtis Enis (39) scored the game-winning TD on a 26-yard run in the fourth quarter.

Tight end Brad Scioli caught an 18-yard pass. Enis, who finished with 211 yards on 23 carries, scampered for 24, then 3 yards. Cuncho Brown, another tight end, made an 8-yard reception. Jurevicius followed with a 9-yard grab. On third-and-one, Harris gained three.

On first down at the Buckeye 26, Enis got the call. He headed right, stopped, made a 90-degree cut left and darted downfield, running out of the grasp of one Buckeye before entering the end zone.

"Like Amtrak," an emotional Enis said, "I was only going one way."

So were the Lions.

Even down by two scores, confidence remained high on the Penn State sideline.

"Honestly, I never thought we would lose the game," Nelson said. "That never entered my mind."

The Penn State defense thwarted Ohio State's would-be rallies, ending one possession on Lee's sixth career interception and the final one when four straight Germaine passes fell incomplete. Cornerback David Macklin punched one ball from the grasp of wideout Dee Miller. Lee broke up another,

on fourth-and-10 with 2:24 to play.

"A lot of people were saying this team wasn't tough enough," said defensive end Chris Snyder, who sacked Germaine twice. "I don't think toughness was a question today."

Toughness wasn't a question. Emotion was.

The Nittany Lions, who tried to downplay the importance of this game last week, let their feelings show after it.

"It means so much," said a teary-eyed Jurevicius, who a team-high five passes for 59 yards. "I don't think there's any question of what Penn State can do. I think we proved it."

Of his weepy teammates, especially Enis who is also an Ohio native, Jurevicius smiled. "Those," he said, "are tears of joy."

Enis, who last year said he choked in a 38-7 loss at Ohio State, reveled in his effort this time.

The junior tailback got stronger as the game wore on. For the first time this season he played in the fourth quarter. His per-carry average was a lofty 9.2 yards.

"You can't tackle him," Paterno said, "unless you use everything you've got in you."

Perfect Michigan Beats Bucks, Wins Big Ten Title

BY ANGELIQUE S. CHENGELIS
The Detroit News

Ann Arbor, Mich. | November 22, 1997

Ohio State	0	0	7	7 —	14
Michigan	0	13	7	0 —	20

It is easy to think about perfection and what it should be like. But it is something else to reach that point and then try to describe it.

The top-ranked Michigan Wolverines completed their first perfect regular season since 1971, relying heavily on their defense in a 20-14 victory over No. 4-ranked Ohio State today. But they could not find the words to illustrate their emotions.

Michigan will be ranked No. 1 in The Associated Press and the ESPN/USA Today polls, thanks to its victory and to Florida's 32-29 victory over Florida State. Florida State was ranked No. 1 in the ESPN/USA Today poll entering today, and Michigan was No. 2. U-M was No. 1 in The Associated Press poll.

The Wolverines didn't hide their emotions. The Wolverines remained on the field following their victory that gave them their first Big Ten title since 1992. They will face Pac-10 co-champion Washington State in the Rose Bowl. The Wolverines ran with roses in their hands, some clenching roses between their teeth as an appreciative Michigan Stadium-record crowd of 106,982 celebrated with them.

The victory was Michigan's third straight over the Buckeyes, and OSU coach John Cooper is 1-8-1 against the Wolverines. It was a brilliant day for Heisman trophy candidate Charles Woodson, who returned a punt for a touchdown, intercepted a pass in the end zone, broke up a pass and had three tackles.

"I'm still emotionally out of it," U-M safety Marcus Ray said. "This was my dream -- to go undefeated, beat Ohio State at home and go to the Rose Bowl. That's why I came here, that's why my teammates came here, too."

Said U-M coach Lloyd Carr, 3-0 against the Buckeyes: "For us, it's truly a dream season. It was their determination, more than anything else, to have a great season ... they won because they had the resolve to win."

The Wolverines did not beat Ohio State because of gaudy offensive numbers. They played the second half without leading tailback Chris Howard, who was injured when he was hit in the head in the first half, and starting left tackle Jeff Backus, who reinjured his right tackle.

Michigan finished with 189 yards of offense, including quar-terback Brian Griese's 147 passing yards. Only one of the Wolverines' touchdowns was generated by the offense, a 1-yard run by freshman tailback Anthony Thomas in the second quarter to give them a 7-0 lead.

Woodson gave the Wolverines a 13-0 lead — Kraig Baker's extra-point attempt was blocked — on a 78-yard punt return late in the second quarter.

"I had been asking the coaches to run that wall left all season, and finally he gave it to me," Woodson said. "The whole team did a great job blocking. I was just able to run down the sideline. I ran out of gas. I locked up. It was a great feeling to finally get the punt return."

Woodson prevented a sure Ohio State touchdown on the opening drive of the second half, when he intercepted Stanley Jackson's pass intended for Dee Miller in the end zone.

"I just cut underneath the pass, and Stanley Jackson threw me a great pass," Woodson said.

"The Wolverines built a 20-0 lead with 10:29 left in the third quarter, when cornerback Andre Weathers intercepted a Jackson pass and returned it 43 yards for the touchdown.

The Buckeyes, who had 252 yards of offense, made their move late in the third quarter when David Boston beat Woodson for a 56-yard touchdown pass from Joe Germaine with 4:50 remaining. Boston punctuated the score by backpedaling the final four yards while yelling at Woodson.

Suddenly, it was a game.

"This was the kind of game we wanted," Ray said. "We wanted a dogfight for the championship.

And the Wolverines got it. Early in the fourth quarter, the Buckeyes made the score 20-14 after Griese made his one mistake of the game, turning the ball over deep in Michigan territory. Griese was blind-sided by Gary Berry, who forced a fumble that was recovered and returned to the 2-yard line by Jerry Rudzinski. Pepe Pearson scored on a 2-yard run.

The Michigan defense, as has been the case all season, preserved the victory.

Charles Woodson's 78-yard punt return late in the second quarter gave Michigan a 13-0 lead at halftime.

Irvin & Spartans Shock No. 4 Nittany Lions

BY DAVE DYE
The Detroit News

East Lansing, Mich. | November 29, 1997

Penn State	0	7	7	0	—	14
Michigan State	7	7	14	21	—	49

After those blocked punts, missed field-goal attempts and disappointments, Michigan State salvaged its season today with a shocking 49-14 victory against No. 4 Penn State.

The Spartans (7-4, 4-4 in the Big Ten) accepted an invitation to the Aloha Bowl on Christmas in Honolulu. MSU needed to win today to get the bid, according to Aloha Bowl CEO Leonard Klompus. The Spartans could have been shut out from a bowl bid if they had lost.

The Spartans scored five touchdowns in the final 23 minutes after Penn State (9-3, 6-2 in the Big Ten) tied the game at 14. MSU had 596 yards total offense, including 452 rushing.

The Aloha Bowl spot opened because the Big 12 doesn't have enough bowl-eligible teams to fulfill its commitment. ABC-TV, which televises the Aloha Bowl, made a big push to get MSU to create a Big Ten-Pac 10 matchup. The deal was completed with 10 minutes remaining after the Spartans opened a large lead.

Some of the players found out late in the game that they were on their way to paradise.

Saban got a call on his cellular phone in the locker room after the game. When he was asked by an Aloha Bowl representative if MSU would accept the bid, Saban said he wanted the players to give the answer. Saban held up the phone, and asked them if they wanted to go. The players went crazy.

MSU likely knocked Penn State out of an Alliance bowl (Sugar or Orange) which will cost the Big Ten several million dollars.

Sedrick Irvin scored four touchdowns — three by running and one by pass — and rushed for 238 yards. Marc Renaud rushed for 203 yards and one touchdown. Quarterback Todd Schultz completed 17 of 23 for 144 yards and two TD's.

Irvin and Renaud became the second duo in NCAA history to each rush for more than 200 yards in a game. It was also done by Tulsa's Gordon Brown (214 yards) and Steve Gage (206) against Wichita State in 1985.

The Spartans' domination in the line of scrimmage led to a 14-0 lead, with Garl Scott scoring on a 19-yard pass from Schultz with 56 seconds left in the first quarter and Renaud running 42 yards for a TD with 3:48 remaining before halftime. But Penn State scored late in the first half on a 54-yard run by Curtis Enis and early in the second half on a 14-yard pass from Mike McQueary to Joe Jurevicius for a 14-14 tie.

It had all the makings of a typical fold by the Spartans, similar to the way they had lost to Penn State in recent years.

But this time was different. The Spartans didn't get scared after losing the early lead. They came right back with a 78-yard scoring drive, with Irvin running 19 yards for the TD to regain the lead. Moments later, Robaire Smith forced a fumble on a sack that was recovered by Desmond Thomas deep in Penn State territory. And the rout was on with Irvin scoring on an 8-yard pass and on runs of 1 and 30 yards. Leroy McFadden's 2-yard run with 2:44 remaining finished the Spartans' scoring.

MSU's seven victories is the most for the Spartans since finishing 8-3-1 in 1990 with a 17-16 victory over Southern California in the John Hancock Bowl.

Dr. Merritt Norvell Jr. pumped a fist in the air and screamed like a kid breaking for afternoon recess.

****

"Yeeessssssss!!! Get in there Babyyyyy!!," Norvell, Michigan State University's athletic director, shouted on the sidelines of Spartan Stadium, as backup runningback Leroy McFadden pounced in to the end zone to wrap up Michigan State's stunning 49-14 victory over Penn State.

A few yards away, Sedrick Irvin danced. Tight end Josh Keur held back tears. Ike Reese bearhugged anyone who strayed within 10 feet of him. Finally. A Spartan Day.

"This was a program win," Norvell said. "It came against the fourth-ranked team. We set a lot of records and we are going to a bowl. It was a good day."

Marc Renaud (26) ran for 203 yards and 1 TD against Penn State. Sedrick Irvin added 238 yards rushing and 4 TD's to lead MSU past the No. 2-ranked Lions.

Michigan State Surges Past No. 1 Buckeyes

BY DAVE DYE
The Detroit News

Columbus, Ohio	November 7, 1998					
Michigan State	3	6	9	10	—	28
Ohio State	17	0	7	0	—	24

Michigan State wanted to shock the world. It did. The Spartans overcame overwhelming odds - they were 27 point underdogs — to upset No. 1-ranked Ohio State, 28-24, today at Ohio Stadium.

MSU (5-4, 3-2 in the Big Ten) rallied from a 24-9 third-quarter deficit to beat a previously undefeated and seemingly invincible Buckeyes team.

The Spartans did the same thing to an undefeated Ohio State team in 1974. They also toppled No. 1 Michigan in 1990.

"Funny things happen in football when a team plays possessed," MSU coach Nick Saban said. "We played like we had nothing to lose. I told the team it was going to be a 15-round fight, and we needed *Rocky* in the 15th round. It's a great win for our program."

The Buckeyes (8-1, 5-1 in the Big Ten) were supposed to be on their way to play for the national championship in the Fiesta Bowl. They appeared superior to any team in college football. The Spartans didn't appear to be going to any bowl.

But that's the beauty of college football.

"They looked flat," MSU center Jason Strayhorn said of Ohio State. "They were pointing into the stands during warm-ups. In the first half, we heard them talking about some parties after the game."

The Buckeyes celebrated wildly after strong safety Damon Moore returned an interception 67 yards for a touchdown to build a 24-9 lead in the third quarter.

Logic suggested the Spartans would fold at that point. They have done it so many times in the past against far inferior competition.

"Some teams go in the tank there," MSU receiver Lavaile Richardson said. "It's happened with us, but we've learned to fight through it."

Back-to-back Ohio State turnovers — one on a misplayed punt when the ball hit an unknowning Buckeye in the back, and the other on a fumble by tailback Michael Wiley — led to an MSU touchdown and a field goal to cut the deficit to six.

The Spartans took their first lead, 25-24, on Paul Edinger's extra point following Sedrick Irvin's 3-yard run with 14:20 remaining.

Ohio State's fifth turnover — a fumble by quarterback Joe Germaine — led to Edinger's fifth field goal, a 42-yarder, for a 28-24 lead with 9:26 left to play.

That meant the Buckeyes had to score a touchdown, and MSU's defense wouldn't yield.

Linebacker T.J. Turner stopped running back Joe Montgomery on a fourth-and-1 at MSU's 21 with under four minutes left.

Cornerback Renaldo Hill's interception helped clinch it after the Buckeyes again moved deep into MSU territory with a minute left.

Spartans quarterback Bill Burke finished with 18 completions on 46 attempts for 323 yards, a touchdown and an interception.

Edinger went 5-for-5 in field goals for the second straight game, breaking a Michigan State record and tying two others.

Edinger's 10 straight set a new MSU record for consecutive field goals. The previous mark of eight was tied by several kickers.

He also tied John Langeloh (1988) for the most field goals in a season with 18. His five field goals — 33, 43, 22, a career-best 49, and 42 yards — tied the record for most in a game for the second consecutive week. He had five last week against Northwestern.

MSU Wins vs. No. 1 Teams

Michigan State is 3-12-1 against the No. 1 team in the AP poll since it began in 1936. Listed below are the Spartans' wins against the top-ranked teams:

Year	Opponent	Site	MSU Ranking	Result
1974	Ohio State	Home	No. 16	Win, 16-13
1990	Michigan	Away	Unranked	Win, 28-27
1998	Ohio State	Away	Unranked	Win, 28-24

Spartans kicker Paul Edinger went 5-for-5 field goals for the second straight game. This feat broke a Michigan State record and tied two others.

Illinois' 4th Quarter Rally Defeats Michigan

By Gary Reinmuth
Chicago Tribune

When it was over, several Illinois players took turns leaping into a small crowd of delirious fans who had crunched up against the brick retaining wall at the south end of Michigan Stadium. The scene took place only a few feet from the end zone where the Illini had scored all but seven of their points.

Up above, the blue and gold scoreboard was still displaying the final score today: Illinois 35, Michigan 29.

Make that one small leap for the Illini and one giant leap for Coach Ron Turner's program.

"I told the guys how proud I am of them," Turner said. "Nobody believed. And I do mean *nobody*. Except the guys in that locker room."

As big as the victory was, however, it wasn't nearly as big as the giant leap of faith Illinois (4-3, 1-3 in the Big Ten) took to get there. To knock off the No. 9 Wolverines (5-2, 2-2 in the Big Ten) on their own field, in front of 110,188 fans and a national television audience, was off-the-charts huge.

The Illini had to erase the fact that they were 24-point underdogs. They had to forget that only seven days ago. Minnesota had thrashed and embarrassed them, 37-7, in Champaign. They had to ignore history — Illinois is 21-60-2 all time against the Wolverines. They had to rally from a 27-7 deficit with six minutes left in the third quarter. And they had to take to heart a rousing motivational speech by Turner.

No. The Illini had no chance win today.

But they did. Thanks to a locker room full of heroes:

■ Almost from out of nowhere, speedy tailback Rocky Harvey re-emerged. Harvey, a forgotten man of late, carried 17 times for 106 yards and scored two touchdowns. The first came on a 59-yard pass from quarterback Kurt Kittner with 2 minutes 42 seconds left that put Illinois ahead, 28-27. The second was a 54-yard run up the middle with 59 seconds to go in the game.

■ Looking calm all day, Kittner completed 24 of 33 passes for 280 yards and four touchdowns without an interception. His TD passes to Harvey (59 yards), Jameel Cook (6 yards),

Ann Arbor, Mich. | October 23, 1999

Illinois	7	0	7	21	—	35
Michigan	7	13	7	2	—	29

Walter Young (31 yards) and Brian Hodges (3 yards) brought the Illini back from a 20-point deficit. Kittner has thrown 16 TD passes this season to 11 different receivers.

■ Finally, not to be forgotten was the defense's four sacks and two interceptions of Michigan quarterback Tom Brady; the blocked extra point and blocked field goal by defensive end Fred Wakefield; and Muhammad Abdullah's fumble recovery in the end zone for a safety that all but snuffed out the Wolverines' final drive with nine seconds left in the game.

"Coach challenged us," senior linebacker Eric Guenther said as he trudged off the field with a big bandage on his forehead. "He challenged us to believe."

Turner did more than that. He told them a story Friday night about what happened when he was as assistant on Dennis Green's staff at Stanford in 1991. Turner told them how the Cardinal went into South Bend, fell behind, 24-7, at halftime and rallied to stun Notre Dame.

"The games were very similar," Turner said. "It was the third year of the program. We had played horrible the week before."

Illinois played its best game in many seasons to beat Michigan for the first time since 1993.

After Kittner hooked up with Cook to give the Illini an early 7-0 lead. Brady (23 of 38 for 307 yards) and the Wolverines ran off 27 unanswered points.

A 6-yard pass to Marquis Walker tied it. A 31-yard pass to Marcus Knight made it 14-7. And 25- and 1-yard TD runs by Anthony Thomas seemed to foreshadow a rout.

But Wakefield's block of the extra point after the third TD and his block of a 46-yard field-goal indicated the Illini weren't giving up the fight.

Helped by a 25-mph wind, Illinois roared back. Harvey's back-to-back TD's seemed to ice the upset, but Michigan wasn't through.

In the final minute the Wolverines marched to the Illini 16.

On third-and-10 from there, however, Tony Francis intercepted Brady with nine seconds left. Francis was hit near the goal line and fumbled the ball back into the end zone, where Abdullah recovered for a safety. The game ended with a squib kick by Neil Rackers from the 20 and a desperation pass by Brady that fell incomplete.

"How big was this win?" Wakefield laughed. "It was huge. I really liked the Louisville one, but this one blows Louisville out of the water. This just skyrockets our chances."

Chances? That's right. Suddenly, the Illini are back in bowl contention, provided they beat Iowa and Northwestern.

Danny Clark said Turner's pep talk rated a "perfect 10."

"Did we worry when we were behind, 27-7? No," the senior linebacker said. "Our belief took care of that. A lot of guys didn't even know the score at halftime. Today wasn't about the score. It was about fighting to win."

LEFT and BELOW: Rocky Thompson's 59-yard TD catch put the Illini ahead, 28-27, with less than 2 minutes left to play.

Gophers' Late FG Beats No. 2-Ranked Penn State

BY MARK CRAIG
Minneapolis Star-Tribune

State College, Penn. | November 6, 1999

Minnesota	3	6	6	9	— 24
Penn State	7	7	3	6	— 23

How many times had Tyrone Carter lowered his head and grabbed a teammate's hand in silent prayer, pleading for that one break, or miracle, that would put Minnesota back on the college football map?

And how many times had the senior strong safety watched as the other team's all-Americans got to dance and smile and run all over the field after beating the Gophers?

"You have to keep fighting, keep praying," Carter said. "It shows your character. This team has a lot of character."

With many of the 96,753 fans at Penn State's Beaver Stadium screaming for Gophers kicker Dan Nystrom to miss a last-second 32-yard field goal, Carter was quietly sprawled on the sideline face down. Next to him was defensive tackle Dyron Russ, in the same position, beside kneeling cornerback Jimmy Wyrick. They joined hands.

"I thanked the Lord for giving us another opportunity," Carter said. "Then I kept my head down. I couldn't look at the field goal."

Nystrom put it down the middle, giving the Gophers the upset of the college football season, 24-23, over the No. 2 Nittany Lions.

"I knew it was good when players started jumping up and down, and one of them hit me," Carter said. "Then I thanked the Lord."

As the Gophers charged the field and hugged everything maroon, the Lions were grieving. Linebacker LaVar Arrington, perhaps the best player in college football, collapsed and cried after failing to block the kick.

"Minnesota played a great game today," Arrington said.

The victory — a first by the Gophers (6-3, 3-3 in the Big Ten) in five Governors' Cup contests against Penn State — clinches a winning season for the Gophers for the first time since 1990 and makes them eligible for their first bowl since 1986. Penn State, 9-1 and ranked No. 2 in the BCS rankings, saw its Sugar Bowl invitation dissolve.

Even Coach Glen Mason, the architect of the Gophers' three-year rebuilding project, admitted it was more satisfying to become bowl eligible in Beaver Stadium against the No. 2 team in the country than it would be against Indiana or Iowa in the final two weeks of the season.

"This is going from a loser to a winner in kind of spectacular fashion," Mason said. Typically, losing programs don't win one at the wire like this."

Mason called it the biggest victory of his 14-year head-coaching career. It also was the Gophers' most important victory in at least that long. Their last victory over a Top 5 team came against Michigan in 1986."

The Gophers' fortunes began to change before Nystrom kicked the winning field goal. After three consecutive Penn State scoring drives, the Gophers' defense forced a punt that sailed into the end zone with 1:50 remaining, giving them the ball at their 20-yard line.

"We went to call a play and I said, 'No, we're going to play the Hail Mary,' " Mason said. "We're going to go for it now. We're not going to play it cautious."

Quarterback Billy Cockerham launched a bomb down the right sideline that receiver Ron Johnson leaped and grabbed for a 46-yard gain.

Three plays — two incompletions and a 6-yard sack by Arrington — left the Gophers in a fourth-and-16 at the Penn State 40.

That's when Carter and his buddies started praying, and when Mason decided to look away, fearing another heart-breaker.

Another desperation Hail Mary fluttered 27 yards downfield. The ball bounced off Johnson's chest, heading for the ground when receiver Arland Bruce, in a slow-motion moment, dived and caught it.

First down at the Lions' 13-yard line.

"After Ron tipped it, I just saw the ball hanging in the air saying, like, 'Come get me, come get me!' " Bruce said. "I just grabbed it. It was meant for us to be on top today."

Three plays later, after a Gophers timeout with two seconds remaining. Nystrom knelt to pray, then entered the game.

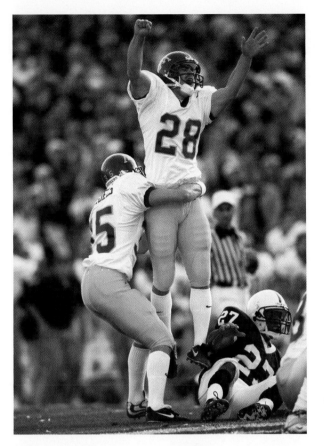

"I was so happy, I don't know what I did; I think I jumped outside of myself," said running back Thomas Hammer, who ran for 96 yards and caught three passes for 58 yards, including a 49-yard touchdown.

"Getting this win definitely validates what we've been thinking about ourselves for a long time," said Cockerham, a senior who threw for a career high 277 yards.

The Gophers gained 391 yards with backup left tackle Jake Kuppe playing the whole game in place of Adam Haayer (ankle injury). They also didn't turn over the ball and committed only one penalty.

Penn State alternated quarterbacks Kevin Thompson and Rashard Casey, but little worked. And the Gophers, who lost three games to ranked Big Ten opponents by a combined 11 points, finally got a chance to celebrate.

"I kept praying," Carter said. "I knew we'd get there one day."

LEFT: Minnesota kicker Dan Nystrom, a freshman, celebrates his game-winning 32-yard field goal over No. 2-ranked Penn State. BELOW: Gophers coach Glen Mason joins in the post-game excitement on the field. It was Minnesota's biggest win since defeating No. 2-ranked Michigan in 1986.

Badgers Win 2nd Straight Big Ten Crown

BY TOM MULHERN
Wisconsin State Journal

Madison, Wisc. | November 13, 1999						
Iowa	0	3	0	0	—	3
Wisconsin	13	14	7	7	—	41

It was the only thing missing for the University of Wisconsin football team last season, a tiny thorn in an otherwise glorious Rose Bowl championship season.

That team shared the Big Ten Conference title with Michigan and Ohio State and needed tie-breakers to get to Pasadena, Calif. This year there is no doubt.

No. 9-ranked Wisconsin claimed its first undisputed Big Ten title since 1962 today with a 41-3 victory over Iowa at Camp Randall Stadium, improving to 9-2 overall and 7-1 in the conference with its seventh straight win.

With the help of Michigan's win over Penn State earlier in the day, UW will be going to a second straight Rose Bowl unless it somehow finishes in the top two in the final Bowl Championship Series rankings, which seems unlikely.

Or, as defensive tackle Wendell Bryant said: It's like you're a prize fighter. Undisputed heavyweight champion. That's what we are. We are the best and it feels really, really good to say that."

On a day when UW tailback Ron Dayne became the Division I-A career rushing leader by gaining 216 yards, to give him 6,397 for his career, the likely trip to the Rose Bowl almost took second billing. It shouldn't.

Although UW coach Barry Alvarez didn't want to call it a bigger accomplishment than going to the Rose Bowl last season, repeating is always more difficult. It's the first back-to-back titles for UW since it won the Western Conference in 1896 and 1897. The last Big Ten team to go to back-to-back Rose Bowls was Michigan in 1991 and 1992.

Given that UW lost its opening conference game to Michigan, it is a more stunning achievement. "Winning the league was the most important thing (this year), it wasn't going back to Pasadena, because we couldn't control that," Alvarez said. "Had we tied Penn State and not played them, they would have gone (based on tie-breakers).

"It's important right now because we can make history. No other Big Ten school has won two (Rose Bowls back to back) and we'll have that opportunity."

The outcome, and the rushing record — jobs No. 1 and 2, respectively — were never really in doubt.

The Hawkeyes threw everything they had on defense to stopping Dayne. On his first 10 carries, Dayne gained just 37 yards. But UW still led, 13-0, thanks to quarterback Brooks Bollinger.

For awhile, it looked like Bollinger was trying to outrush Dayne. The defense was so focused on stopping Dayne, every time Bollinger ran a bootleg he was almost alone. He completed seven of eight passes for 115 yards and three touchdowns as UW built a 27-3 halftime lead. Bollinger also rushed for 96 yards in the first half on his way to a season-high 113 for the game.

Bollinger, in turn, opened things up for Dayne, as he has all season since becoming the starter at the beginning of this winning streak in the second conference game.

"That takes a lot of heat off Ron and makes them play things honest and loosen up inside," Alvarez said.

Dayne finally got going on UW's third series, with a 37-yard run through left guard that seemed to relax everybody.

"It was definitely on all of our minds," Tauscher said of the rushing record. "In the beginning it was kind of a struggle. I think it was maybe getting to us a little bit that we were getting 2, 3 yards a shot and weren't breaking any (long runs). Then we got a few big hits and the tension eased off a little bit and we started going."

On first-and-10 from the UW 17-yard line, Dayne broke the record with a 31-yard run through right guard with 4 minutes 32 seconds left in the half and was mobbed by his teammates — which broke the all-time rushing mark held by Ricky Williams, the former University of Texas halfback.

All that was left was to enjoy the dual celebrations of the record and the title. Both events shared the podium after the game, as well they should. The Big Ten trophy was presented to the UW captains and Dayne's name and number was unveiled on the façade of the upper deck.

It capped an amazing day that may never be topped.

Ron Dayne (33) ran for 216 yards to boost his career rushing total to an NCAA-record 6,397 yards. The win gave Wisconsin its second straight Big Ten title. A few weeks later, Dayne would win the Heisman Trophy.

Tight end Scooter Badgus' 2-yard TD catch gave the Gophers a 17-3 first quarter lead. The win gave Minnesota its first victory in Ohio Stadium since 1949.

Gophers Shock Buckeyes, Break Longtime Jinx

BY MARK CRAIG
Minneapolis Star-Tribune

Columbus, Ohio	October 14, 2000						
Minnesota	17	6	0	6	—	29
Ohio State	3	7	0	7	—	17

A cool kid from California that no Minnesotan had heard of eight months ago entered Ohio Stadium today. He looked out at 98,120 screaming homecoming fans and across the field at the Big Ten's No. 1 defense and No. 6 team in the nation.

Then he led his team, the Gophers, to a feat not accomplished by Minnesota since 1949, when Bud Grant was the MVP, Billy Rye was the running back and a guy named Bernie Bierman walked the sideline.

Yes, the Gophers, 11-point underdogs at kickoff, shocked the undefeated Buckeyes, 29-17. They ended a 15-game losing streak at the Horseshoe and a 16-game losing streak overall against Ohio State dating to 1981. The victory also put the Gophers into a first-place tie in the Big Ten.

Minnesota's last win in Ohio Stadium was a 27-0 rout of the Buckeyes in 1949.

"This shows this team is capable of going places," linebacker Sean Hoffman said. "To stand on that field and see 99,000 people sitting on their hands, that's awesome. And to think it's our first win here in 51 years ... man, my dad wasn't even born then."

The Gophers have won three in a row, all behind quarterback Travis Cole, a transfer from Foothill (Calif.) Junior College.

Now, before you can say bye-bye Micronpc.com Bowl, Minnesota is 5-2 overall, 3-1, in the Big Ten and tied for first place in the league with Michigan, Purdue and Northwestern.

Expect the Gophers to appear in The Associated Press Top 25 tomorrow.

"It's hard not to think about a bigger bowl, but we can't worry about that," said receiver Ron Johnson, who caught season-high eight passes for 163 yards and one touchdown, the school-record 18th of his career.

"We've got something good going right now. We have to get rid of Indiana first. If we take them for granted. Just like Ohio State might have mistaken us for a lightweight, everything we worked for at this point wouldn't matter."

Whether Ohio State (5-1, 2-1 in the Big Ten) took the Gophers for granted, the fact is Minnesota, especially its offensive line, simply overpowered the same defense that last week notched nine sacks and 17 tackles for loss in a victory at Wisconsin.

The Gophers gained 381 yards, including 138 rushing, both season-highs for an Ohio State opponent. Running back Tellis Redmon rushed for 118 yards, including a 20-yard touchdown that capped an impressive 13-play, 74-yard that clinched the game with four minutes 51 seconds remaining.

Miami of Ohio, with 132 yards rushing, is the only team to run for more yards against OSU than Redmon ran for today.

"They just pushed us around," Buckeyes defensive and Brent Johnson said. "They just kept hammering it to us. They ran just base plays, but we couldn't stop them."

Cole completed 16 of 28 passes for 243 yards and two touchdowns. On third down, he was nine of 12 for 176 yards. On third down in the first half, he threw six passes to the 6-3 Johnson, who used a 4-inch height advantage over cornerback Nate Clements to catch six passes for 145 yards and a 3-yard touchdown.

The air show led to the Gophers leading, 10-0, before Ohio State had a second first down, 17-3, after the first quarter and 23-10 at the half.

"Cole was unconscious today," Gophers coach Glen Mason said.

Defensively, the Gophers held Ohio State to season lows in total yards (200), yards rushing (70) and first downs (13). Ten of the Buckeyes' points were set up by a strip-sack of Cole and an 81-yard kickoff return by Ken-Yon Rambo.

"We didn't do anything," running back Jonathon Wells said.

The Gophers took the opening kickoff and silenced the crowd, driving 71 yards in 15 plays and 6 minutes 35

Minnesota's Ron Johnson (3) had six receptions for 145 yards and 1 touchdown against the Buckeyes.

seconds. They had first-and-goal at the Ohio State 4, but had to settle for a 23-yard field goal by Dan Nystrom.

The Gophers went ahead, 10-0, with 5:12 left in the first quarter following a blocked punt by Jermaine Mays. Cole's 2-yard touchdown pass to tight end Scooter Baugus after an excellent play-fake capped a 20-yard drive.

Ohio State closed the gap to 17-10 and 23-17 with 12:24 left. The Gophers defense held Ohio State without a first down on its next possession and the offense took over and took nearly six minutes off the clock with a long touchdown drive.

"It's been a long time since we got the ball at the end of the game and were able to run it out," said Mason, whose only other trip here as Gophers coach was a 45-15 loss in 1998. "I'm so proud of our guys. Everything hasn't gone our way this season, but they've hung in there. All the credit goes to the players.

By design, the Gophers didn't get overly excited on the field after the game, as they did last season when they upset then-No. 2 Penn State on the road.

But that doesn't mean there weren't plenty of smiles to go around.

"This is great," said linebacker Curtese Poole, a Columbus native. "I don't have to hold my head high and pat them on the back and say, 'Tough luck,' like they do to me every year."

Yes, for the first time in 51 years, everybody came home to Minnesota from Ohio Stadium with their heads held high.

Purdue wide receiver Vinny Sutherland (14) dives for a fourth-quarter TD to give the Boilermakers a 24-20 lead.

Purdue's Brees & Co. Rally to Defeat Ohio State

BY TOM KUBAT
Journal and Courier

West Lafayette, Ind.	October 28, 2000					
Ohio State	0	3	17	7	—	27
Purdue	0	7	3	21	—	31

Quarterback Drew Brees admitted today that after Purdue lost to Penn State four weeks ago, he looked at the remaining schedule and was very discouraged. Then came a miracle second-half rally to beat Michigan. That was followed by victory over Northwestern, the first on the road against a ranked team under fourth-year coach Joe Tiller.

In last week's stunning victory at Wisconsin, Purdue won in overtime on a blocked field goal that was returned for a touchdown.

How do you top that? Easy.

You have Drew Brees pass 64 yards to Seth Morales with 1:55 left to play for a thrilling 31-27 victory over Ohio State in the most important Purdue football game in two decades.

So, is this band of miracles workers a team of destiny? Are they destined to win the Big Ten Conference championship and play in the Rose Bowl.

"I guess so," Brees said. "What happened at the end I'm still a little biy in shock."

Know this. The No. 16-ranked Boilermakers (7-2 overall, 5-1 in the Big Ten) grabbed the rest of the Big Ten by the throat with today's victory over No. 12-ranked Ohio State (6-2, 3-2 in the Big Ten).

All that stands between them and Pasadena are a pair of second division teams, Michigan State and Indiana.

But it took a 21-point fourth quarter and the last gasp Brees to Morales touchdown pass to get it done.

Just seconds before, Brees was blitzed by Ohio State line-backer Joe Cooper and his long pass in the right flat was intercepted by Buckeyes safety Mike Doss, who returned it 33 yards to the Purdue 2-yard line.

"That was terrible," said Brees, who was picked off four times. "I was just trying to complete the pass. I was just trying to throw it away, into the ground. But I was surprised their linebacker came in so quick up the middle, and the ball slipped out of my hand and sailed high."

It was like a gift from heaven for Doss.

"We were in man-to-man coverage, Drew tried to throw the ball away and I just made the catch," he said. "It was like God said, "here's the ball," and I caught it."

When Jerry Westbrooks scored on a 2-yard run with only 2:16 on the clock to give Ohio State a 27-24 lead, it looked as if the Buckeyes were the ones who could start thinking of making reservations in Pasadena.

Until Doss quickly went from hero to goat.

Knowing the main thing the Buckeyes didn't want to do on Purdue's next possession was let a Boilermaker receiver get behind the secondary — and that's exactly what Doss did.

He jumped up to cover A.T. Simpson on an underneath route, and Morales sprinted past him, catching the ball 5-10 yards behind the OSU secondary.

"I know exactly what I'm supposed to do, and I never looked back to the other side," Doss said. "He just threw it over the top of me. I take the blame for that."

"Drew Brees is a great quarterback. If you intercept him four times, you'd think you would win the game."

Brees passed for 455 yards. His 39 completions in 65 attempts, both were the second most in his career, behind only his 55 for 83 night against Wisconsin in 1998.

But until the fourth quarter, Ohio State's defense was keeping the Boilermakers out of the end zone. The Buckeyes took a 13-10 lead in the final 15 minutes, with Purdue's points coming on a 2-yard run by Steve Ennis, following Akin Ayodele's interception of a deflected pass at the OSU 45-yard line, and a 34-yard Travis Dorsch field goal.

Brees finally got the offense untracked with a great individual play two minutes into the final quarter. On third and goal from the 5, Brees was flushed from the pocket to his left and, while backpedaling to avoid the rush, he passed to John Standeford for a touchdown.

Now the offense was really warming up.

On Purdue's next possession, the Boilermakers converted on four third-and-5 situations, driving 90 yards in 13 plays. Brees passed 19 yards to Vinny Sutherland for a 24-20 lead with

5:18 remaining to play.

Sutherland had just returned to the game after going to the locker room to receive fluids intravenously after cramping. Sutherland caught the pass in the right flat, and then flashed his famous speed, outracing a Buckeye defender into the corner of the end zone.

While Brees called his four interceptions "terrible," Ohio State wasn't able to capitalize on its three picks in the first half, going three-and-out each time.

Morales, Sutherland and tight end Tim Stratton each had 100 or more yards receiving or more yards receiving, marking only the second time that three Purdue receivers had reached a century mark in a game.

Stratton caught a career-high 12 catches for 100 yards, Sutherland had 10 for 142 and Morales seven for 142.

But it was that 64-yarder that will go down in history.

"That took my breadth away," Sutherland said of the game-winning pass. "You fight the whole game, and losing the close ones hurt. But winning the close ones are great."

But Sutherland stopped short of calling the 2000 Boilermakers a team of destiny.

"I'm destined for a good time tonight," he said. "That's as far as it goes."

Seth Morales gathers in a 64-yard TD pass from Drew Brees with 1:55 left to play, which gave Purdue a 31-27 win.

Northwestern's Sam Simmons' 11-yard TD catch with 20 seconds remaining gave the Wildcats a 52-51 lead.

Kustok Rallies Wildcats to Stunning Victory

BY SKIP MYSLENSKI
Chicago Tribune

Evanston, Ill. | November 4, 2000						
Michigan	14	14	17	6	—	51
Northwestern	7	16	13	18	—	54

Northwestern coach Randy Walker emerged from the crowd outside his team's locker room today, and there waiting for him was his wife, Tammy. He reached out and grabbed her hand, took a few steps and then leaned down to give her a soft kiss. "Oh, man," he said as he resumed walking. "I don't know what to say, and that's hard for a guy like me. I usually know what to say.

"I'm almost speechless," Walker reiterated moments later, now standing behind a lectern and in front of countless cameras. "I know for some of you that's hard to believe."

He was correct. Yet Walker being speechless was no harder to believe than the game that had just ended, a wondrous, amazing game that finished with his Wildcats beating No. 12-ranked Michigan, 54-51, at sold-out Ryan Field.

The analogy is overused and often abused, but here it is appropriate; this was a battle between two talented heavyweights who staged a bloodletting worthy of a championship fight.

Both loaded up right at the start, and from the moment Northwestern took the opening kickoff 85 yards for a touchdown, they whaled on each other with a series of withering blows. Noses would be bloodied and knees would buckle and each would take a turn down on the canvas, and then came the counter-puncher that assured matters wouldn't be settled until the very end.

It was fitting then, that only 1 minute 44 seconds remained when the climax began to play itself out with Michigan leading, 51-46. On fourth-and-goal from the Wolverines' 12-yard line, NU quarterback Zak Kustok faked a sweep left to Damien Anderson, then rolled right as Anderson, unattended, loped unnoticed toward the left flag. Kustok, under a heavy rush, threw him a Texas Leaguer.

Anderson had been superb all afternoon, finishing with 268 rushing yards and two touchdowns. But here, all alone, he dropped Kustok's pass at the goal line, and now the ball belonged to Michigan.

"It was a great play by Michigan," Walker said, "absolving the mishap. "They came with heat and Zak had to throw a lot faster than he wanted to."

Said Anderson: "I had to make an adjustment on the ball and I lost it a little bit in the lights. But that's no excuse. It hit me in the hands. I have to make that catch."

The Wolverines had been lethal all afternoon, scoring seven touchdowns and kicking a field goal on 11 previous possessions. Quarterback Drew Henson had been spectacular and finished 23-of-35 for 312 yards and four touchdowns. David Terrell and Marquise Walker torched the NU secondary, each catching nine passes, and running back Anthony Thomas rushed 37 times for 199 yards and three touchdowns.

Now, on second-and-3 from his 19, Thomas took a handoff, burst through the line and prepared to accelerate into an open field. But as he did, Wildcats safety Sean Wieber dove at him from the left and swiped at the ball, knocking it free. "All I had in mind was the first down, but tried to get a little too much," a crestfallen Thomas said later.

"I thought the A-Train was gone," Weber acknowledged. "I think what happened, he came through the hole and no one else was there, I think he saw 80 yards in front of him and probably started swinging his arms a little too much. I just dove at him and got a hand on the ball."

NU safety Raheem Covington pounced on the fumble. "I was surprised when he dropped the ball, but I thought, 'They're not going to get it from me. They have to rip my arms off to get it from me. They have to rip my arms off to get it from me,' " Covington said.

With the ball at the Michigan 30, Kustok dumped a pass to Anderson for 5 yards and then hit Teddy Johnson for a quick slant from the left for 14 more. All through this day he had matched Henson's magic with some of his own — he finished 27-of-40 for 322 yards and two touchdowns and scrambled for 55 yards and more touchdowns.

Now, on first-and-10 from the 11, he dropped back for the final time and threw a dart toward Sam Simmons, who was breaking toward the post. He collected Kustok's throw a step into the end zone to put the Cats up, 52-51, with 20 seconds left to play.

"We were getting outside coverage in that scoring zone and that's pretty sound defense," Walker said. "It took real good timing and real good placement to make that shot. It was a tight window."

The catch was Simmons' 12th for 124 yards. "When they called it I could see it was open," he said. "The defensive

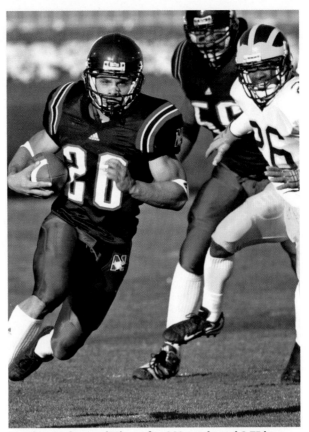
Damien Anderson (20) ran for 268 yards and 2 TD's.

back was outside and the linebacker was nowhere. I just knew I had to run it almost vertical."

Said Kustok: "We'd been going to the boundary (the sideline) the whole came, so I really think they were guarding the boundary I saw Sam with an open lane in the middle and just squeezed it in there."

That was the play that served as the exclamation point, and all that came now was more denouement. The Cats' two-point conversion, Kustok to Johnson, two Henson completions that carried the Wolverines to the Northwestern 39; and the botched hold on what would have been a 57-yard field goal attempt to tie the game and send it into overtime.

They were like after-dinner mints to a sumptuous dinner, and when it was officially over, Northwestern fans stormed the field and tried unsuccessfully to bring down a goal post. "We need to get some of those students in the weight room," Walker joked.

He could afford to after Northwestern (7-2, 5-1 in the Big Ten) kept itself in the Rose Bowl race. Michigan (6-3, 4-2 in the Big Ten) fell out of it.

"You don't want it to come down to that," Covington said. "You'd like it to be easier. But when it does come down to it like that, you can't control yourself. I can't, anyway."

Williams, Hoosiers Run Wild on Wisconsin

BY ANDY GRAHAM
Hoosier Times

Madison, Wisc. | October 6, 2001

Indiana	32	10	14	7	—	63
Wisconsin	0	17	8	7	—	32

It was if Indiana's football team released five years' worth of pentup frustration in one day. Or even one quarter. It's hard to imagine a more dazzling quarter in the whole history of Hoosier football than the 32-0 start of what became a 63-32 IU romp this afternoon over Wisconsin's Badgers.

The Indiana dominance in all three phases of the game — offense, defense and special teams — was almost beyond belief, and probably, considering Indiana's 0-3 record entering the game, beyond the wildest imaginings of anybody in a stunned crowd of 79,264.

If the game had to be seen to be believed (and this one wasn't on television), it was a product of the Hoosiers believing in themselves.

"I don't think the Lord decides on whether it's Wisconsin or Indiana who wins the game — I don't think He cares — but He has really blessed us with a group of kids who kept believing in us," said IU coach Cam Cameron. "I think we're extremely blessed to have the kind of kids and staff we have on our team.

"There is nothing more important than players hanging in there and just being able to block out all the negative and continue to believe in what we're doing. It's not easy, but we've been able to get it done until this point."

What the Hoosiers got done today was simply staggering.

Senior tailback Levron Williams scored six touchdowns to set an IU record and tie the Big Ten record. He carried 20 times for a career-high 280 yards, the second-highest total ever for a Hoosier ball-carrier. His yardage total ranks behind only the 377 yards amassed by current Indiana running backs coach Anthony Thompson in a 1989 game against Wisconsin in Camp Randall Stadium — an NCAA record at the time and still the Big Ten record. The six touchdowns erased another Thompson record: five, against Northwestern in 1989.

Indiana's 631 yards rushing and passing was its highest total since a record-setting 650 against Kentucky in 1994. The Hoosiers averaged 8.3 yards per carry compared to Wisconsin's 2.7.

The point total was the Hoosiers' highest ever in a Big Ten game (previously 52, against Iowa in 1945 and Purdue in 1988). The 95-point game total also was an IU record.

The 32-0 blitz in the game's first 12 minutes included dominant play by both IU's offense and defense.

Cameron thought the game's first play set the mood. Wisconsin quarterback Brooks Bollinger threw long and Hoosier cornerback Sharrod Wallace matched receiver Lee Evans stride-for-stride and knocked the ball away when it arrived.

"That was a great play," Cameron said. "We haven't made that play in four years. I think that play set the tone, because that was what we had talked about. We made critical plays and had guys playing with an aggressive frame of mind.

"I told them, 'guys, we've tried that other way and it doesn't work. I mean, standing out there thinking too much, playing hesitantly, it doesn't work. Just turn yourselves loose. I want to see every guy trying to make a play. If you get beat (on a play), it's on me — go make a play. There is no way to play the game if you're hesitant.' "

There was absolutely no hesitation to Indiana this day, in any respect — and certainly not on the part of a lightning-strike offense.

None of IU's 10 scoring drives took more than six plays, or took more than 2:50 off the clock.

Wisconsin, which through 32-0 had needed an offside penalty to get its only first down, finally got a first down on a 12-yard run by Robert Williams on the next series, and got on the scoreboard with 11:57 left in the half on a 22-yard field goal from Mark Neuser.

Which made IU quarterback Randle El mad.

"I just wanted us to keep going," he said. "That's where I was at. It was 32-0, but then they scored three points and I got upset. I said, 'Let's keep going.' "

After Wisconsin cut the lead to 32-10 with a 43-yard flea-flicker TD pass from Bollinger to Evans. IU took off again. A

Levron Williams ran for 280 yards and six touchdowns against the Badgers. His 6 TD's set a new NCAA record.

77-yard drive capped by an 8-yard Williams TD run, then a career-first 28-yard field goal by Robertson restored the 32-point lead.

"First, let me commend Indiana for playing such a fine football game," Wisconsin coach Barry Alvarez said. "I thought, offensively, they were outstanding. I really can't put a finger on why we played like we did today. I guess I have to be at fault for not having the team ready to play.

"It seemed like every time we'd get some light, they'd answer and they'd answer fast. So if you had light, they took it away from you. It's hard to believe what you've seen, and you've seen it before. This happened to them up here two years ago (in a 59-0 Wisconsin win), same thing — six plays and its 21-0. I haven't been in many games like that. It's a helpless feeling.

"The important thing, as a coach, is to keep your players

into it. I thought our offense tried to stay in it, guys on the bench tried to stay in it, but they always had an answer for us out there."

Wisconsin got a 1-yard sneak from Bollinger for a score with 1:05 left in the half, and the Hoosiers weren't complacent with a 42-17 halftime lead.

"We came in at halftime and said, 'Hey, it ain't over,' " Randle El said. "And we came out that second half and tried to maintain that same attitude, trying to put points on the board."

The Hoosiers opened the second half with an 81-yard scoring drive that sent a clear message: there would be no Badger comeback this day. Williams capped the drive with an 8-yard touchdown run. He added scoring runs of 7 and 51 yards before he was through and just missed a seventh touchdown when he ran 48 yards to the Wisconsin 1-yard line and had to leave the game temporarily. Brian Lewis replaced him and scored from there.

"My buddy," Randle El said of Williams. "Levron went out and played really well. And I think a lot of it had to do with the offensive line, too. The way they blocked, the holes were open for us, and he'd make the safeties miss. There is always one guy left, but he made that safety miss a bunch of times. It started with the offensive line, then he did the rest.

"He's been running hard all season. And that's what I like. Especially between the tackles — that's what we've been wanting him to do better and do more often, with more play calls having him running inside, taking it in there, making guys miss, and taking it to the house."

Randle El had a 284-yard total-offense day: 102 yards rushing and 182 (on 8-for-13) passing. His first-quarter touchdown pass to Aaron Halterman gave him the school career record with 36.

Wisconsin's second-half touchdowns came on a 10-yard pass from Bollinger to tight end Mark Anelli in the third quarter and — after Indiana starters had been pulled — a 26-yard run with a fumble recovery by Joey Boese with 4:24 to play.

Cameron already was looking to next week, when 4-1 Illinois visits for Indiana's homecoming game.

"This was just one game," Cameron said. "That's a good (Wisconsin) football team. We've lost to three pretty good teams, too. North Carolina State is pretty good. Utah is pretty good. Ohio State is pretty good. And that's why I kept saying, 'We're not a bad football team, because we've lost to some good people, but we can be good. But I don't think you are good until you put some of these things back-to-back-to-back."

Lions Roar as Paterno Gets Career Win 324

By Ray Parrillo
Special to the Centre Daily Times

State College, Pa. | October 27, 2001

Ohio State	7	6	14	0	—	27
Penn State	6	3	13	7	—	29

The trappings that surround a famous football coach never much mattered to Joe Paterno. He has lived in the same modest home here for more than three decades. He buys suits in outlet stores. And he wheels around in a five-year-old automobile that's as bland as the uniforms worn by his Penn State Nittany Lions.

But those trappings come too easily for an earnest man like Paterno. Instead, he prefers to bask in the struggles of the game, the relentless attention to detail required in the pursuit of victory.

So it seemed fitting today that the win that placed Paterno atop the career list of major-college coaches was hard-earned, one that required his team to keep getting off the canvas after another staggering punch from Ohio State.

It also seemed fitting that the win was gained by perhaps the most maligned of the 36 teams he has coached in Happy Valley.

And after quarterback Zack Mills' clutch run for a first down in the closing minutes sealed the thrilling 29-27 Big Ten Conference win over the Buckeyes before 108,327 at Beaver Stadium, Paterno was given a well-deserved salute. He was hoisted onto the shoulders of some of his players as the crowd roared, chanting "324" and "JoePa, JoePa."

Paterno then stood on a portable stage with his wife, Sue, and his five children and nine grandchildren. Behind those thick tinted glasses, Paterno's eyes welled as the crowd chanted his name, family members took turns hugging him, and a tasteful video presentation of his career was displayed. Meantime, several of his players embraced one another on the field. More than anyone, they know how difficult it was to get Paterno victory No. 324.

"I can't put into words how I really feel about this football team, this university and you fans," Paterno said as he addressed the crowd. "I've had 52 of the greatest years anyone could ever want."

The win pushed Paterno ahead of Paul (Bear) Bryant, who invited Paterno and the Nittany Lions to play in the first Sugar Bowl that took place in the Louisiana Superdome on New

Year's Eve, 1975. "Paul knew he could beat us," Paterno said, laughing, while recounting the story Friday night. Bryant's Alabama teams defeated Paterno's Penn State teams all four times they met.

Paterno needed two wins to break the record when the season began, but the Nittany Lions (2-4 overall, 2-3 in the Big Ten) lost their first four games for the first time in the 115 years of Penn State football. With each loss, the 74-year-old coach's pursuit of the record seemed to be pushed aside by concerns that perhaps his time had come and gone.

With each loss that followed last year's 5-7 season, Paterno appeared more determined to turn things around.

"They could have thrown in the towel a long time ago," Paterno said of his players. "They could have called it quits. But they've hung in there, and I think we're getting pretty good."

For the second straight game, Penn State's offense, moribund in the first four games, percolated under the guidance of Mills, the redshirt freshman who came off the bench and drove the Nittany Lions to a 38-35 win at Northwestern last week.

Today, Mills accounted for three TDs and a school-record 418 of Penn State's 531 yards. He ran 69 yards for a touchdown to resurrect his team after Ohio State (4-3, 2-2) took a 27-9 lead on Derek Ross' 45-yard run with an interception with 12 minutes, 16 seconds remaining in the third quarter. On the interception, Mills hit wide-open Eddie Drummond in the hands on a flare pass, but Drummond couldn't handle it and the ball caromed to Ross.

Mills never flinched. Less than a minute later, he was racing into the end zone to finish Penn State's longest run from scrimmage since a 70-yarder by Chafie Fields against Arizona on opening day in 1999.

"It was supposed to be a 7- or 8-yard play," Paterno said. "He just took off. He has good speed."

Later in the third quarter, Mills tossed a 26-yard TD pass to

Joe Paterno celebrates after getting his 324th career victory, which pushed him ahead of Paul (Bear) Bryant.

Tony Johnson, and the Nittany Lions were within 27-22. Shawn Meyer's fumble recovery set up the TD. On Penn State's next possession, Mills moved the team 90 yards on 10 plays. The eventual game-winner was a 14-yard TD throw to Eric McCoo. It was the same play that beat Northwestern with 22 seconds to go. The Nittany Lions had rubbed out an 18-point deficit in little more than 12 minutes.

"It's really special to get that win for him (Paterno)," said Mills, who replaced starter Matt Senneca after Senneca threw three incomplete passes during the opening drive. "Pretty much everyone doubted us except him, and I can't say enough about him."

Mills, a 19-year-old lefthander from Jamsville, Md., ran for 138 yards on 15 carries and completed 17 of 32 passes for 280 yards. Paterno said he planned to play both Senneca and Mills, but Mills played too well to be replaced.

"Mills is the quarterback with the most potential," Ohio State coach Jim Tressel said. "He was the one who worried us the most on film. He has shown all year he can make plays under pressure."

Has Mills finally earned the starting job? "I don't think it's right to answer that until I talk to the players," Paterno said.

Before the Nittany Lions found the end zone, freshman Robbie Gould chipped away at Ohio State's early lead with field goals from 23, 46 and 46 yards. For the Buckeyes, who last year handed Penn State its most lopsided loss of the Paterno era (45-6), it was pretty much all or nothing. They scored touchdowns on a 66-yard pass from Steve Bellisari to Michael Jenkins, a 65-yard run by Jonathan Wells, and Ross' interception return.

For a while, it appeared Paterno might have cost his team a win by choosing to kick for the PAT rather than go for two points after Penn State took a 28-27 lead. But Paterno was spared when Jimmy Kennedy blocked a 34-yard field-goal attempt by Mike Nugent with 2:55 remaining in the fourth quarter, and Mills ran 34 yards for the first down that enabled Penn State to run down the clock.

"I almost blew it by not going for two points," Paterno admitted.

But his decision was long forgotten in the aftermath of his historic victory. In the locker room after the game, senior defensive end Bob Jones presented Paterno with a diamond-studded ring that had No. 324 inscribed on it.

"It's a great day, a beautiful day," linebacker Shamar Finney said. "He's the man now. Bottom line: He's the best coach ever."

Rocky Harvey's 13-yard TD in the game's final two minutes gave the Illini a 33-28 come-from-behind victory.

Harvey's TD Run Keys Illini Rally Against Lions

BY GARY REINMUTH
Chicago Tribune

Champaign, Ill. | November 10, 2001					
Penn State	14	7	0	7	—	28
Illinois	0	7	7	19	—	33

With 1 minute 19 seconds remaining on the clock, Illinois settled the long-running debate once and for all. When these never-say-surrender Illini are asked someday which *Rocky* movie is their all-time favorite, none of the Sylvester Stallone "epics" will stand a chance.

The most beautiful cinematic moment in their memories lasted only three seconds. In it, senior tailback Rocky Harvey bursts through a huge hole in the middle of the line, hurdles a pile of would-be tacklers and dances 13 yards into the end zone for the winning touchdown in today's come-from-behind again 33-28 victory over Penn State at Memorial Stadium.

Chicago's Bears may own the broadcast rights to fantastic finishes this season, but after claiming its fourth come-from-behind win of the season, its third in the last three weeks and

its first win over Penn State since 1960, Illinois (8-1, 4-1 in the Big Ten) is gaining.

"Once again this team showed its heart and character," Coach Ron Turner said after a victory that kept the Illini tied with Michigan for first place in the Big Ten, kept them alive for a BCS bowl berth and improved their record to 8-1 for the first time since 1983. "This team has the attitude it's not going to be denied, no matter what happens."

Following a script that's getting more predictable every week, Illinois fell behind, 21-7, at halftime, scored 20 straight points to grab a 27-21 lead with 3:47 left in the game, let Larry Johnson return a kickoff 97 yards to put Penn State (3-5, 2-4 in the Big Ten) back in front, 28-27, with 3:29 to go and then marched 80 yards in nine plays for the win on Harvey's second touchdown of the game.

Harvey, who finished with 51 yards in 11 carries, was in the game because his tailback partner, Antonio Harris, broke his wrist midway through the fourth quarter after rushing for 98 yards in 20 carries to spark the comeback. Harris is scheduled to have surgery tomorrow and is lost for the season.

"When we were in the huddle everyone was saying, 'Let's at least get the field goal,' " Harvey said. "But the hole opened wide and I just tried my best to hurry into the end zone."

When cornerback Christian Morton intercepted quarterback Matt Senneca's pass with 59 seconds left to end Penn State's last hope, Harvey and his teammates were as relieved as they were excited. The Illini overcame a dreadful first half by quarterback Kurt Kittner and the offense, a 71-yard punt return by Bruce Branch that gave Penn State a quick 7-0 lead, a 63-yard halfback pass for a TD from Eric McCoo to Tony Johnson and enough missed tackles, assignments and opportunities to scare every bowl scout in attendance.

Kittner blames himself for the first half, during which he completed only seven of 20 passes for 105 yards and threw two interceptions.

"I don't think I'm doing anything different," he said. "All my mechanics are the same. I'm just not hitting them. It wasn't anything they were doing. It's that we weren't executing. It was three-and-out, three-and-out. You can't play much worse in the first half than we did."

At halftime, Turner told his players they were trying to do too much. "We weren't screaming and shouting," he said. "I just talked to the offense and said 'Relax. It's a game. Smile. Have some fun.' "

After the break, Illinois found a way to do just that part. Led by cornerback Eugene Wilson's three interceptions, the defense teed off on backoff quarterback Senneca, who was on in relief of starter Zack Mills, who left with an injured ankle. The offense took it from there. Harvey started it with a 20-yard touchdown run to cut the deficit to 21-14. Behind Harris, who ran for 46 yards, Kittner drove his team 81 yards in 12 plays and sneaked over from the 1 to tie the game at 21-21.

Two field goals by Peter Christofilakos made it 27-21 with 3:47 left, and not even Johnson's 97-yard kickoff return after the second kick could deter Illinois. After Aaron Moorehead and fullback Carey Davis dropped Kittner's first two passes, he found Brandon Lloyd along the sideline for a clutch 30-yard gain on third-and-10.

"It was a broken play," Lloyd said of his only reception. "The pocket really collapsed. I was supposed to go across the field, but I saw Kurt was in trouble and I turned and he dropped the ball off to me. It was a great play. There isn't a quarterback in the nation we'd rather have. "

Kittner followed with a 13-yard pass to Moorehead and then handed off to Davis on four straight plays. It was third-and-2 at the 13. A capacity crowd of 70,904 was probably thinking, "One more play and kick the field goal," but Kittner and Harvey had a better idea.

"We said to ourselves, 'We won't lose, we will finish,' " Kittner said. "No one got down. A lot of teams would have been discouraged, but our team is not like other teams."

Illini kicker Peter Christofilakos booted two field goals — a 30-yarder and a 31-yarder — against the Lions.

Jermelle Lewis, a backup tailback, ran for 109 yards and 2 TD's against the Wolverines.

Hawkeyes Whip No. 8 Michigan in the Big House

By Andrew Logue
Des Moines Register

Ann Arbor, Mich. | October 26, 2002						
Iowa	10	0	14	10	—	34
Michigan	0	6	3	0	—	9

It was a moment Dallas Clark wanted to share with Iowa football players past and present.

Michigan Stadium — once filled with 111,496 spectators — was nearly empty after the No. 13-ranked Hawkeyes had humbled the No. 8-ranked Wolverines, 34-9, this afternoon. Those who remained were wearing black and gold.

They gathered in the stands near the south end zone, joining Clark and his teammates to sing the Iowa fight song.

Clark, a junior tight end, wished he could share the celebration with the generation of former Hawkeyes who had their Rose Bowl dreams crushed in the same historic venue.

"Impressive," Clark said after Iowa handed Michigan its worst home loss since 1967.

"I'll never forget it," he added. "This was for all the people who played for the Hawks, who wore the Tigerhawk and couldn't beat Michigan."

This year's Hawkeyes, 8-1 overall and 5-0 in the Big Ten, had a swagger when they entered the Big House.

Coach Kirk Ferentz's team was greeted by the largest crowd ever to watch an Iowa football game — the sixth largest in the 75-year history of Michigan Stadium.

"We got here (Friday) and walked into the Big House to see how big it was," receiver Mo Brown said. "We weren't really impressed with it. We liked Penn State better."

Penn State gave Iowa a better game, too, taking the Hawkeyes to overtime last month. Against Michigan, Iowa dominated most of the first half, overcame a botched punt attempt just before intermission, and left with the school's largest margin of victory ever at Ann Arbor.

The Hawkeyes remain atop the Big Ten standings, but will need help to secure a trip to the Rose Bowl. No. 4-ranked Ohio State escaped with a 13-7 victory over Penn State today to join Iowa as the Big Ten's only unbeaten teams.

Iowa could share the league title with Buckeyes but miss out on a trip to Pasadena, Calif., because Ohio State would have a better overall record. The Hawkeyes and the Ohio State don't play each other this season.

"I don't know if we're thinking that far ahead," Iowa offensive lineman Bruce Nelson said. "I don't even know who we play this week."

It's Wisconsin, at Kinnick Stadium in Iowa City.

Michigan began today with Rose Bowl aspirations, but now find itself in a position to help Iowa when the Wolverines meet Ohio State in November.

"Any type of loss is bad, especially at home," Michigan linebacker Victor Hobson said. "We had goals coming in here and didn't reach them."

Iowa, meanwhile, enhanced its status as a Bowl Championship Series contender. The Hawkeyes could play in one of the four BCS bowls if they win their remaining three games. They would need to finish among the Top 12 teams in the final BCS standings.

"We just proved we can play with anybody," Brown said. "(Michigan) has got the big names and the big recruits. We've just got guys that play football."

Michigan (6-2, 3-1 in the Big Ten) focused on stopping Iowa's running game, which was netting 218.5 yards per game and succeeded for most of the three quarters. Hawkeyes tailback Fred Russell averaged just 1.4 yards on his first 20 carries before leaving with a hand injury.

That's when Jermelle Lewis, who began last week as Iowa's third-string running back, began a breakout performance.

Lewis finished with 109 yards on 18 rushes. His first touchdown came on a 5-yard run to put the Hawkeyes ahead, 24-9, with less than 3 minutes left in the third quarter. He caught a shovel pass from Brad Banks moments later and ran for 23 yards for another score. I never thought I'd be playing in the Big House, in the biggest game in my life, with the best guys in the world," said Lewis, who replaced Russell six weeks earlier against Utah State and gained 109 yards.

The Wolverines tried to intimidate Lewis, who moved up on the depth chart when Aaron Greving left the team late in the week.

"Nothing came easy," Lewis said. "They were out there

flying around and hitting. I was at the bottom of the pile and they were poking their fingers in my mouth, trying to grab my neck."

Eventually, Lewis left the Wolverines bickering among themselves.

"They were out there arguing with each other," he said. "It was like 10 guys missed their assignment, and only one guy got it right. I just said, 'You guys need to get it together.' "

Iowa succeeded in shutting down Michigan's ground game and harassing quarterback John Navarre. The Wolverines had just 22 rushing yards and Navarre threw for 112 passing yards.

"They pinned their ears back and came at us all day long," Navarre said.

The last three Iowa teams to win at Michigan all went to the Rose Bowl. Ferentz downplayed the Hawkeyes' postseason possibilities, but a pleasant aroma floated through the Iowa locker room after the game.

"I'm smelling the roses," receiver C.J. Jones said.

Iowa tight end Dallas Clark caught 5 passes for 68 yards.

Buckeyes Beat Michigan, Fiesta Bowl & Miami Next

BY JOHN ERADI
The Cincinnati Enquirer

The Olentangy River flowed backward, hills were raised out of the flat plain known as Cow Town, and Woody Hayes came back from the dead to praise the maize and blue on High Street.

If any of those things had really happened when the clock at Ohio Stadium read 0:00 this afternoon, nobody would have noticed.

That's because everybody in Ohio Stadium was either looking at the heavens or rushing the field when Ohio State finally beat arch rival Michigan when it really, truly mattered.

With everything on the line — a trip to the Fiesta Bowl national championship game on Jan. 3 in Tempe, Ariz., a record 13-0 season and a share of the Big Ten championship — the Buckeyes turned history and the game statistics on their head and shocked the supremely confident Wolverines, 14-9, before a stadium-record 105,539 fans.

"It felt great to hear the bell ring," said second-year Ohio State coach Jim Tressel, referring to the 150-foot high Victory Bell in the stadium's south tower that peels loud and long after OSU victories.

For most of the game, the Buckeyes were hearing bells, and they had to be wondering if they tolled for thee.

Michigan (9-3, 6-2 in the Big Ten) owned the game until OSU running back Maurice Hall took an option pitch from quarterback Craig Krenzel with 4:47 on the clock and ran it 3 yards — it seemed like 300 to long-frustrated Buckeyes fans — into the end zone for a 14-9 lead.

The touchdown was set up by a 26-yard pass to freshman Maurice Clarett on a pattern just added this week to the playbook.

Nobody in scarlet and gray felt safe about the lead. The Wolverines had swaggered their way up and down the field all day. They knew they could throw the ball when it counted (247 yards to OSU's 124), control the clock to wear down a vaunted defense (35 minutes to OSU's 25) and win the third-down conversion battle by calling the right plays on offense and guesiing right on defense (12-of-22 to OSU's ugly-as-it-sounds 1-for-7).

Columbus, Ohio | November 23, 2002

Michigan	3	6	0	0	— 9
Ohio State	7	0	0	7	— 14

"I thought we were the most balanced team that (OSU) had faced all year," said Michigan coach Lloyd Carr. "When you look at the game from a statistical standpoint, we out-played them. But we knew we were going to need a touchdown to win the game."

UM burned up more than 4 minutes on its first scoring drive — a 36-yard field goal by Adam Finley; weathered a 10-play, 76-yard TD drive by OSU that gave the Buckeyes a 7-3 lead, then had seven- and eight-minute drives in the second quarter capped by Finley's 35- and 22-yard field goals to take a 9-7 halftime lead.

As usual, Ohio State got what it needed, when it needed it: Clarett, gritting his way past a terribly painful shoulder stinger, entered the game on OSU's second offensive possession, immediately caught a screen pass for nine yards and had four rushes for 38 yards, the last 2 for a TD to put the Buckeyes up, 7-3.

What the Wolverines didn't know — what nobody *ever* knows — is whether they would suffer a turnover at a critical time or be detoured into the magical world that had been OSU's trademark all season.

Starting from its 20 and trailing, 14-9, Michigan went on another ball-control drive to OSU's 30 before big-game disaster struck: Wolverines quarterback John Navarre was stripped of the ball by Darrion Scott and Will Smith recovered it with 2:49 left to play.

OSU went three plays, then punted, with the Wolverines getting the ball on their 20-yard line with 58 seconds left. Navarre cooly managed the clock with sideline throws, moving the ball to the Buckeyes' 41 with 19 seconds left. A pass interference call helped the Buckeyes push Michigan back to the 24.

"It was so loud, we couldn't hear a thing," said OSU safety Donnie Nickey. "We were all saying to ourselves: Make a play! Make a play!"

Two plays later, safety Will Allen did, picking off a pass near the goal line as time expired.

Buckeyes quarterback Craig Krenzel, who completed 10 of 14 passes for 124 yards, outruns a Michigan defender.

Northwestern's Noah Herron scores on a 3-yard run in overtime to give the Wildcats a 33-27 win over Ohio State.

Northwestern Stuns Buckeyes in OT Thriller

BY JOHN MULLIN
Chicago Tribune

Evanston, Ill.	October 2, 2004						
Ohio State	3	7	7	10	0	—	27
Northwestern	3	10	7	7	6	—	33

Northwestern defensive tackle Luis Castillo matter-of-factly described the Ohio State offense last week as "mediocre." Before a Buckeyes-dominated crowd of 47,130 tonight at Ryan Field. Castillo and his teammates made the assessment stand up with a 33-27 overtime victory.

The victory was Northwestern's first over Ohio State since 1971 and the first in Evanston since 1958.

Ohio State's offense, outgained 419 to 305 in regulation, scored 10 unanswered points in the fourth quarter, driving 69 yards in five plays and 1 minute 29 seconds to tie Northwestern (2-3, 1-1 in the Big Ten) in regulation.

Mike Nugent, who converted 9 of 10 previous field-goal attempts, missed from 40 yards on the first overtime series.

Brent Basanez ran 21 yards on Northwestern's second overtime play to the Ohio State 3-yard line. Two plays later, Noah Herron blew through a huge hole in the middle of the Buckeyes' defense for the victory.

"If you want to know what responding looks like, you just saw it," Northwestern coach Randy Walker told his players.

What no one would have predicted was that the Northwestern offense would render the defense of the No. 7-ranked Buckeyes (3-1, 0-1 in the Big Ten) pretty mediocre as well. The Wildcats took a 27-17 lead on the first play of the fourth quarter when Herron wedged in from 1 yard out to match Northwestern's highest point total against Ohio State since 1982.

But Ohio State shut out the Wildcats the rest of regulation while its offense was chipping away at Northwestern's lead.

It was a game of nearly violent momentum changes, all in the closing minutes.

Ohio State tied the game, 27-27, with 1:54 remaining. Justin Zwick threw 21 yards to Santonio Holmes for the tying score after Northwestern had strung together a run of plays that kept taking the game away from the team that had beaten them 24 straight times.

Ohio State faced third-and-goal from the Northwestern 4-yard line, but linebackers John Pickens and Nick Roach combined for a 7-yard sack of Zwick to force a 29-yard field goal by Nugent for a 27-20 score. It was Roach's second partial sack of the game and was an emphatic statement by Pickens, who in his first game back from a spring shoulder injury also forced a fumble.

Pickens then sacked Zwick for a 13-yard loss after a potentially devastating interception that had given Ohio State the ball at Northwestern's 22-yard line. But cornerback Jeff Backes made a diving interception on the next play — the first of Backes' collegiate career — with just under five minutes left.

Ohio State forced an NU punt and moved into Wildcats territory. Zwick then found Holmes for the tying score. Zwick finished 18 of 38 for 211 yards, a touchdown and an interception.

The Wildcats limited Ohio State to 281 yards, while Northwestern's offense gained 446 yards. Herron topped 100 rushing yards, finishing with 113.

Northwestern led, 13-10, at halftime and expanded that edge when senior Mark Philmore took a flanker screen from Basanez 27 yards for the first touchdown of his NU career on the first drive of the third quarter. Philmore went over 100 receiving yards for the third time this season, with 134.

In what may have been the key move of the week, NU coaches held Basanez out of practices Tuesday and Wednesday to rest his bruised shoulder. They also devised an offensive game plan that had Basanez rolling to both sides away from pressure.

At the same time, the Northwestern offensive line held Ohio State without a sack through three quarters while consistently controlling one of the nation's most feared attacking defenses all along the line of scrimmage.

The result: Basanez completed 14 of 25 passes in the first half for 141 yards against a unit that ranked eighth in the country, allowing only 137 per game. Basanez threw for 278 yards, completing 24 of 44 for two touchdowns and two interceptions.

Brian Huffman made a pair of field goals, the first matching his career best of 41 yards and the second from 40 yards.

Mark Philmore had 11 receptions for 134 yards and 1 TD.

Penn State Upsets No. 6 Buckeyes, Leads Big Ten

BY JEFF RICE
Centre Daily Times

State College, Pa. | October 8, 2005

Ohio State	3	7	0	0	—	10
Penn State	0	14	3	0	—	17

They met at about the 35-yard line, the respective leaders of Penn State's offense and defense, and embraced, knowing the win was simply the next installment of their master plan but recognizing its significance all the same. The giddy mob of players and students and cameramen swarmed around Michael Robinson and Paul Posluszny, who lived in memorable fashion the stories of two different halves that added up to the Nittany Lions' 17-10 defeat of No. 6 Ohio State.

Robinson led Penn State (6-0 overall, 3-0 in the Big Ten) to an early 14-3 lead against one of the nation's top defenses before Posluszny and his charges showed the Nittany Lions, the conference's lone unbeaten Saturday after Wisconsin's loss at Northwestern, have a defense that deserves just as much attention.

The 109,839 in Beaver Stadium stayed until the end, shaking the stadium to its core from Derrick Williams' second-quarter touchdown jaunt until Tamba Hali separated Buckeyes quarterback Troy Smith from the football and Scott Paxson recovered it with 81 seconds to play.

For Penn State coach Joe Paterno, who won his eighth straight game and the 349th of his career, it was a good, tough win over a good, tough team, and little more.

"We got one more touchdown than they did," Paterno said, reminding the assembled media that his team visits Michigan next week. "But I thought it was a heck of a football game."

For the Buckeyes (3-2, 1-1 in the Big Ten), perennial Big Ten title contenders, it was the latest in a long line of will-testers, a prime-time bout with a tough, balanced squad in a hostile environment.

But for the Nittany Lions, it represented a shot at something bigger, a chance to silence what critics remained even after a 5-0 start and prove themselves as, at the very least, legitimate contenders for the Big Ten title.

Penn State, which defeated the Buckeyes for just the second time in five seasons but for the fifth time in the last seven in Beaver Stadium, never trailed and was turnover-free for the second straight week.

But there was a sense, particularly in the second half, that the Nittany Lions were getting sucked in to the same old Ohio State trap. They increased their lead to a touchdown early in the third quarter but the Buckeyes, so accustomed to pulling out close games, remained frighteningly calm, sticking to their game plan and daring Penn State to put them away. A.J. Hawk and the gritty Buckeye defense got nastier as the night wore on and kept their erratic offense in the game. Penn State had just 22 net yards over the final 23 minutes.

It became evident that Penn State's defense was going to have to win this one. And it did.

Penn State's offense stepped up just enough early on.

The teams traded punts and possessions like heavyweights feeling each other out during the first few possessions, the Buckeyes drawing first blood.

After an 11-yard punt from Jeremy Kapinos, the Buckeyes drove 44 yards in 12 plays to the Penn State 13, where Josh Huston kicked a 30-yard field goal to put Ohio State ahead, 3-0, with 6:41 remaining in the first quarter.

Seven minutes later, the Nittany Lions found the burst that would clinch the game, but they couldn't have known it then.

A 25-yard burst from tailback Tony Hunt (16 carries, 64 yards) drove the Nittany Lions deep into Buckeye territory, while Robinson, who evaded heavy pressure from the Ohio State front seven all night, scrambled 16 yards to the Buckeye 13-yard line.

Williams, who had a mostly quiet evening, took a pitch from Robinson, got a great clear-out block from right tackle Andrew Richardson, squeaked past a lunging A.J. Hawk and darted 13 yards into the end zone — directly in front of the Ohio State contingent of fans — and the Nittany Lions led, 7-3.

Then, as Zombie Nation blared from the loudspeakers, Beaver Stadium began to rumble. Three plays later, Smith was intercepted by Calvin Lowry, who returned the ball 36 yards to the Ohio State 2-yard line. Three plays after that, Robinson took it in on an option keeper.

Michael Robinson, who ran for 52 yards and passed for another 78, tries to escape from two Buckeye defenders.

Penn State 14, Ohio State 3. Seven minutes and 55 seconds remained in the second quarter.

The Buckeyes were not about to fold as easily as Minnesota had here the week before in a 44-14 loss. A pair of Smith completions to tight end Ryan Hamby got the Buckeyes into Penn State territory, where Tressel returned to the ground game. Smith, Antonio Pittman and fullback Brandon Schnittker took turns churning Ohio State to the 10 before Smith bulled his way into the end zone, stretching the ball across the goal line with 33 seconds left in the half to pull the Buckeyes to within four.

But that was it for Smith and Ohio State, which never got speedy receiver Ted Ginn (three catches, 40 yards) going and never really threatened in the second half, despite forcing four straight three-and-outs by the Nittany Lions.

The Penn State pass rush, led by Tamba Hali, increased its pressure on Smith, while Posluszny, who led all defenders with 14 tackles, was there at every turn.

"I don't think you can play any better football than he played today," Paterno said.

Robinson, meanwhile, led Penn State to its lowest yardage total (195 of the season), but was at his best with Hawk or another Buckeye directly in his face, avoiding the rush for big

scrambles or clutch passes when it looked as though he was in for a hefty loss.

Kevin Kelly's 41-yard field goal on Penn State's opening drive of the half increased the lead to 17-10 with 11:10 remaining in the third. Then both offenses shut down. The Buckeyes could do little with the football but the Nittany Lions kept giving them chances.

"I was scared to death the whole time," Paterno admitted with a smile. "One play."

But the Buckeyes never got that play from Ginn, or from his brash fellow wideout Santonio Holmes. Pittman was held to 58 yards rushing and the Buckeyes only got into Penn State territory once in the fourth quarter. The game was the defense's to win or lose, and Penn State's came through — narrowly.

"I ain't satisfied until all the time is off the clock," Zemaitis said.

When the final seconds had ticked off, and fans began planning for Ann Arbor and a bowl (the Nittany Lions' sixth win made them postseason-eligible), its leaders allowed themselves a brief moment, a few seconds to smile before getting back to work.

This night, on this grand stage, they had both earned it.

Michigan's Miracle Win Stuns Lions on Final Play

By ANGELIQUE S. CHENGELIS
The Detroit News

Ann Arbor, Mich. | October 15, 1997

Penn State	0	0	3	22	—	25
Michigan	0	3	7	17	—	27

Again, Michigan has found its pulse.
Sometimes faint this season, the unranked Wolverines, teetering on the brink of a losing season, looked more energized, more determined and steely than ever.

Trailing with one second remaining against No. 8-ranked and unbeaten Penn State, Michigan quarterback Chad Henne completed a 10-yard touchdown pass to freshman receiver Mario Manningham for a 27-25 victory before a boisterous Michigan Stadium crowd.

The players sprinted from the Michigan sideline to join their offense in the end zone and then took the celebration over to the student section to rejoice.

"We just wanted to get the play off and do what we had to do to come out with the win," Manningham said. "We didn't do anything different. We just executed the play. Chad just put it right there."

Michigan (4-3, 2-2 in the Big Ten) has won seven straight against Penn State (6-1, 3-1 in the Big Ten).

There were four lead changes in the fourth quarter, which Michigan entered leading with a 10-3 lead.

"That's as wild a game as I've ever been in," Michigan coach Lloyd Carr said. "Just unbelievable."

Henne's touchdown pass culminated an edge-of-your-seat eight-play, 53-yard drive in the final 42 seconds. Steve Breaston set the drive up on a stunning 41-yard kickoff return to give Michigan possession on its 47.

"I just wanted to get the ball downfield as far as I could," said Breaston, who had 169 all-purpose yards, including 156 on returns. "Everybody was just into the game and they kept telling me, 'Steve, make a play. Just go out there.' I just had to do my job, and everybody did their job (blocking) up front."

The Wolverines had 42 seconds left and were trailing, 25-21, after Penn State's go-ahead touchdown. Starting tailback Mike Hart, who had 23 carries for 108 yards and a touchdown, said the final huddle was upbeat and positive.

"We just said it's going to be a great victory," Hart said.
Henne opened the series with a 17-yard completion to Jason

Avant, who finished with eight catches for 75 yards. Two plays later, on third-and-1, Hart gained 11 yards.

Michigan reached the Penn State 10 with 1 second left.

"They didn't bring any blitzes, so we just stuck with our regular protection," said Henne, who was 21-of-36 for 212 yards and two touchdowns.

"They gave us the coverage we wanted for that play. They matched the inside receiver and were one-on-one with the outside. Mario made a great stick, and I just went after the throw and put it there in front of him."

Breaston was the first read on the play and Manningham, who had two touchdown receptions, was the second. Michigan coach Lloyd Carr praised his sophomore quarterback.

"When it's one second on the clock and the game's on the line, and there's millions and million's of people watching on TV, and there's 111,000 people in the stadium, and you take the ball and throw it perfectly with people who are trying to sack you, I'd say that's a lot of poise," Carr said. "It isn't like there's going to be any second chances."

There were plenty of chances in the second half, particularly the fourth quarter.

Michigan built a 10-0 lead early in the second half after getting its first third-quarter touchdown of the season on a 2-yard run by Hart.

After Penn State and Michigan exchanged punts on the next two series, the Nittany Lions started their second possession of the quarter at their 29. On third-and-5, quarterback Michael Robinson fumbled the snap, picked up the ball, faced extreme pressure from Michigan's Alan Branch but managed to complete a pass to Terrell Golden for 56 yards. The Wolverines held Penn State to a 25-yard field goal by freshman Kevin Kelly, who missed two field-goal attempts in the first half.

Penn State tied the score at 10 early in the fourth quarter after Tony Hunt broke a 61-yard run to the Michigan 2-yard

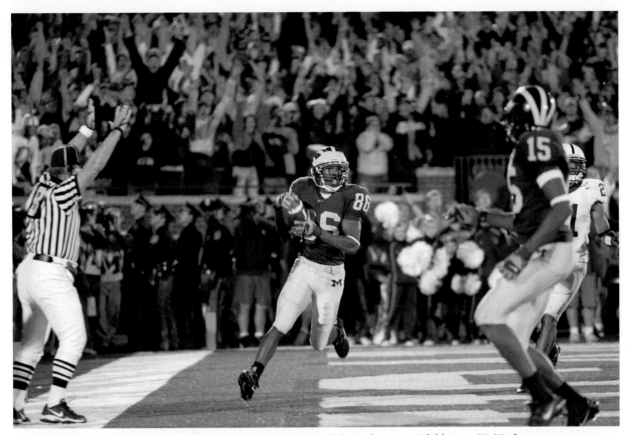

Mario Manningham's 10-yard touchdown catch on the game's last play gave Michigan a 27-25 victory.

line. On fourth down, Robinson scored on a four-yard quarterback option. This was the first of three straight touchdowns scored within the first 5:28 of the fourth quarter.

On the first play of Michigan's ensuing drive, Henne scrambled with the football in his right arm and dropped his shoulder as he tried for extra yardage against cornerback Alan Zemaitis.

Zemaitis hit Henne hard and stripped him of the ball, running 35 yards for the touchdown, his second of the season.

Penn State added two points on a broken play when the snap for the extra-point attempt was fumbled. Kelly took the football and ran in for the conversion, giving the Nittany Lions their first lead, 18-10, with 11:39 left.

The Wolverines tied the score on a 33-yard touchdown pass from Henne to Manningham, whom he found deep in the left corner of the end zone. Hart ran in to tie the score at 18 with 9:32 left. Garrett Rivas hit a 47-yard field goal, tying a career high, with 3:45 remaining to give U-M a 21-18 lead.

Michigan's defense came through on Penn State's next possession when Leon Hart intercepted Robinson. But the Wolverines were assessed a 10-yard holding penalty on Grant Mason on Hall's return, which proved exceptionally costly.

Michigan began on its 40, but was forced to punt giving Penn State, which used all three of its timeouts during the Wolverines' drive, possession with 2:46 remaining in the game.

"If we had lost this game, I would have blamed myself," Carr said. "What I should have said, is 'Let's throw the ball in the end zone.' We were concerned with making Penn State use their timeouts and maybe kicking a field goal, we left them (the defense) out there."

Penn State marched back after starting on its 20. Robinson completed a key second-down pass to Jordan Norwood for 28 yards to the Michigan 42.

U-M forced Penn State into fourth-and-7 after a replay review showed that Robinson's 8-yard pass to Deon Butler was incomplete. Robinson converted on fourth down, running left after being forced out by linebacker David Harris for a 9-yard gain and a first down.

On third down, Michigan suffered a breakdown as Hall was called for pass interference, giving Penn State a first down at the Michigan 3-yard line. Robinson got the go-ahead score, an exclamation point to cap a 13-play drive that gave the Nittany Lions a 25-21 lead.

Hart said he had never experienced a victory like this.

Continuing a Legacy

By Pat Fitzgerald
Special to Chicago Tribune

Obviously this was my dream job. But it came under the worst circumstances ever imaginable.

When everything happened (with Coach Walker's death), it was such a roller coaster of emotions, from the deepest valley you could possibly be in to lose such a great coach and a great mentor and great friend, an unbelievable man and unbelievable family man.

My personal memory that really stands out is every time he and I were alone on the road recruiting and we'd have private time together, where you're talking about more than just football. We were talking about life, we were talking about our families, talking about where I was going and what I wanted to do and where he saw himself.

At the same time, Coach always talked to us about responding. I know that our entire staff and our players have a call to duty and we will respond.

We've got a great plan here in place. It's successful. We're a consistent winner; we're 14-10 in the Big Ten over the last three years. Now is there a different guy blowing the whistle to change the drills and talk to the team after practice? You better believe it. But as far as what we do, I learned from arguably the best guy in the coaching profession, and its my job and our staff's and our entire university's job to continue that legacy. That's what we're taking forward one day at a time.

Our goal is to win the Big Ten championship and go to the Rose Bowl. That will never change.

Neither of my parents went to college. My Dad started off working for Illinois Bell and putting phones in people's houses. He ended up retiring in middle management. (He is) Very close to me, very private.

He takes care of our headphones on the sidelines. He's done that for three years now. It's really a special treat to be a coach and be in a hotel the night before a game and to be able to sit there and have dinner and snack with your Dad. I don't know how many coaches have that chance in America, but I know how blessed and fortunate I am.

I was in the second grade playing for the Orland Park Pioneers — the Pee-Wees. I think it was called — and you could play up to the 6th grade as long as your weight was below whatever the weight limit was. I was second grader my first year, playing tackle football with 6th graders, you know?

And I was out there getting my lips knocked off. I had no idea how to play and I'd come home and I'd go, "I don't know if I want to do this." My Mom would say, "You're going back. You're going back."

My Dad never coached us because he was at work. That was the Fitzgerald work ethic: If you start something, you're going to finish it, whether it was playing sax in the band or football in the 2nd grade.

There were times when I was pulled off the field when grade reports came back that weren't very good. I was making poor decisions about being rambunctious in the classroom. Even when I went to Sandburg I was taken off the practice field when (my) grades weren't in order.

When you're 10 years old and you're growing up in Chicago and the Chicago Bears win the Super Bowl, I don't know if it gets a whole lot better than that team.

I remember watching Mike Singletary and Walter Payton and listening to those guys speak about what the game of football taught them and what they had to overcome to become great players.

I remember Jay Hilgenberg came to football registration for the Pioneers and I thought that was the greatest thing in the world. I still have the picture.

If you sacrifice and come together as a team, then anything can happen.

That's my picture of 1995.

And we weren't surprised that it happened because we had worked so hard to get there. It was fun to change the attitude of the nation toward Northwestern football.

I'm forever grateful (to Gary Barnett) because he was the man and his staff that gave me the chance to attend Northwestern as a student-athlete and earn a degree. I wouldn't be here as the youngest head football coach in America, at 31, without the opportunity (I had) to attend Northwestern.

Whether you're in this profession for one year or 50 years, if you've been paying attention and learning from your mentors, you're prepared to be a head football coach. Just be confident and trust (in) who you are.

I've learned that life is extremely fragile and you need to live life everyday like it may be your last, and to really truly love the people who are close to you and that they know that you love them. And communicate to the people around you how important they are in your life because you never know when they're not going to be there.

Northwestern coach Pat Fitzgerald and his 2006 Wildcats enter the playing field to begin a new era.

Remembering Biggie Munn

By Mike Bynum

Clarence (Biggie) Munn was one of those rare coaches who forever changed the course of a college football program.

Munn played on Fritz Crisler's 1930 and 1931 Minnesota Gophers teams, where he earned All-Big Ten honors as a guard. In 1931, he was named the Big Ten's MVP and was selected as an all-American. Munn was also the best punter in the country in 1931.

He wasn't big at six feet and 215 pounds, but was gifted with great speed and determination.

Following his playing career, Munn worked as an assistant to Bernie Bierman in building those memorable powerhouse Gophers teams.

Following an 8-0 season in 1934, Munn became the head coach at Albright College in Reading, Pa. In two seasons, his teams put together a record of 13-2-1.

He became an assistant at Syracuse in 1937 and then worked as a line coach for his Crisler at the University of Michigan from 1938 to 1943.

In 1944, he returned to Syracuse as an assistant, then after Ossie Solem retired following the 1945 season, Munn took over as head coach at Syracuse. In his only season there — in 1946 — he led the Orangemen to a 4-5-0 record.

It was at Syracuse that he reunited with his college teammate, Bud Wilkinson, who would later become the great coach at Oklahoma. He also had an opportunity to coach Duffy Daugherty, who would one day be his assistant and successor in East Lansing.

In 1947, Munn accepted the head coaching job at Michigan State and quickly installed the single wing offense and to put his team on the college football map.

He first began to win, going 20-5-0 in his first three seasons.

In 1950, he was successful in persuading Father Cavanaugh, the University of Notre Dame president, to get the Fighting Irish to put the Spartans on their schedule.

He then lobbied to get Michigan State into the Big Ten to fill the spot left vacant by the University of Chicago.

In his meteoric seven year coaching career in East Lansing, Munn's teams 54 games, lost nine and tied 2. They also won a pair of national championships in 1951 and 1952.

He then led the Spartans to a Big Ten co-championship in their first season in the league and a 28-20 win over UCLA in the Rose Bowl.

His Spartans had put together a 28-game streak, that began in 1950 and wasn't interrupted until a 6-0 loss to Purdue on October 24, 1953 in West Lafayette.

Following the triumphant 1953 campaign, Munn took over for Ralph Young as the school's athletic director and promoted Duff Daughtery to replace him. He would serve as the Spartan's AD until 1971.

Munn was named Coach of the Year following the 1952 season and was elected to the College Football Hall of Fame in 1959. He coached 18 first-team all-Americans.

The hockey arena at Michigan State was built in 1974 and named in his honor.

He passed away the next year at the age of 66.

Biggie Munn's Michigan State teams won the 1951 and 1952 national championship and tied for the Big Ten title in 1953, the Spartans' first year in the league.

Big Ten Champions

Year	School	Conference Record	Overall Record	Coach
1896	Wisconsin	2-0-1	7-1-1	Phil King
1897	Wisconsin	3-0-0	9-1-0	Phil King
1898	Michigan	3-0-0	10-0-0	Gustave Ferbert
1899	Chicago	4-0-0	12-0-2	Amos Alonzo Stagg
1900	Iowa	2-0-1	7-0-1	Alden Knipe
	Minnesota	3-0-1	10-0-2	Henry L. Williams
1901	Michigan	4-0-0	11-0-0	Fielding H. Yost
	Wisconsin	2-0-0	9-0-0	Phil King
1902	Michigan	5-0-0	11-0-0	Fielding H. Yost
1903	Michigan	3-0-1	11-0-1	Fielding H. Yost
	Minnesota	3-0-1	14-0-1	Henry L. Williams
	Northwestern	1-0-2	9-2-3	Walter McCormack
1904	Michigan	2-0-0	10-0-0	Fielding H. Yost
	Minnesota	3-0-0	13-0-0	Henry L. Williams
1905	Chicago	7-0-0	10-0-0	Amos Alonzo Stagg
1906	Michigan	1-0-0	4-1-0	Fielding H. Yost
	Minnesota	2-0-0	4-1-0	Henry L. Williams
	Wisconsin	3-0-0	5-0-0	Dr. C.P. Hutchins
1907	Chicago	4-0-0	4-1-0	Amos Alonzo Stagg
1908	Chicago	5-0-0	5-0-1	Amos Alonzo Stagg
1909	Minnesota	3-0-0	6-1-0	Henry L. Williams
1910	Illinois	4-0-0	7-0-0	Arthur Hall
	Minnesota	2-0-0	6-1-0	Henry L. Williams
1911	Minnesota	3-0-1	6-0-1	Henry L. Williams
1912	Wisconsin	5-0-0	7-0-0	William Juneau
1913	Chicago	7-0-0	7-0-0	Amos Alonzo Stagg
1914	Illinois	6-0-0	7-0-0	Bob Zuppke
1915	Illinois	3-0-2	5-0-2	Bob Zuppke
1916	Ohio State	4-0-0	7-0-0	J.W. Wilce
1917	Ohio State	4-0-0	8-0-1	J.W. Wilce
1918	Illinois	4-0-0	5-2-0	Bob Zuppke
	Michigan	2-0-0	5-0-0	Fielding H. Yost
	Purdue	1-0-0	3-3-0	Butch Scanlon
1919	Illinois	6-1-0	6-1-0	Bob Zuppke
1920	Ohio State	5-0-0	7-1-0	J.W. Wilce
1921	Iowa	5-0-0	7-0-0	Howard Jones
1922	Iowa	5-0-0	7-0-0	Howard Jones
	Michigan	4-0-0	6-0-1	Fielding H. Yost
1923	Illinois	5-0-0	8-0-0	Bob Zuppke
	Michigan	4-0-0	8-0-0	Fielding H. Yost
1924	Chicago	3-0-3	4-1-3	Amos Alonzo Stagg
1925	Michigan	5-1-0	7-1-0	Fielding H. Yost

Year	School	Conference Record	Overall Record	Coach
1926	Michigan	5-0-0	7-1-0	Fielding H. Yost
	Northwestern	5-0-0	7-1-0	Glenn Thistlewaite
1927	Illinois	5-0-0	7-0-1	Bob Zuppke
1928	Illinois	4-1-0	7-1-0	Bob Zuppke
1929	Purdue	5-0-0	8-0-0	James Phelan
1930	Michigan	5-0-0	5-3-1	Harry Kipke
	Northwestern	5-0-0	7-1-0	Dick Hanley
1931	Michigan	5-1-0	8-1-1	Harry Kipke
	Northwestern	5-1-0	7-1-1	Dick Hanley
	Purdue	5-1-0	9-1-0	Noble Kizer
1932	Michigan	6-0-0	8-0-0	Harry Kipke
1933	Michigan	5-0-1	7-0-1	Harry Kipke
1934	Minnesota	5-0-0	8-0-0	Bernie Bierman
1935	Minnesota	5-0-0	8-0-0	Bernie Bierman
	Ohio State	5-0-0	7-1-0	Francis Schmidt
1936	Northwestern	6-0-0	7-1-0	Lynn Waldorf
1937	Minnesota	5-0-0	6-2-0	Bernie Bierman
1938	Minnesota	4-1-0	6-2-0	Bernie Bierman
1939	Ohio State	5-1-0	6-2-0	Francis Schmidt
1940	Minnesota	6-0-0	8-0-0	Bernie Bierman
1941	Minnesota	5-0-0	8-0-0	Bernie Bierman
1942	Ohio State	5-1-0	9-1-0	Paul Brown
1943	Michigan	6-0-0	8-1-0	Fritz Crisler
	Purdue	6-0-0	9-0-0	Elmer Burnham
1944	Ohio State	6-0-0	9-0-0	Carroll Widdoes
1945	Indiana	5-0-1	9-0-1	Bo McMillin
1946	Illinois	6-1-0	8-2-0	Ray Eliot
1947	Michigan	6-0-0	10-0-0	Fritz Crisler
1948	Michigan	6-0-0	9-0-0	Bennie Oosterbaan
1949	Michigan	4-1-1	6-2-1	Bennie Oosterbaan
	Ohio State	4-1-1	7-1-2	Wes Fesler
1950	Michigan	4-1-1	6-3-1	Bennie Oosterbaan
1951	Illinois	5-0-1	9-0-1	Ray Eliot
1952	Purdue	4-1-1	4-3-2	Stu Holcomb
	Wisconsin	4-1-1	6-3-1	Ivy Williamson
1953	Illinois	5-1-0	7-1-1	Ray Eliot
	Michigan State	5-1-0	9-1-0	Biggie Munn
1954	Ohio State	7-0-0	10-0-0	Woody Hayes
1955	Ohio State	6-0-0	7-2-0	Woody Hayes
1956	Iowa	5-1-0	9-1-0	Forest Evashevski
1957	Ohio State	7-0-0	9-1-0	Woody Hayes
1958	Iowa	5-1-0	8-1-1	Forest Evashevski
1959	Wisconsin	5-2-0	7-3-0	Milt Bruhn
1960	Iowa	5-1-0	8-1-0	Forest Evashevski
	Minnesota	5-1-0	8-2-0	Murray Warmath

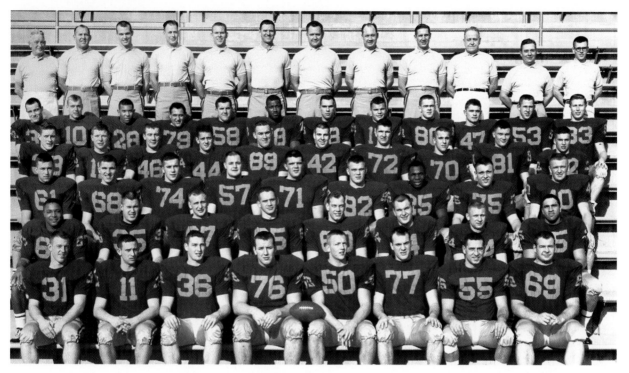

The 1960 Minnesota Gophers tied for the Big Ten title with Iowa, but still won the national championship.

Year	School	Conference Record	Overall Record	Coach
1961	Ohio State	6-0-0	8-0-1	Woody Hayes
1962	Wisconsin	6-1-0	8-2-0	Milt Bruhn
1963	Illinois	5-1-1	8-1-1	Pete Elliott
1964	Michigan	6-1-0	9-1-0	Bump Elliott
1965	Michigan State	7-0-0	10-1-0	Duffy Daugherty
1966	Michigan State	7-0-0	9-0-1	Duffy Daugherty
1967	Indiana	6-1-0	9-2-0	John Pont
	Minnesota	6-1-0	8-2-0	Murray Warmath
	Purdue	6-1-0	8-2-0	Jack Mollenkopf
1968	Ohio State	7-0-0	10-0-0	Woody Hayes
1969	Michigan	6-1-0	8-3-0	Bo Schembechler
	Ohio State	6-1-0	8-1-0	Woody Hayes
1970	Ohio State	7-0-0	9-1-0	Woody Hayes
1971	Michigan	8-0-0	11-1-0	Bo Schembechler
1972	Michigan	7-1-0	10-1-0	Bo Schembechler
	Ohio State	7-1-0	9-2-0	Woody Hayes
1973	Michigan	7-0-1	10-0-1	Bo Schembechler
	Ohio State	7-0-1	10-0-1	Woody Hayes
1974	Michigan	7-1-0	10-1-0	Bo Schembechler
	Ohio State	7-1-0	10-2-0	Woody Hayes
1975	Ohio State	8-0-0	11-1-0	Woody Hayes
1976	Michigan	7-1-0	10-2-0	Bo Schembechler
	Ohio State	7-1-0	9-2-1	Woody Hayes

Year	School	Conference Record	Overall Record	Coach
1977	Michigan	7-1-0	10-2-0	Bo Schembechler
	Ohio State	7-1-0	9-3-0	Woody Hayes
1978	Michigan	7-1-0	10-2-0	Bo Schembechler
	Michigan State	7-1-0	8-3-0	Darryl Rogers
1979	Ohio State	8-0-0	11-1-0	Earle Bruce
1980	Michigan	8-0-0	10-2-0	Bo Schembechler
1981	Iowa	6-2-0	8-4-0	Hayden Fry
	Ohio State	6-2-0	9-3-0	Earle Bruce
1982	Michigan	8-1-0	8-4-0	Bo Schembechler
1983	Illinois	9-0-0	10-2-0	Mike White
1984	Ohio State	7-2-0	9-3-0	Earle Bruce
1985	Iowa	7-1-0	10-2-0	Hayden Fry
1986	Michigan	7-1-0	10-1-1	Bo Schembechler
	Ohio State	7-1-0	10-3-0	Earle Bruce
1987	Michigan State	7-0-1	9-2-1	George Perles
1988	Michigan	7-0-1	9-2-1	Bo Schembechler
1989	Michigan	8-0-0	10-2-0	Bo Schembechler
1990	Illinois	6-2-0	8-4-0	John Mackovic
	Iowa	6-2-0	8-4-0	Hayden Fry
	Michigan	6-2-0	9-3-0	Gary Moeller
	Michigan State	6-2-0	8-3-1	George Perles
1991	Michigan	8-0-0	10-2-0	Gary Moeller
1992	Michigan	6-0-2	9-0-3	Gary Moeller
1993	Ohio State	6-1-1	10-1-1	John Cooper
	Wisconsin	6-1-1	10-1-1	Barry Alvarez
1994	Penn State	8-0-0	12-0-0	Joe Paterno
1995	Northwestern	8-0-0	10-2-0	Gary Barnett
1996	Northwestern	7-1-0	9-3-0	Gary Barnett
1997	Michigan	8-0-0	12-0-0	Lloyd Carr
1998	Michigan	7-1-0	10-3-0	Lloyd Carr
	Ohio State	7-1-0	11-1-0	John Cooper
	Wisconsin	7-1-0	11-1-0	Barry Alvarez
1999	Wisconsin	7-1-0	10-2-0	Barry Alvarez
2000	Michigan	6-2-0	9-3-0	Lloyd Carr
	Northwestern	6-2-0	8-4-0	Randy Walker
	Purdue	6-2-0	8-4-0	Joe Tiller
2001	Illinois	7-1-0	10-2-0	Ron Turner
2002	Iowa	8-0-0	12-1-0	Kirk Ferentz
	Ohio State	8-0-0	13-0-0	Jim Tressel
2003	Michigan	7-1-0	10-3-0	Lloyd Carr
2004	Iowa	7-1-0	10-2-0	Kirk Ferentz
	Michigan	7-1-0	9-3-0	Lloyd Carr
2005	Penn State	7-1-0	11-1-0	Joe Paterno
	Ohio State	7-1-0	10-2-0	Jim Tressel

Chicago Tribune Silver Football Award (Big Ten MVP)

Year	Player	Position	School
1924	Red Grange	Halfback	Illinois
1925	Tim Lowry	Center	Northwestern
1926	Benny Friedman	Quarterback	Michigan
1927	Ken Rouse	Center	Chicago
1928	Chuck Bennett	Halfback	Indiana
1929	Willis Glassgow	Halfback	Iowa
1930	Wes Fesler	End	Ohio State
1931	Clarence Munn	Guard	Minnesota
1932	Harry Newman	Quarterback	Michigan
1933	Joe Laws	Quarterback	Iowa
1934	Pug Lund	Halfback	Minnesota
1935	Jay Berwanger	Halfback	Chicago
1936	Vernon Huffman	Quarterback	Indiana
1937	Corbett Davis	Fullback	Indiana
1938	Howard Weiss	Fullback	Wisconsin
1939	Nile Kinnick	Halfback	Iowa
1940	Tom Harmon	Halfback	Michigan
1941	Jack Graf	Fullback	Ohio State
1942	Dave Schreiner	End	Wisconsin
1943	Otto Graham	Halfback	Northwestern
1944	Les Horvath	Halfback	Ohio State
1945	Ollie Cline	Fullback	Ohio State
1946	Alex Agase	Guard	Illinois
1947	Chalmers Elliott	Halfback	Michigan
1948	Art Murakowski	Fullback	Northwestern
1949	Bob Wilson	Center	Wisconsin
1950	Vic Janowicz	Halfback	Ohio State
1951	Bill Reichardt	Fullback	Iowa
1952	Paul Giel	Halfback	Minnesota
1953	Paul Giel	Halfback	Minnesota
1954	Alan Ameche	Fullback	Wisconsin
1955	Howard Cassady	Halfback	Ohio State
1956	Kenny Ploen	Quarterback	Iowa
1957	Jim Pace	Halfback	Michigan
1958	Randy Duncan	Quarterback	Iowa
1959	Bill Burrell	Guard	Illinois
1960	Tom Brown	Guard	Minnesota
1961	Sandy Stephens	Quarterback	Minnesota
1962	Ron Vander Kelen	Quarterback	Wisconsin
1963	Dick Butkus	Center/Linebacker	Illinois
1964	Bob Timberlake	Quarterback	Michigan
1965	Jim Grabowski	Fullback	Illinois

Year	Player	Position	School
1966	Bob Griese	Quarterback	Purdue
1967	Leroy Keyes	Halfback	Purdue
1968	Ron Johnson	Halfback	Michigan
1969	Mike Phipps	Quarterback	Purdue
1970	Mike Adamle	Halfback	Northwestern
1971	Eric Allen	Halfback	Michigan State
1972	Otis Armstrong	Halfback	Purdue
1973	Archie Griffin	Halfback	Ohio State
1974	Archie Griffin	Halfback	Ohio State
1975	Cornelius Greene	Quarterback	Ohio State
1976	Rob Lytle	Tailback	Michigan
1977	Larry Bethea	Defensive Tackle	Michigan State
1978	Rick Leach	Quarterback	Michigan
1979	Tim Clifford	Quarterback	Indiana
1980	Mark Herrmann	Quarterback	Purdue
1981	Art Schlichter	Quarterback	Ohio State
1982	Anthony Carter	Wide Receiver	Michigan
1983	Don Thorp	Defensive Tackle	Illinois
1984	Keith Byars	Tailback	Ohio State
1985	Chuck Long	Quarterback	Iowa
1986	Jim Harbaugh	Quarterback	Michigan
1987	Lorenzo White	Tailback	Michigan State
1988	Anthony Thompson	Tailback	Indiana
1989	Anthony Thompson	Tailback	Indiana
1990	Nick Bell	Halfback	Iowa
1991	Desmond Howard	Split End	Michigan
1992	Lee Gissendaner	Wide Receiver	Northwestern
1993	Brent Moss	Halfback	Wisconsin
1994	Kerry Collins	Quarterback	Penn State
1995	Eddie George	Halfback	Ohio State
1996	Orlando Pace	Offensive Tackle	Ohio State
1997	Charles Woodson	Cornerback	Michigan
1998	Joe Germaine	Quarterback	Ohio State
1999	Ron Dayne	Halfback	Wisconsin
2000	Drew Brees	Quarterback	Purdue
2001	Antwaan Randle El	Quarterback	Indiana
2002	Brad Banks	Quarterback	Iowa
2003	Chris Perry	Halfback	Michigan
2004	Braylon Edwards	Wide Receiver	Michigan
2005	Michael Robinson	Quarterback	Penn State

Woody Hayes, Ohio State

Bill Mallory, Indiana

Dave McClain
Coach of the Year

Year	Coach	School
1972	Bo Schembechler	Michigan
1973	Woody Hayes	Ohio State
1974	Denny Stolz	Michigan State
1975	Woody Hayes	Ohio State
1976	Bo Schembechler	Michigan
1977	Darryl Rogers	Michigan State
1978	Jim Young	Purdue
1979	Earle Bruce	Ohio State
1980	Bo Schembechler	Michigan
1981	Hayden Fry	Iowa
1982	Dennis Green	Northwestern
1983	Mike White	Illinois
1984	Leon Burtnett	Purdue
1985	Bo Schembechler	Michigan
1986	Bill Mallory	Indiana
1987	Bill Mallory	Indiana
1988	John Mackovic	Illinois
1989	John Mackovic	Illinois
1990	Hayden Fry	Iowa
1991	Gary Moeller	Michigan
1992	Gary Moeller	Michigan
1993	Barry Alvarez	Wisconsin
1994	Joe Paterno	Penn State
1995	Gary Barnett	Northwestern
1996	Gary Barnett	Northwestern
1997	Joe Tiller	Purdue
1998	Barry Alvarez	Wisconsin
1999	Glen Mason	Minnesota
2000	Randy Walker	Northwestern
2001	Ron Turner	Illinois
2002	Kirk Ferentz	Iowa
2003	John L. Smith	Michigan State
2004	Kirk Ferentz	Iowa
2005	Joe Paterno	Penn State